ECONOMICS AND THE VIRTUES

Economics and the Virtues

Building a New Moral Foundation

Edited by
JENNIFER A. BAKER
and
MARK D. WHITE

OXFORD
UNIVERSITY PRESS

OXFORD
UNIVERSITY PRESS

Great Clarendon Street, Oxford, OX2 6DP,
United Kingdom

Oxford University Press is a department of the University of Oxford. It furthers the University's objective of excellence in research, scholarship, and education by publishing worldwide. Oxford is a registered trade mark of Oxford University Press in the UK and in certain other countries

First Edition published in 2016

Published in the United States of America by Oxford University Press
198 Madison Avenue, New York, NY 10016, United States of America

British Library Cataloguing in Publication Data
Data available

Library of Congress Control Number: 2015945360

ISBN 978–0–19–870139–2

Acknowledgments

Our first and deepest thanks go to Adam Swallow and Terry Vaughn at Oxford University Press, both of whom supported this project from the beginning, solicited enough reviewers to put Aristotle's golden mean to the test, and made our proposal much better in the process. We commend these editors as well as Oxford University Press for their continued dedication to edited collections and the conversations and collaborations that flourish because of them.

We think of Deirdre McCloskey as a guardian angel over this project, and her own work is a tremendous stimulus to all that follows. Also, her scribbled notes to us while we presented our work alongside her at conferences proved invaluable to our own thinking, as did her unfailing encouragement. Jonathan Wight and Thom Brooks were also very supportive throughout the life of the project, as were so many others in our professional and personal circles.

We would like to thank the International Network for Economic Method and the Allied Social Science Associations for hosting a conference session featuring early versions of several chapters in this volume; it was after that session that we first approached Oxford about a volume on economics and virtue. We would also like to thank the American Association for the Philosophic Study of Society for hosting another conference session featuring some early work on the book at the Eastern Division meetings of the American Philosophical Association.

Finally, we would very much like to express our continued gratitude to our authors. We were delighted when they agreed to write for us and were even more delighted to read what they wrote. They produced work that, frankly, dazzled us—and this, despite us having no small estimation of their talents in advance. So thank you, Michael Baurmann, Christian Becker, Geoffrey Brennan, Jason Brennan, Ginny Choi, Tim O'Keefe, Jim Otteson, David Rose, Eric Schliesser, Virgil Storr, Christine Swanton, and Andrew Yuengert. It is your efforts here and in general which help illuminate so much that would otherwise remain hidden.

Table of Contents

Contributors

Jennifer A. Baker is Associate Professor of Philosophy at the College of Charleston. She attempts to update ancient virtue ethics for use today. Though most of her work is in ethical theory, her publications on how virtue can be related to economics include "Visible Hands: The Justification of the Market and Moral Agency" in *Of Sympathy and Selfishness: The Moral and Political Philosophy of Adam Smith* (Charlotte C.S. Thomas (ed.), Mercer University Press); "Virtue Ethics and Practical Guidance" in *Social Philosophy and Policy* (2013); "Don't Let the Best Be the Enemy of the Good: A Stoic Defense of the Market," in *Accepting the Invisible Hand* (Mark D. White (ed.), Palgrave, 2010); and "Virtue and Behavior" in *Review of Social Economy* (2009).

Michael Baurmann studied sociology, philosophy, and law. After being assistant professor and lecturer at the faculties of law at the Universities of Frankfurt and Mainz, he was appointed to a chair for sociology at the University of Düsseldorf in 1997. He has been visiting professor in Australia (ANU), Mexico (ITAM), and the United States (New York University), and was senior research fellow at the Alfried Krupp Wissenschaftskolleg in Greifswald in the years 2009/2010 and 2013. His main research interests are general theory of sociology, rational choice theory, the role of morality in modern market societies, and the societal preconditions of liberal societies and the rule of law. Recently he has been working on a theory explaining fundamentalist beliefs within the framework of rational actor theory and social epistemology. Since 2014 he has been a member in a research project dealing with citizen participation via internet tools. He has been co-editor of *Analyse & Kritik: Journal for Social Theory* for 30 years.

Christian U. Becker studied mathematics, economics, German literature, and philosophy in Germany. He earned his Ph.D. in economics from Heidelberg University (2003) and his Habilitation in philosophy from Kaiserslautern University (2010). Since 2013, he has been a faculty member at the College of Business at Colorado State University. His primary research and teaching interests are in theoretical and applied ethics, the history of economic thought, philosophy of economics, environmental philosophy, and sustainability studies. He is the author of *Nature and Economics in Romanticism* (Metropolis, 2003, in German) and *Sustainability Ethics and Sustainability Research* (Springer, 2012). He has published various papers on philosophical and economic topics in journals such as *Archives for Philosophy of Law and Social Philosophy*; *Ecological Economics*; *Ethics, Policy, and Environment*;

Environmental Values; *European Journal for the History of Economic Thought*; and *Journal for Business, Economics, and Ethics*.

Geoffrey Brennan self-identifies as a PPE person (Philosophy/Politics/Economics). He originally trained as an economist but now works across the three disciplines. Mid-career, he worked with Nobel Laureate James Buchanan and produced two books with him, *The Power to Tax* (1980) and *The Reason of Rules* (1985). He has written extensively on the "expressive" theory of voting behavior, most notably with Loren Lomasky in *Democracy and Decision* (1993), and on the implications of that account of voting for institutional design, with Alan Hamlin in *Democratic Devices and Desires* (2000). He is also author, with Philip Pettit, of *The Economy of Esteem* (2004). His most recent book is *Explaining Norms* (2013) with Lina Eriksson, Robert Goodin, and Nicholas Southwood.

Jason Brennan is Robert J. and Elizabeth Flanagan Family Chair and Associate Professor of Strategy, Economics, Ethics, and Public Policy at the McDonough School of Business, and by courtesy Associate Professor of Philosophy, at Georgetown University. He is the author of *Markets without Limits* with Peter Jaworski (Routledge, 2015), *Why Not Capitalism?* (Routledge, 2014), *Compulsory Voting: For and Against* with Lisa Hill (Cambridge, 2014), *Libertarianism* (Oxford, 2012), *The Ethics of Voting* (Princeton, 2011), and *A Brief History of Liberty* with David Schmidtz (Blackwell, 2010). He is currently writing *Against Politics* (Princeton University Press) and *Global Justice as Global Freedom* with Bas van der Vossen (Oxford University Press). His research focuses on democratic theory, civic virtue, and the moral foundations of markets.

Seung (Ginny) Choi is a Ph.D. candidate at George Mason University's Department of Economics and a Dissertation Fellow at the Mercatus Center at George Mason University. She is also affiliated with the Interdisciplinary Center for Economic Science, an experimental economics center at George Mason University. She received her M.A. in economics from New York University and her B.A. in economics from Emory University. Originally from South Korea, she received her primary and secondary education in Jakarta, Indonesia. Her research is in applied microeconomics, with a specialization in the design and analysis of economic experiments: her primary interest is to understand how institutional features impact the formation of social networks in economic and non-economic environments and how individuals repurpose these networks to achieve new economic goals. Her dissertation explores the interplay between trust and markets in the formation of dyadic social bonds and identifies some features of institutions that promote trusting behavior.

Tim O'Keefe is Associate Professor of Philosophy at Georgia State University. He specializes in ancient philosophy, particularly Hellenistic philosophy. He has published extensively on Epicureanism, including two books, *Epicurus on Freedom* (Cambridge University Press, 2005) and *Epicureanism* (University of California Press/Routledge, 2009), and papers on topics such as the Epicureans on the mind–body relation, freedom of action, the ontological status of sensible qualities, friendship, justice, and death. But his interests range broadly, and he has also published on the Pyrrhonian skeptics, the ethics and epistemology of the Cyrenaics (a group of hedonists who were skeptical of our ability to gain knowledge of the external world), Aristotle's cosmology, and the spurious Platonic dialogue the *Axiochus*, in which Socrates retails inconsistent arguments against the fear of death. Current research interests include Anaxarchus (a sophist and compatriot of Pyrrho), Aristotle on shame, and the dubious Platonic dialogue the *Clitophon*.

James R. Otteson is executive director of the BB&T Center for the Study of Capitalism and the Thomas W. Smith Presidential Chair in Business Ethics at Wake Forest University. He received his B.A. from the University of Notre Dame and his Ph.D. from the University of Chicago, and he has taught previously at New York University, Yeshiva University, Georgetown University, and the University of Alabama. He writes on political economy, political philosophy, business ethics, and liberalism. His publications include *Adam Smith's Marketplace of Life* (Cambridge, 2002); *The Levellers: Overton, Walwyn, and Lilburne* (ed.), 5 vols. (Thoemmes, 2003); *Actual Ethics* (Cambridge, 2006), which won the 2007 Templeton Enterprise Award; and *Adam Smith* (Bloomsbury, 2013). His most recent books are his edited collection *What Adam Smith Knew* (Encounter, 2014) and *The End of Socialism* (Cambridge, 2014).

David C. Rose is a professor of economics at the University of Missouri-St. Louis. His research focuses on behavioral economics, political economy, the theory of the firm, and ethics. He has published scholarly articles in a wide range of areas. He has one book, *The Moral Foundation of Economic Behavior* (Oxford University Press, 2011), which explored the role that moral beliefs play in the development and operation of free market societies. He is currently working on another book for Oxford University Press, *Why Culture Matters Most*, which explores how culture uniquely solves the most daunting obstacle to individual and collective human flourishing: individual rationality undermining the common good. He also frequently contributes to policy debates through radio interviews, television interviews, and op-eds on topics ranging from social security reform, health care reform, monetary policy, fiscal policy, and judicial philosophy. He earned a bachelor's degree in economics from Missouri State University and a Ph.D. in economics from the University of Virginia.

Eric Schliesser is Professor of Political Theory in Political Science at the University of Amsterdam Netherlands. In addition, he is Visiting Professor,

Philosophy & Moral Sciences, Ghent University, Belgium. He has published widely on early modern philosophy and its relationship to physics and political economy, with numerous articles on Spinoza, Huygens, Newton, Berkeley, Hume, Adam Smith, Kant, and Sophie de Grouchy, among others. He has co-edited volumes on Adam Smith and Isaac Newton, and recently edited *Sympathy: A History* for Oxford University Press. He also writes about the philosophy of economics with a special interest in the rise and fall of Chicago economics and the role of economic expertise in political context.

Virgil Henry Storr is a Senior Research Fellow and the Director of Graduate Student Programs at the Mercatus Center, a Research Associate Professor of Economics in the Department of Economics, George Mason University, and the Don C. Lavoie Fellow in the F.A. Hayek Program in Philosophy, Politics, and Economics at the Mercatus Center, George Mason University. His book *Understanding the Culture of Markets*, published by Routledge, explores how culture shapes economic activity and describes how social scientists (especially economists) should incorporate considerations of culture into their analysis. His forthcoming book with Palgrave Macmillan, *Community Revival in the Wake of Disaster: Lessons in Local Entrepreneurship* with Stefanie Haeffele-Balch and Laura E. Grube, argues that entrepreneurs promote community recovery after disasters by providing necessary goods and services, restoring and replacing disrupted social networks, and signaling that community rebound is likely and, in fact, underway. His writings in political economy have been published or are forthcoming in *Small Business Economics*, *Public Choice*, *Rationality & Society*, *Journal of Urban Affairs*, *Cambridge Journal of Economics*, *American Journal of Economics and Sociology*, *Review of Austrian Economics*, and other scholarly publications.

Christine Swanton is in the Philosophy Department at University of Auckland, New Zealand. In 2015 she published *The Virtue Ethics of Hume and Nietzsche* with Wiley Blackwell, and her earlier book *Virtue Ethics: A Pluralistic View* was published by Oxford University Press in 2003. Recent and forthcoming work includes papers on virtue ethics and role ethics, and virtue ethics and particularism.

Mark D. White is Chair and Professor in the Department of Philosophy at the College of Staten Island/CUNY, where he teaches courses in philosophy, law, and economics. He is the author of *Kantian Ethics and Economics: Autonomy, Dignity, and Character* (Stanford University Press), *The Manipulation of Choice: Ethics and Libertarian Paternalism*, and *The Illusion of Well-Being: Economic Policymaking Based on Respect and Responsiveness* (both from Palgrave Macmillan), as well as over 50 journal articles and book chapters. He has edited or coedited a number of books, including *The Thief of Time: Philosophical Essays on Procrastination* (with Chrisoula Andreou) and

Retributivism: Essays on Theory and Policy, both from Oxford University Press. He also writes often on philosophy for wider audiences, most recently in his book *The Virtues of Captain America: Modern-Day Lessons on Character from a World War II Superhero* (Wiley Blackwell, 2014).

Andrew M. Yuengert is the Blanche E. Seaver Professor of Social Science and a Professor of Economics at Seaver College, Pepperdine University. Before coming to Pepperdine in 1994, he was a research economist at the Federal Reserve Bank of New York. Professor Yuengert has made research contributions in several fields: economic philosophy, Catholic Social Teaching, the empirical study of religion, labor economics, and finance. He is a former President of the Association of Christian Economists and editor of its journal, *Faith & Economics*. He has published three books: *The Boundaries of Technique: Ordering Positive and Normative Concerns in Economic Research* (Lexington, 2004), *Inhabiting the Land: A Case for the Right to Migrate* (Acton Institute, 2004), and his most recent book, *Approximating Prudence: Aristotelian Practical Wisdom and Economic Theories of Choice* (Palgrave Macmillan, 2012).

Introduction

Jennifer A. Baker and Mark D. White

As the twenty-first century marches on, economics is being pulled in a number of directions. The exponential increase in computing power and "Big Data" is expanding the ability of mathematical and computational economists to model and predict the behavior of individuals, industries, and economies. At the same time, advances in game theory, experimental economics, and behavioral economics point to the complexity of economic behavior and social interaction in light of psychology and neuroscience, some of which washes out when data are aggregated and averaged, but some of which represents valuable information that risks being lost in the wash itself.

But not every recent development in economics has been in terms of technique (*technê*) to the exclusion of prudence (*phronēsis*), to use the terminology of Aristotle. There is also a broader movement to incorporate more explicit ethical thinking into modern economics. This movement picked up considerable steam after the financial crisis began in 2007 and indicted academic economists, professional financiers, and government actors a like. The public began to question the moral basis of financial markets and regulation like never before, and economists started to reflect on the extent to which their profession had become mired in formal, mathematical methods while losing sight of the real world and the people affected by their predictions and recommendations. Ironically, these very modern concerns have inspired people to look back to classical economics, which in its time had not yet been separated from ethics. Adam Smith, the father of modern economics, was well known in his day as a moral philosopher, and stressed the importance of ethics in his *Theory of Moral Sentiments* long before heralding the role of self-interest in markets in *The Wealth of Nations*. John Stuart Mill and David Hume are better remembered today as philosophers, but both made seminal contributions also to economics, as did Aristotle himself.

To be fair, ethics never left economics, although it has been taken for granted for the last century or so. Although John Stuart Mill had the closer link to modern economics, it was Jeremy Bentham's simpler utilitarianism that became embedded in economic practice (and of which Mill himself was very critical). As maximization became the standard technique in economics for the purposes of individual choice, firm behavior, and public policy, utility or welfare took center stage as the natural and rarely questioned *summum bonum* of economics. Eventually, the utilitarian roots of modern economic practice were forgotten, replaced with technical terms such as "cost-benefit analysis" and "Kaldor–Hicks efficiency" that granted Bentham's reform-minded utilitarianism a scientific gloss. As a result, the valuable moral aspects of utilitarianism, such as the concern for human welfare and equality of treatment, were lost. While it would be hyperbole to claim that this negligence of the moral nature of utilitarianism is responsible for the inability of modern economics to predict or effectively remedy the recent financial crisis, it is safe to say that a return to ethics, in all of its varied forms, is called for.[1]

As it happens, the rest of the philosopher–economists mentioned above are not utilitarians, but are associated to some extent with the ethics of *virtue*. Most commonly connected to Aristotle but also represented in different forms by the Stoics, the Scholastics, sentimentalists such as Adam Smith and David Hume, and even non-Western philosophers such as Confucius, virtue ethics is a broad term encompassing views of ethics that focus on persons and character traits, rather than choices or actions (as judged by utilitarians and deontologists), as the locus of goodness (or virtue). Rather than determining the rightness of actions based on their consequences or their adherence to rules or duties, philosophers in the virtue tradition focus on the character of the person performing the action and the dispositions of that person that led to it after being judged appropriate.[2]

In light of the growing dissatisfaction among the public—and even some economists—with the formal, antiseptic methods used in mainstream economics, the ethics of virtue provides a fresh perspective from a time-tested source. A focus on the person, character, and judgment in economics is not unprecedented even today: for instance, many heterodox schools of economics stress a renewed focus on human beings, schools such as social economics, feminist economics, humanistic economics, and post-autistic economics. A small but distinguished number of economists, such as Deirdre McCloskey, Irene van Staveren, and Andrew Yuengert, have engaged with the philosophical literature on virtue to expand the ethical perspective of economics, and a recent survey article in a key mainstream economics journal has exposed even more economists to the concept of virtue.[3]

Economics and the Virtues contributes to this growing literature with a dozen original essays on the importance of virtue ethics for economics. Our contributors, drawn from prominent philosophers and economists around the globe, reveal novel connections between scholars in the virtue tradition, ranging from Aristotle to Alasdair MacIntyre, and economic thought, theory, and methodology. The combination of the time-tested ethics of virtue, with its focus on the person, character, and judgment, with deep thinking on the history, theory, and practice of economics, is certain to further discussion on the moral and humanistic foundation of economics as we continue through the twenty-first century.

This book is divided into three parts. The essays in Part I, "Approaches to Virtue and Economics," focus on both the proven and potential impact on economics of five key thinkers or schools within the ethics of virtue. In "Aristotelian Virtue Ethics and Economic Rationality," Christian Becker, with one eye on today's economic methodology, submits for analysis Aristotle's seminal contribution to economics and human reasoning. In "The Epicureans on Happiness, Wealth, and the Deviant Craft of Property Management," Tim O'Keefe offers up the Epicurean method of reconciling economics and virtue, one rarely considered today, despite the influence of the approach's hedonism and materialism. In "Economic Good as Indifferent: The Stoics' Radical Approach," Jennifer A. Baker suggests that only a Stoic approach, with its account of virtue along with an account of goods "indifferent" to virtue, can reconcile ethics to behavior in markets. In "Adam Smith on Virtue, Prosperity, and Justice," James Otteson walks readers through the complexities of Smith's account of ethics and then defends the viability of Smith's own notion of economic justice against modern arguments based on social justice. Finally, in "The Virtues of a Kantian Economics," Mark D. White defends a reading of Immanuel Kant's ethics as "virtue-ous" and offers an account of moral judgment, based on Kantian ethics as well as the jurisprudence of legal philosopher Ronald Dworkin, which focuses on character, a key concern of virtue ethicists.

The essays in Part II, "Virtue and Economics in Theory," examine the history, methodology, and theory of economics and find numerous threads of virtue in past writing and future developments. In "On Virtue Economics," Michael Baumann and Geoffrey Brennan argue, against previous claims to the contrary, that virtue is of relevance to economics in several different ways and for both normative and explanatory reasons. In "The Separation of Economics from Virtue: A Historical–Conceptual Introduction," Eric Schliesser takes us from Sidgwick to twentieth-century debates over economic methodology in order to explain why virtue, in the Smithian sense, is no longer considered germane to economics (though virtue of a sort still is). Finally, in "The Space Between Choice and Our Models of It: Practical Wisdom and Normative Economics," Andrew Yuengert carefully describes the gap between the formal analysis of choice in economic modeling and the reality of human decision-making, emphasizing the practical significance of this gap, and suggesting that the Aristotelian notion of practical rationality might fill the breach.

The essays in Part III, "Virtue and Economics in Practice," explore the interrelationships between markets, profits, and justice, all in the context of virtue and vice. In "Virtues of Productivity versus Technicist Rationality," Christine Swanton challenges the omission of productive virtues from modern accounts of virtue ethics, referencing both Alasdair McIntyre and Ayn Rand in her critique of an overly "technicist" read of practical rationality and, in the process, expanding the way we think about reason and virtue. In "Virtues as Social Capital," David Rose proposes that we conceive of virtue both as social capital and as a public good, predicting when certain types of virtue will be underprovided and how we can address this. In "Can Trust, Reciprocity, and Friendships Survive Contact with the Market?" Ginny Choi and Virgil Storr revisit claims made in the eighteenth century by Montesquieu, Paine, and Smith concerning whether commercial society can enhance social bonds and have an "ameliorative" effect on our baser instincts. Finally, in "Do Markets Corrupt?" Jason Brennan looks at the same issue through the perspective of market critics, responding to their arguments with empirical research, which he claims is missing from popular critiques of the market as corruptive of private and civic virtues.

We hope that this collection will advance the ongoing discussion of economics and the virtues, in theory as well as practice. If economics is to retain its identity as a humanistic social science, it needs a humanistic core of ethics to support both its positive and normative aspects. Technique is of crucial value, but that value is greatly reduced if it is not joined with prudence. Knowing what to do is necessarily prior to knowing how to do it, and an ethics of virtue is ideally suited to helping us decide what we ought to do.

NOTES

1. For important work in ethics and economics in general, see, for example, Amartya Sen, *On Ethics and Economics* (Oxford: Blackwell, 1987); Daniel M. Hausman and Michael S. McPherson, *Economic Analysis, Moral Philosophy, and Public Policy*, 2nd ed. (Cambridge: Cambridge University Press, 2006); Irene van Staveren and Jan Peil (eds.), *Handbook of Economics and Ethics* (Cheltenham, UK: Edward Elgar, 2009); and Amitava Krishna Dutt and Charles K. Wilber, *Economics and Ethics: An Introduction* (New York: Palgrave Macmillan, 2010).
2. For presentations of virtue ethics, we recommend Daniel Russell's *Practical Intelligence and the Virtues* (Oxford: Oxford University Press, 2009); Julia Annas, *Intelligent Virtue* (Oxford: Oxford University Press, 2011); Lawrence Becker, *A New Stoicism* (Princeton, NJ: Princeton University Press, 2001); Rosalind Hursthouse, *On Virtue Ethics* (Oxford: Oxford University Press, 2001); Mark LeBar, *The Value of Living Well* (Oxford: Oxford University Press, 2013); and any number of collections of classic readings and contemporary perspectives, many of them cited through this volume.

3. For example, see Deirdre McCloskey, *The Bourgeois Virtues: Ethics for an Age of Commerce* (Chicago: University of Chicago Press, 2006) and "Adam Smith, the Last of the Former Virtue Ethicists," *History of Political Economy* 40(2008): 43–71; Irene van Staveren, *The Values of Economics: An Aristotelian Perspective* (London: Routledge, 2001) and "Beyond Utilitarianism and Deontology: Ethics in Economics," *Review of Political Economy* 19(2007): 21–35; and Andrew Yuengert, *The Boundaries of Technique: Ordering Positive and Normative Concerns in Economic Research* (Lanham, MD: Lexington, 2004) and *Approximating Prudence: Aristotelian Practical Wisdom and Economic Models of Choice* (New York: Palgrave Macmillan, 2012). The survey article mentioned is Luigino Bruni and Robert Sugden, "Reclaiming Virtue Ethics for Economics," *Journal of Economic Perspectives* 27(2013): 141–64.

Part I

Approaches to Virtue and Economics

1

Aristotelian Virtue Ethics and Economic Rationality

Christian U. Becker

One can broadly define the economy as "the entirety of actions, institutions, and organizations dealing with the production, distribution, consumption, and disposal of goods and services to satisfy human needs and desires in a rational way."[1] Given this definition, every individual is, in various ways, involved in the economy, and many aspects of daily life and actions are related to the economy. On a different level, virtue ethics assumes that individuals develop and act according to virtues. A virtue can generally be defined as an excellent (and durable) character trait that enables someone to act and get along with other people in an exemplary way.[2] Typically, virtues are not considered to be inborn capacities, but acquired dispositions. Virtues need to be developed over time through experience within certain contexts of practice and within a community of interaction and feedback.[3] However, for an excellent character trait to be considered an ethical virtue, it must also be part of, and contribute to, some general conception of good. Thus, ethical virtues cannot be developed and determined in isolated sub-communities, but ultimately, require a reference to a broader context of society or humankind and a conception of the good within this broader context.[4]

Given the substantial involvement of individuals in economic contexts and actions, one may ask what role virtues play in economic practices. Recent literature in business ethics and psychology provides some evidence that virtues have a crucial function in business and that one can identify specific business virtues or economic virtues. Robert Solomon discusses several business virtues, such as "honesty, fairness, trust and toughness," as crucial character traits for acting in an excellent way in business contexts.[5] Such virtues may be specific to business or may be modifications of general virtues and are important factors in economic actions and decisions. Deirdre McCloskey argues that a set of "bourgeois virtues" such as "prudence, temperance, justice, courage, love, faith and hope" are crucial for the capitalist economy, both supporting this type of economy and being reinforced by it.[6] Empirical research from business ethics, psychology, or experimental economics also provides some evidence for links between economic spheres of action and individual virtues. Some studies focus on the impact of the economic sphere on individual self-identity and character formation, for example, the impact of consumerism on individual self-identity and well-being.[7] Other empirical studies reveal the role of specific character traits for economic actions,[8] and insights of experimental economics about the impact of certain normative dispositions, such as fairness, on economic decisions could also be interpreted as reflecting virtue.[9]

The various indications of links between virtues and the economic sphere raise important questions for economics and philosophy. In this chapter, I discuss potential ways for a more systematic analysis of the relationship between virtues and economic spheres in the context of virtue ethics and economics. I will consider two interrelated perspectives. First, I explore into the *internal* role of virtues for economic actions, the formation and stability of economic systems, and concepts of excellence and self-identity within business. This includes questions such as: Do economic practices generate specific economic or business virtues? How do virtues impact economic decisions and actions? Do virtues support and stabilize economic institutions and organizations? The economic function of virtues is potentially important for explaining economic actions and systems, and thus, falls into the realm of economics. I particularly focus on the question of what economics can (or cannot) say about the role of virtues in the economy, and discuss the possibility of an economic theory of (economic) virtues.

Second, I explore the question of how the internal role of virtues in economic spheres is related to spheres *external* to business and economic life, that is, overarching conceptions of human excellence and broader societal frameworks the economy is embedded in. This topic is of particular interest for virtue ethics, and includes two sets of questions. A first set is about the individual person and the relationship between individual virtues and economic spheres: In what ways and how far do economic spheres of action contribute to virtue development of individuals? What virtues do economic spheres support (or suppress)? How do (potential) economic virtues fit into overall sets of individual virtues? How do they fit into overall conceptions of individual identity and good life? A second set of questions is about the relevant frameworks and communities for individual virtue development and their (theoretical and practical) constitution: What are relevant economic spheres for virtue development and how does their constitution influence individual virtue development? What is the relation between economic spheres and other spheres of human action and life? Is the constitution of today's economic spheres and the individual virtues developed within compatible with existing and new societal or individual conceptions of excellence and the good? How must the economy of the future be constituted to meet new societal (global) norms and future (economic) challenges and to allow individuals to develop virtues and self-identities accordingly?

The internal and the external aspects of the relations between virtues and economic spheres are interconnected and need to be approached in an integrated way. Virtues are embedded in broader contexts of life, and to explain the specific function of virtues in the economy and the meaning of economic practices for virtue formation, one must consider the relation between economic spheres and non-economic spheres of life as well as overarching conceptions of human excellence and good life.

My core thesis is that the crucial link between virtues and economic actions or spheres is *rationality*, and that integrative approaches to the relationship between virtues and economic activity need to be based on a substantial understanding of the role of rationality for both. Rationality is a core methodological element of modern economics, and it also plays a crucial role in virtue ethics. For exploring the systematic linkage between virtue ethics and economics, the relationship between economic rationality and ethical rationality (as it matters for virtue ethics) is crucial. I generally define rationality as "the ability to be in accordance with *ratio*," whereby *ratio* is understood by the two core meanings of the Latin term: first as translation of the Greek term *logos*, and second as calculable order. I use this definition as a general basis for my analysis and discuss more specific definitions of rationality in the course of this chapter.

My approach is based on an Aristotelian perspective. I refer to the ethical and economic thought of Aristotle to demonstrate the crucial role of rationality for linking virtues and economic spheres and to further explore the role of rationality for linking virtue ethics and economic thought.[10] My analysis of Aristotle's ethical and economic thought will serve as a backdrop for exploring potentials to develop a modern economic theory of virtues and its integration into a modern virtue ethics perspective on the economy. Against the backdrop of Aristotle's thought, I discuss modern economic rationality concepts and their potential to address virtues in economic contexts. I argue that the standard economic rationality concept is not feasible, but that alternative research on bounded rationality concepts may serve as a methodological basis for an economic theory of virtues that could be part of an integrated approach of virtue ethics and economics.

Further, I discuss the current economy with its specific characteristics and new challenges from a virtue ethics perspective. Specifically, I explore relevant economic spheres for individual virtue development, identify and discuss the relevant societal and global frameworks of these economic spheres, and discuss potential new conceptualizations of the good that meet the new challenges of the twenty-first century and can serve as normative orientation for a future economy. My example here is sustainability, and I argue that sustainability constitutes a widely shared new conception of the good that has implications for individual (economic) virtues and the future role of the economy.

The chapter is structured as follows. Section 1 analyzes Aristotle's economic thought and its link to virtue ethics, and demonstrates that the key to this link is Aristotle's conception of economic rationality. Against the backdrop of Aristotle's thought, Section 2 critically discusses the established rationality concept of modern economics and resulting limitations for analyzing economic virtues, and considers bounded rationality as a potential alternative methodological basis for developing systematic economic approaches to virtues and their meaning in economic spheres. Section 3 explores a modern virtue ethics perspective on individual excellence that adequately refers to the various modern spheres of economic life and action. In Section 4, I discuss what modern societal and global frameworks need to be considered to determine (economic) virtues and their overall meaning. Section 5 discusses sustainability as a normative concept and potential basis for economic virtues that adequately consider future challenges of the economy, and I conclude in Section 6.

1. ARISTOTLE AS A REFERENCE POINT FOR FURTHER DISCUSSION

Aristotle is a crucial reference point for virtue ethics and philosophical analyses of virtues.[11] At the same time, Aristotle is considered to represent the beginning of systematic economic thought.[12] Moreover, Aristotle has developed a sophisticated theory of rationality that is an important backdrop of both his virtue ethics and his economic theory.[13] In the following I demonstrate how far Aristotle provides a theoretical framework for the link between virtues and the economy, and in what way rationality—particularly Aristotle's definition of economic rationality—plays a crucial role for this linkage, which I will discuss by closely examining the role of the *logos* in Aristotle's conception of the economy. The results of this analysis of Aristotle's thought will serve for discussing implications for modern economics and economic virtues in the rest of the chapter.

1.1 Aristotle's conception of the economy

For Aristotle, the economy is an important basic sphere of human life. Aristotle considers the human being as a social being (*zoon politicon*) that, as such, has elementary needs. As a natural being (*zoon*), the human being has, like any other animal, the need for basic provisions such as shelter and food (*Pol* 1256a20ff). Moreover, as social beings, humans cannot live by themselves but necessarily require certain basic relationships with other humans. Humans, however, cannot address their need for provisions and basic relationships in a predetermined way as other (social) animals can by inborn instincts and given capacities. Humans are unique beings insofar as they are rational beings: they are the only beings that have the capacity of *logos* (reason, language) (*Pol* 1253a9). As such, humans address their basic needs by the faculties of the *logos*—by their rationality.

Sequentially, Aristotle understands the economy as the rational way of dealing with the basic needs of the human being as a social animal: the need for basic relationships with other humans and the need for basic provisions.[14] The crucial institution for the economy is the *oikos* (the household). With assistance of *logos*, the *oikos* gets a *nomos*, an order, which ensures the proper satisfaction of all elementary needs of the members of the household.[15]

Aristotle, however, has a rather differentiated conception of human rationality. *Logos* (reason) encompasses actually five different potentials: theoretical rationality (*episteme*), which is relevant for recognizing unchanging truth, such as in mathematical subjects; practical rationality (*technê*), which is relevant for knowing how to produce or create something, such as in art and crafts; practical wisdom (*phronēsis*) that guides how to act properly and live well; the overarching capacity of *nous*, the ability for insight into the first principles; and *sophia* (wisdom), which integrates episteme and nous (*NE* 1139b17–1143b17). Thus it is important to determine the rational abilities that are relevant for the economy. What exactly is the role of logos in the economy? How is economic rationality defined and how does it work in addressing the basic needs?

1.2 Aristotle on economic rationality

Aristotle defines economic rationality primarily by referring to *phronēsis*, practical wisdom. Aristotle considers the economy to be not a theoretical but a practical matter. Therefore, it is not theoretical rationality but practical rationality that is relevant. Moreover, Aristotle argues that economic activity is primarily defined by action and not by bringing forth, producing, or creating something (*Pol* 1258a19ff). Therefore, practical wisdom (*phronēsis*), not know-how (*technê*), is the primary rational ability that matters for the proper organization of the economy and guidance of economic activities (*NE* 1140b10).

Generally, Aristotle defines *phronēsis* as the rational ability by which one "is able to deliberate . . . what conduces to living well as a whole" (*NE* 1140a26). *Phronēsis* is "a true and practical state involving reason, concerned with what is good and bad for a human being" (*NE* 1140b5). While production (bringing forth) is focused on some end or product distinct of the activity by which the process of bringing forth is achieved, *phronēsis* focuses on activities themselves: "the end here is acting well itself" (*NE* 1140b7). With regard to the economy, the end of economic activity is not defined by achieving certain products or outcomes, but rather by acting well within the context of the economy. Excellent leaders are "practically wise [and] can see what is good for themselves and what is good for people in general; and we consider household managers . . . to be like this" (*NE* 1140b10). Economic rationality thus is the general ability of *phronēsis* applied to the specific situation and context of the household. Given this, however, economic rationality actually encompasses four tasks which must simultaneously be considered and integrated:

1. Taking into account and adequately developing and actualizing the general function of *phronēsis* as ability of ethical guidance with regard to virtue development, right actions, and good life.
2. Considering and adequately addressing the specific internal context of the household and its challenges.
3. Properly linking the household to the external context in which it is embedded (that is, the well-ordered community of the polis—the city-state) and considering the relevance of this external context for the well-ordered household and the well-being of its members.
4. Adequately utilizing further rational abilities that are relevant to satisfy the elementary needs in the economy.[16]

I discuss these four tasks and their challenges in more detail in the following four subsections.

1.2.1 *The general function of* phronēsis *and its relevance for ethics*

Economic rationality is based on *phronēsis* and requires the general development and use of this rational ability. The main task of *phronēsis* is to guide one's own development of ethical virtues and to ensure acting according to virtues in order to live well. Aristotle bases his considerations about virtues on a specific concept of the human soul and its distinct parts: a part of reason (*logos*) and a part of inborn desires and affects. In the latter part, Aristotle further distinguishes a part of desires, appetites, and emotions that can "obey and listen" to reason and a "vegetative part [that] has no share at all in reason" (*NE* 1102b28). Inborn desires, affects, and emotions can be educated over time and through experience and, by this, can be transformed into virtues, that is, excellent character traits (*NE* II). This is a practical matter, not a theoretical one, and *phronēsis* is the crucial ability of the logos that guides the process of virtue development and virtuous actions (*NE* 1107a1).

Phronēsis is a context-related rational ability in two respects. First, *phronēsis* must refer to each unique situation and train ethical virtues by reflecting on the attitude and action in relation to the situation. Second, the social context matters for the determination and development of ethical virtues. *Phronēsis* needs to refer to consultation and feedback on attitudes and actions from the societal framework in order to develop ethical virtues.[17] It is important to understand that *phronēsis* is not a given capacity of the mind, but rather an excellent trait (state) that also must be developed over time and, for this, experience and societal consultations are crucial.[18] Overall, *phronēsis* can be considered as ethical rationality insofar as it guides the development and actualization of ethical virtues. By this, *phronēsis* ultimately aims at living-well, as, for Aristotle, living-well is constituted by acting according to virtues.

Economic rationality is based on *phronēsis*; therefore, one needs to properly develop *phronēsis* in order to be able to decide and act economically rational. This means that economic rationality cannot be separated from ethical rationality and the overall development of *phronēsis* and virtues in the societal context of the *polis*. In other words, only the good citizen—in the sense of the person that has developed practical wisdom and virtues within the broader societal and political context—can be an excellent rational economic actor.

1.2.2 The internal function of economic rationality in the household

Economic rationality is *phronēsis* applied to the specific internal situation and challenges of the household. This means that economic rationality must address the main internal tasks of the household: proper development of its internal relationships, guidance of its members, and satisfaction of the basic needs. To realize these internal tasks in an excellent way, one must properly understand the role of *phronēsis* within the household, the characteristics of the specific relationships in the household, and the specific needs and capacities of its members.

For his conception of the internal function of economic rationality, Aristotle employs an analogy between the household and the soul: the head of the household, the household manager, is considered to be the "*logos*" of the household, and all other members must listen to him in order to develop themselves and the proper order of the household.[19] The head particularly guides the development of virtues of all members according to their roles in the household and their individual abilities and, with this, develops the basic relationships that define the household. For Aristotle, three basic relationships essential for humans as social beings are taken care of in the household and must be properly developed and guided by the household manager: the relationship between him and his wife (Aristotle considers the head to be male), between parents and children, and between master and slaves (*Pol* 1253b). Each relationship has its specific nature, and each partner of the different relationships must be guided according to his or her abilities for developing virtues and pursuing tasks. A particular aspect here is the education of children who, depending on age and ability, must develop different kinds of virtues. This is clearly a matter of practical wisdom: the right judgment of individual abilities and the ever-changing situations of education of children depending on age, individual character, and situation. With regard to the guidance of children, the household is an important place for the socialization of future adult members of the state.[20]

Aristotle considers the proper management of relationships and guidance of the development of the individual members as primary tasks and responsibilities of the household manager and the economy (*Pol* 1259b19f). In addition, the economy is about the acquisition of goods and the just distribution of goods and tasks in the household according to each member's abilities and claims. Overall, household management is a specifically ethical matter of guiding virtue development and realizing justice in the household and its constituting basic relationships.

However, neither justice nor virtues can be defined and developed within the context of the household alone, but only with regard to the societal context in which the household and the economy is embedded, that is, with reference to the *polis*. Likewise, not all basic needs can be satisfied within the household; the household depends on external acquisitions and protection, for which the broader context of the *polis* is crucial. Therefore, the household manager must consider the external relations of the household and how to properly refer to them in order to internalize justice, virtues, and means in the household.

1.2.3 The external function of economic rationality regarding the context and societal embedment of the household

Economic rationality has to consider both how to link the household properly to the external context in which it is embedded as well as the relevance of this external context for the well-ordered household and the well-being of its members. The relevant external context for the economy is the societal community of the *polis* (*Pol* 1260b15–30). Virtues and justice can only be determined and developed in the *polis*, and individual good life can only be realized within the *polis*. The meaning and function of the economy, the proper management of the economy, and what is economically rational can ultimately only be determined in the context of the *polis*. The head of the household must refer to and participate in the societal life of the *polis*, and must make sure that he translates the general ethical principles of the polis properly into the economy. Only this secures right guidance of virtue development and just distribution in the household. In this regard it is important to recognize that the meaning of *logos* is also speech or language. *Logos* does not only refer to the mind's internal capacity for reflection—that is, to reason—but also to the external possibility of reflection—that is, to consultation and discussion with other members of the community based on the human capacities of speech and language.[21] External consultation and advice on one's actions and attitudes play a crucial part in the determination and individual development of virtues in a community, and the *polis* is the broader framework that matters for the general definition of virtues that the household manager needs to transfer to the household.

Furthermore, the household needs external protection, which is also guaranteed by the *polis*, and external acquisitions of goods that cannot be produced by the household itself (*Pol* 1321b 15). With regard to the acquisition of goods, Aristotle argues that there is a limit to means and that acquisition is not, and should not, become an end in itself, but instead must always be oriented on what is necessary for living well, that is, what is necessary for developing and acting according to virtues (*Pol* 1256b26–35). However, there is no objectively defined "set" of such necessary means, and Aristotle recognizes that one may need substantial means to act virtuously in society (*NE* 1178a,b). The consideration of the right balance—the proper amount of means—is a matter of practical wisdom which considers the role of goods and means for a good life. Therefore, Aristotle distinguishes a necessary (natural) art of acquisition that is limited and is part of household management from an unnecessary art of acquisition, that is, money-making, which is unlimited and should not be considered an economic task (*Pol* 1256a–1259a). Aristotle thinks that the latter misses the ultimate goal of a good life, which the economy must ultimately serve. Money-making actually can endanger a good life and the stability of the society if it becomes an end in itself. In this case money-making serves no other end and has no limit, and it becomes an expression of *pleonexia* (insatiability, voracity), a dangerous vice (*NE* 1129a 36ff). *Pleonexia* is in contrast to self-sufficiency, which Aristotle considers a crucial characteristic of happiness and good life. Also, *pleonexia* endangers the stability and justice of society. Aristotle considers the overall amount of goods that nature provides for humans to be limited and the person who wants to have more and more takes something away from others. There is a danger of confusing means and ends and missing the ultimate ends of the economy: "some persons are led to believe that making money is the object of household management, and that the whole idea of their lives is that they ought to increase their money without limit, or at any rate not to lose it. The origin of this disposition on men is that they are intent upon living only, and not upon living well" (*Pol* 1258b40).

1.2.4 *Utilizing further rational abilities under the guidance of* phronēsis

Economic rationality must bring the economy into orientation with the ultimate end of a good life within a stable and just society, and must carefully consider what means need to be acquired to serve this end. This is a matter of *phronēsis*. However, for the acquisition and generation of the means itself, other rational abilities are relevant. Aristotle mentions the important role of *technê* (know-how) in this regard. The good household manager must develop a rational ability for, and knowledge of, trade and production. Aristotle considers both trading and producing goods arts, and therefore the relevant rational ability for succeeding in both is *technê*, which is a rational ability to be trained over time and through experience in doing those activities. The household manager particularly must acquire knowledge about potential opportunities of buying and selling, and must have know-how in basic areas of production, such as agriculture, fishery, forestry, and mining (*Pol* 1258b12ff), and recognize "universal economic laws," such as the mechanisms of monopoly (*Pol* 1259a5–35). With regard to such universal economic laws, *sophia* (wisdom) is the rational ability that is needed to recognize them and, with this, *nous* (the ability to understand the first principles) and *episteme* (the ability to recognize universal, unchanging laws) are relevant.[22] This comes closer to the approach of modern economics and its understanding of economic rationality. However, the roles of *technê* and *episteme* in the economy are limited. *Technê* and *episteme* can only fruitfully serve the economy under the lead of *phronēsis*. They are additive rational elements that contribute to economic rationality, of which *phronēsis* constitutes the core part.

2. RECONSIDERING ECONOMIC THEORY AND ECONOMIC VIRTUES IN LIGHT OF ARISTOTLE

There is no distinct theory or substantial research explicitly addressing the role of virtues for economic decisions and actions within mainstream economics. I will argue that this is not an accidental neglect but reflects a systematic inability of economics to address virtues grounded in the methodological foundation of standard economic theory,[23] more precisely, in its modeling of the economic actor and specific definition of economic rationality.[24] Established economics considers economic actors as *rational utility maximizers*. Rationality here means the ability of the economic actor to completely and consistently order its own preferences[25] and to maximize its own utility function with regard to given constraints.[26] The origin, formation, justification, and content of preferences are not considered to be the subject matter of economics. Rather, in economic theory, preferences are taken as given. Furthermore, preferences are considered to be independent: they are not influenced by the preferences of other individuals and, thus, in particular, are independent of the societal contexts and communities of which the individual is part.

These assumptions about the economic actor are not a sufficient theoretical basis for analyzing the formation and role of virtues in economic actions and decisions. To refer to virtues in economic actions would require considering either the impact of economic actions on the formation of specific durable preferences or a conception of character formation that influences the rational decision-making process and behavior in economic settings. This would require considering a conception of development of economic character and individual decision capacity over time and through experience—a conception of a broader "rationality" as a personal capacity that guides economic actions. This is beyond the standard economic theory that assumes economic actors and their basic characteristics as given in a static sense. Economic actors do not "develop" rationality or preferences—they simply *are* rational and *have* preferences (in the economic sense), both of which completely define the character and identity of the actor in economic theory. Thus, standard economics cannot capture the idea of development of character (including rationality and preferences) and the guidance of actions by formed character traits, which are important elements of virtue theory. Also economic theory relies on the independence of preferences, which neglects the relevance of societal contexts of practice that are crucial for most virtue ethics theories.

The rationality assumptions of standard economic theory outlined above are an important theoretical basis of economics. However, there has also been substantial research within economics on alternative rationality conceptions, particularly in the field of behavioral economics. This has led to variations, extensions, or alternatives of the standard economic rationality concept, particularly in terms of bounded rationality.[27] Research on bounded rationality has prominent roots in the work of Herbert Simon.[28] With regard to this tradition, "the term *bounded rationality*... refers to the rational principles that underlie nonoptimizing adaptive behavior of real people."[29] Standard economic rationality assumes that human actors engage in a full optimization calculus that requires a huge amount of information (about given alternatives, prices, constraints, probabilities of outcomes, and so forth) in order to determine an economic decision and pursue an economic action. Theories of bounded rationality, in contrast, model more simple rational decision procedures that can be observed empirically: for instance, simplified heuristic procedures that base rational decisions on a few observable parameters. Gigerenzer and Selten provide a basic example for heuristic rationality with reference to baseball. A player who wants to catch a ball that comes in high does not decide the direction and speed of his running using a complex theoretical calculation of the course of the ball based on physical laws and data, such as speed and spin of the ball, wind speed, and so forth. Rather, he operates with a simple heuristic: "he adjusts [his] running speed so that the angle of gaze—the angle between the eye and the ball—remains constant."[30] It is not theoretical rationality and optimization that matter here but *practical* rationality. In terms of Aristotle, this rationality could be considered *technê* (know-how), a practical rational ability which someone develops over time through experience and training.

However, approaches to economic decision-making processes that refer to bounded rationality are more complex. Herbert Simon considers a heuristic process of searching alternatives of action instead of decisions about a given set of alternatives.[31] An economic actor will search for possible actions or decisions until she finds a satisficing alternative that meets or exceeds a targeted aspiration level, rather than trying to conduct an overall maximization exercise considering all possible alternatives and outcomes. However, bounded rationality also includes the rational ability to adjust the aspiration level throughout the process of searching by the information gained about available alternatives.[32] This more complex bounded rationality, which would be typical for, say, executive decision-making processes, includes the rational ability for finding fruitful alternatives, judging about satisficing, and judging if the goals themselves are appropriate. This ability seems more comparable to Aristotle's concept of practical wisdom, by which such judgments can be made in light of what is good for the entire firm with regard to the specific context and also by consultation with other executives.

The term "bounded rationality" is, thus, misleading, suggesting some kind of a restricted version of an ideal economic rationality. This certainly reflects the original motivation of Herbert Simon, who considered bounded rationality to be an answer of humans to their "cognitive limitations . . . of both knowledge and computational capacity" and, thus, an answer to their inability to base decisions on full rational optimization.[33] From an Aristotelian perspective, however, bounded rationality should clearly be considered a different *type* of rational ability, practical rather than theoretical, and it would make sense to conceptualize bounded rationality with reference to the concept of practical wisdom.[34]

Bounded rationality comes close to Aristotle's conception of economic rationality and might be a fruitful basis for developing a modern economic theory of economic virtues that could be linked to a modern virtue ethics theory. Some relevant characteristics of bounded rationality are the consideration of contexts of action, judgment about goals and satisficing levels, development of heuristic strategies, and learning through experience. For economics and psychology (and related fields), several empirical questions would be of interest. How does bounded rationality develop over time in different economic and non-economic contexts? Is there a correlation between bounded rationalities observed in different areas of action? Is the ability of bounded rationality correlated with the possession of certain character traits? Answers to these questions could lead to an economic theory of economic virtues, a theory that could analyze and explain the emergence and role of specific virtues in economic contexts and the influence of virtues on the decision-making processes and actions of economic actors.

If bounded rationality can be linked to a virtue theory and to virtue ethics, this could also provide a broader framework that explains the motivation and guidance of bounded rationality procedures for which Gigerenzer and Selten are asking. They assume that individuals possess an "adaptive toolbox," a bundle of heuristics they can choose from and apply to a specific context to make fast and frugal decisions about actions. As they write, this "bundle of heuristics in an adaptive toolbox is orchestrated by some mechanism reflecting the importance of conflicting motivations and goals. This mechanism is not yet well understood."[35] The missing element here might be practical wisdom, which does not merely refer to the situation itself, but also to the overall context of action and life and to guiding normative principles—for instance, some overarching principle of the good. The link to practical wisdom would also provide a theoretical framework for explaining the very "processes of goal formation, construction of alternatives and expectation formation" in decision-making processes.[36]

However, the concepts of virtues and virtue ethics have largely been neglected in most behavioral and experimental economics research, although the conception of virtues could prove fruitful for explaining and understanding economic behavior and its ethical aspects. This holds, for instance, for studies about the role of fairness in economic decisions, a prominent topic in behavioral and experimental economics. Matthew Rabin characterizes fairness exhibited in situations such as the ultimatum game as an "emotion" that is somehow irrational with respect to standard economic rationality.[37] A virtue ethics perspective would explain fairness as a character trait that has developed through the interplay of emotional prepositions and practical wisdom in contexts of practice and community. This would shift the perspective of economic analyses to more systematic studies of the role of virtues in economic systems.

The concept of virtue and the virtue ethics framework could also be of interest for empirical business ethics. In an outline of future research questions in business ethics, Trevino and Weaver state "current models of ethical decision-making behavior . . . focus primarily on ethical judgment and ethical action, neglecting moral awareness, recognition or sensitivity, moral motivation, and moral character. Therefore, future research will need to test more complex models."[38] As they continue on the same page:

> We should also recognize that current ethical decision making and behavior models are highly cognitive in nature . . . however, emotions or affect is likely to

> play a larger role than it has been given credit for in the past. Ethical decision making is not as cold and calculating as these models suggest. Positive emotions, such as joy, pride, and hope, and negative emotions, such as anxiety, guilt, and fear are likely to play a significant role in these processes and may be associated with multiple stages of the ethical decision-making process.[39]

Virtue ethics can provide a theoretical background for further research, particularly as virtue ethics integrates emotions and rationality into a force of ethical motivation and, along with this, provides a theory for the role of personal character within organizations and ethical decision-making processes.

Normative frameworks are difficult to recognize in research that focuses on empirical aspects of human decision-making processes, but they could provide an important supplement to empirical theories of bounded rationality. Normative frameworks need not be virtue ethics frameworks, but virtue ethics seems to be a good fit to bounded rationality concepts and can particularly be fruitful for research that struggles with the impact of emotions and rationality on economic decision-making processes. Combining virtue ethics and bounded rationality research with regard to further empirical analyses of the role of ethics for economic decisions could become a model for the combination of empirical and normative ethical studies that has been asked for in the field of business ethics and is a general need in future applied ethics.

3. MODERN ECONOMIC SPHERES, INDIVIDUAL VIRTUES, AND SELF-IDENTITY

What is the contribution of economic spheres of life and action to the overall development of individual virtues? How does this contribution fit into the contribution of other spheres of life and action? How can we ensure compatibility and avoid problematic frictions? These are important questions from an Aristotelian perspective, especially if we assume a broader context of life and action beyond the economic sphere, and assume also a normative reference point of the good to which all virtues contribute in an integrated and harmonious way. However, before discussing the above questions under these assumptions, it is important to reflect on the influence economic activity and economic theory has on the individual, if there is no broader framework defined—if economic aspects are, or become, the entire horizon of individual development and self-identity. This is a pathological but crucial case for current virtue ethics and the modern economy.

As argued above, virtues are not an explicit subject matter of standard economic theory. However, the standard economic conceptions of the human actor and rationality nevertheless matter for virtue ethics insofar as there is a substantial impact of the theoretical economic model on individual life and self-identity as well as on societal interactions. Theories of social sciences are not neutral tools of analysis and explanation, but potentially influence the subject matter itself. This holds particularly for economic theory, which has become rather influential in policy advice, public discourses, and education. The economic model of the human actor, *homo economicus*, is a theoretical model that cannot refer to virtues and, one might say, cannot develop virtues in a broader sense. However, the *homo economicus* model can influence the self-understanding and actions of individuals and, by this, may become a kind of virtue—a character trait and identity—by itself. Self-interested utility maximization may become a normative concept, and people may train themselves to approximate "perfect" rational utility maximizers. This way, the theoretical model of the *homo economicus*, constructed for the purpose of explaining economic interaction results by mathematical analysis, transforms into a practical guidance or a model for character-formation and self-identity. Economic theory may claim that it merely *assumes* an individual acts as *homo economicus* and does not imply that he or she actually *is homo economicus*.[40] However, in practice, the economic theory may nevertheless result in an individual (aiming at) becoming *homo economicus*. Recent empirical research has shown that economic rationality and characteristic features of *homo economicus* can be trained and developed over time, for example by teaching economics.[41] This means that being economically rational (even in the sense of standard economics) is a kind of character trait or capacity of the mind that is developed over time, similar to virtues of thought in an Aristotelian sense (as described in Section 1.2.1).

It is also important to note that some economists consider the conception of economic rationality to be a general conception of human rationality that guides all human decisions and actions. A prominent example is the Nobel laureate Gary Becker, who expanded the economic theory of rational decision to the sphere of general life and action, which serves to transform economic theory into a universal theory of rational decision and human action.[42] This, however, could be considered a problematic reduction of the human being against broader theories of human existence and life, including most conceptions of virtue ethics.

A large part of the philosophical tradition and of the history of economic thought assumed that the economic sphere is part of a broader set of spheres of human life and actions, which are distinct from economic thought and actions. Among the thinkers that share this position is also Adam Smith, whose *The Wealth of Nations* is considered an important source of modern economic thought.[43] Considering economic action as part of a more complex human existence naturally raises the question of what is the exact place of the economic dimension within the other dimensions of human life, and the history of philosophy and economic thought offers a variety of more or less sophisticated answers to this question.

In terms of virtue ethics, one may reformulate the question as follows: How do economic actions and spheres contribute to the overall set of virtues and ultimately to an overarching conception of the good? However, today we cannot reasonably identify *one* clearly determined economic sphere of which individuals are part, such as Aristotle did with the *oikos*. Rather, we are confronted with many overlapping economic spheres in which individuals participate and act, and which are all relevant for individual virtues and self-identity. On the micro-level, individuals are members of one or more economic organizations. For instance, one may be an employee, consultant, board member, or volunteer of one or more companies or corporations. The cultures of such organizations differ substantially, and individuals can have different roles and positions in an organization. The specific cultural context and the specifics of a role and position matter for the definition of individual excellence and the development of individual virtues and self-identity. This has been discussed, for example by Richard Solomon, who put a particular emphasis on the context of the development of specific business virtues and on the question of how such business virtues may fit into overall individual integrity.[44]

On the macro-level, individuals participate in local and global market systems as consumers, employees, business owners, entrepreneurs, creditors, or debtors. McCloskey recently argued that the capitalist market economy has an overall positive impact on the development—or at least the support—of certain individual virtues such as prudence, temperance, and courage.[45] However, this is a rather optimistic perspective that ignores potential reductionist impacts of the market on individuals, such as the impact of consumerism[46] or the self-fulfillment of the *homo economicus* discussed at the beginning of this section.

The crucial aspect regarding an analysis of individual virtues, their relation to economic spheres of action, and related questions of personal integrity is the identification and analysis of the set of economic spheres relevant to (certain groups of) individuals. The multitude and overlapping of several economic spheres is a complicated matter of integration. This comes also back to the question of rationality, because the judgment of the relevance of the spheres, and how to order them and relate them to an overarching conception of good life and individual excellence, seems also to be a matter of practical wisdom. However, what matters here even more is not the set of economic spheres and their specific constitution, but moreover the embedment of economic spheres into broader frameworks of communities against which the cultures and demands of economic spheres can reasonably be reflected, and virtues be developed.

Crucial from a virtue ethics perspective is the reference point of a conception of individual excellence and the good, which is neither merely subjective (as economic theory assumes) nor reasonably definable within an economic sphere alone, but requires the reference to a broader context. Thus, we need to explore the frameworks of modern economic spheres, and modern shared conceptions of excellence and the good within such frameworks.

4. RELEVANT FRAMEWORKS OF MODERN ECONOMIC SPHERES

Aristotelian virtue ethics considers a broader societal sphere—a broader community—as crucial for the determination and development of individual virtues. A limited system, such as the *oikos* or a modern company, is by itself not a sufficient community for determining and developing virtues, because such limited systems lack sufficient internal free and independent reflection and consultation and have a narrow focus on specific internal (business) purposes rather than on an overarching (societal) good. In Aristotle, the crucial broader community for virtue development is the *polis*, although the context that is relevant for the modern economy and economic actor is certainly no longer the small *polis* Aristotle had in mind. However, one may ask if there are any modern equivalents to the *polis*, modern societal spheres in which economic spheres are embedded and which are the ultimate reference points for human excellence. This seems to be more difficult to determine with regard to today's complex and global economy. Also, the relationship between economic spheres and broader societal contexts can be expected to be more complex than the *oikos–polis* relation in Aristotle's thought.

A company, as a specific and rather clearly defined economic sphere, is part of the society and, increasingly, multiple societies in which it operates. By this, the definition of virtues cannot, and does not, happen in isolation within a company, but in reference to external societal relationships of the company. The relevance of the entire web of societal and global relationships of a company for conducting business has been prominently addressed by *stakeholder theory*, originally developed by Edward Freeman.[47] Freeman argues that modern business is not a matter of analytical optimization under constraints (including societal and ethical requirements), but rather a matter of active interaction with all *stakeholders* of a company, all groups that have a legitimate stake in (claim to) the company. Stakeholders could be employees, unions, investors, shareholders, communities, suppliers, NGOs, and so forth.

From a virtue ethics perspective the concept of stakeholders provides an ethically relevant modern framework of business. Stakeholder management is active management of the relationships with external groups, and altogether stakeholders represent a kind of external reflection and consulting space for business similar to the *polis* in Aristotle. To a certain degree, stakeholder management coordinates internal and external relationships, values and virtues, and minimizes problematic frictions (problematic for the individuals but also for the success of the business itself). The internal constitution and culture of the organization, as well as the values and identities of its members, are constantly related to the external community of stakeholders of the organization and challenged by external perspectives. In this process, however, companies and corporations are not just passively reacting to the external framework, and transferring values or virtues from the external framework to their internal system. Rather, the organization actively participates in, and contributes to, the determination and development of virtues, norms, and values in the broader stakeholder community. An interesting case is global players, international companies that operate in many countries all over the world. Such companies must integrate many different perspectives from a huge number of stakeholders in different cultures. One may say that this integration and the resulting formation of an internal culture and values contribute to a globally oriented business ethos of the corporation.[48] This can then also have effects on the societies and stakeholders in which the corporation operates.

Modern economic spheres, even if we just focus on a company as a clearly defined small sphere, turn out to have a rather complex external framework in which they are embedded and operate. Stakeholder theory is a helpful instrument for identifying and analyzing the relevant external (potentially global) framework of a company, and could be made fruitful for virtue ethics considerations. However, there are other crucial economic spheres of individual life and action that are more difficult and complex. If we consider, for instance, consumption and the related economic spheres in which most individuals participate, we are faced with the sphere of global markets. As consumers, we participate in (a rather large subset) of the global economy, and any precise definition of our global relations in this regard seems to be impossible. It is also difficult to define a broader societal framework in which global markets are embedded. Global markets cross through many different societal and political systems rather than being embedded in one. Therefore, a state or nation is not the relevant framework of global markets. The modern global economy could better be considered as a sphere on its own than a subset of any clearly defined societal framework. There seems to be no modern equivalent or modification of the *oikos–polis* hierarchy that fits this case, and this certainly is a challenge for virtue ethics.

It is important to consider here the perspective of modern economics that provides an elaborated approach to the sphere of markets, which also has practical (political and ethical) implications. At its core, modern economics offers an *invisible-hand explanation* of the market system: all individuals in the market focus on their own preferences and the maximization of their own utility functions, and this automatically results in a social optimum (defined as a Pareto optimum) if the market functions properly.[49] This is one of the most fundamental results of neoclassical welfare economics and the underlying reason for a broad range of policies that focus on market solutions or the curing of market failures. Philosophically this result implies that neither individuals nor politics need to care about details of coordination of the economy and the complex activities within, because the market mechanism itself coordinates the efficient production and distribution of goods and the satisfaction of the various individuals' needs. Individuals can, and should, concentrate on their own interests and preferences and on maximizing their own utility or gain, which will then automatically result in a social optimum. Politics has only to deal with possible market failures, such as those related to public goods, externalities, and so on. In other words, politics has a mere supportive function to markets.

I call this conception of economic markets the specific expression of *systemic rationality*, referring to my general definition of rationality as the ability to be in accordance with *ratio*, here understood as *calculable order* (as discussed above). The market system is rational insofar as it orders the complexity of individual interests and actions in a (calculable) way so that the overall result is Pareto efficient. With this groundbreaking conception of systemic rationality, economics offers a theoretical model that guarantees the overall integration of the economy into societies. It is often not recognized that modern economics provides such a concept of systemic economic rationality (based on its specific conception of individual rationality), and that this perhaps is the most important achievement and contribution of modern economics.[50] However, to think that individual rationality of *homo economicus*, together with systemic economic rationality, would be sufficient for guiding and maintaining economic spheres and integrating them into broader societal contexts, would be a problematic conclusion. Pareto efficiency is not a sufficient or ultimate norm for the economy or the society, and in particular it says nothing about justice and other ethical principles relevant for economic distribution. Also, neither individual nor systemic economic rationality refer to the importance of virtues in supporting and maintaining economic spheres, which McCloskey (for one) intensively discusses.[51] One may even argue that mere *homines economici* will undermine or destroy any system in the long run if there is no expanded further motivation of action or corrective mechanism that supports the system.[52]

Systemic rationality may be an important aspect of modern economic rationality, and the respective design of economic spheres, such as markets, is probably an essential element of a future economy. However, systemic rationality is only one aspect of the rationality of economic spheres, a simplification that must be supplemented by other systemic and individual rational elements. A more abstract solution for an external framework for global markets and the underlying economic rationality would be to embed economic rationality into other layers of rationality that can be actualized on a global scale. Habermas, for example, offers a theoretical framework for such a broader systemic solution.[53] Communicative rationality could reflect on economic rationality and its ultimate purposes on the scale of local and global discourses. This would at least mirror an aspect of the role of *logos* in Aristotle's considerations: the external reflection and consultations that matter for virtue development, although in Habermas this remains on the level of theoretical argument and does not necessarily involve practical wisdom. The problem with such an approach of framing economic spheres is that it actually conserves economic rationality as it is, and says nothing about the role and emergence of economic virtues and their function in economic actions and decision-making.

5. SHARED CONCEPTIONS OF EXCELLENCE AND THE GOOD, NEW CHALLENGES OF THE ECONOMY OF THE TWENTY-FIRST CENTURY, AND THE EXAMPLE OF SUSTAINABILITY

The modern economy and its development since industrialization may be considered a success story in terms of material wealth, at least for part of the world (mainly the northern hemisphere). However, this story has always had its shadow sides that have been criticized. Rising concerns about environmental and social issues (both local and global) in recent decades may make us wonder if this success story is about to come to an end, and if there is the need for remodeling the economic system to meet future economic challenges. A perspective that expresses this concern and exhibits future challenges is expressed by the concept of *sustainability*, which has emerged since the 1980s and has led to various societal, political, and global discourses. I have argued elsewhere that sustainability entails a new normative claim that can be interpreted as leading to new, broadly shared global conceptions of excellence and the good.[54] I will outline this in brief and use it as an example to demonstrate how a modern (Aristotelian) virtue ethics approach can open up new perspectives on the relation between virtues and the economy and, with this, can contribute to the development of the future economy.

The concept of sustainability has spread since the 1980s into various societal, political, and academic discourses. Despite the large variety of use and specific definitions, one can identify three core elements of its meaning. First, sustainability is about the ability to maintain something, such as a process, entity, or system. Second, sustainability has a normative and evaluative meaning (at least in its usage in public and political discourses) in that it is typically considered to be something positive that one should strive for.

Third, sustainability is a relational concept, referring to the relationship between contemporaries, future generations, and nature.[55] The relational dimension of the sustainability concept allows us to further exhibit the normative and evaluative dimension of the concept. Sustainability is good not because we consider the maintenance of something (or everything) in itself to be good, but rather because we consider the maintaining of certain systems, processes, and entities to be good with regard to the relationship among contemporaries, future generations, and nature. Prominent examples are the maintaining of crucial ecosystems and its services, or the maintaining of a stable economy.

From a philosophical perspective, the modern sustainability concept implicitly entails a specific underlying conception of the human being and, by this, implicitly suggests a fundamental paradigm shift with regard to the self-identity and understanding of the modern individual. Sustainability puts the dominant ideal of the modern autonomous individual—which the modern economy and modern economics is essentially based on and supportive of—into question.[56] In its place, sustainability suggests a new normative orientation, a reconsideration of humans as fundamental relational and dependent beings—as timely, socially, and naturally contingent beings. The normative question related to this view of the human being is: How should one act and live as such a fundamentally relational being? This question I call the basic question of *sustainability ethics*.

The virtue ethics formulation of the sustainability ethics questions is: What is human excellence if the human being is understood in this way as a fundamental relational being? I have argued elsewhere that one can deduce a set of *sustainability virtues* that determine excellence in this context and allow one to realize the fundamental relationships of sustainability in an excellent way.[57] The sustainability virtues include basic relational virtues of attentiveness and receptiveness that are crucial for the flourishing of any relationship, as well as a set of more specific virtues such as respect, care, and responsibility, each with respect to natural entities, other contemporaries, and future generations.[58] The rational ability involved in the development of sustainability virtues is a kind of enlightened practical wisdom. This rational ability is based on practical wisdom, which refers to concrete experiences of relationships with natural entities, children as the immediate future generation, and other contemporaries (locally and globally) to guide the development and actualization of sustainability virtues. Enlightened means that, in addition, one needs the ability to reflect on the general relational characteristics of human existence and the resulting ethical implications. The individual who develops, in this way, excellence and self-identity as a relational being, I call a *sustainable person*.

Against the backdrop of sustainability ethics and the concept of the sustainable person, the crucial question regarding the economy concerns the relation between sustainability virtues and the economy: Is the existing economy with its underlying theoretical and ideological foundations compatible with sustainable persons and sustainability virtues? Or do we need some adjustments and modification of the economy? It is important to recognize here that sustainability implies new challenges and normative questions that go beyond traditional economic thought and political philosophy. The primary traditional question was: What is the meaning of the economy for the individual and for the society? The related normative question was: How has the economy to be organized so that it has the best possible positive function for the individual and the society? With regard to sustainability, additional questions are crucial that are new or at least of new relevance for the current and future economy: What is the meaning of the economy for the global community, future generations, and nature? What would be a good way to organize the economy so that it has the best possible overall function for contemporaries, future generations and nature? With regard to the virtue ethics framework formulated above, the question is: What economy would support sustainable persons and their virtues best (or, what would an economy look like in which sustainable persons act and decide)? An economy that would be simultaneously oriented towards the welfare of contemporaries (globally), future generations, and nature, and support the development (and would consequently be an actualization) of sustainable persons, I call a *sustainable economy*.

With regard to these new challenges and the concept of a sustainable economy, the established conceptualization of the economy and its theoretical underpinning in modern economics, including its concepts of the economic actor and individual and systemic economic rationality, comes to its limits. The conception of the economic actor with its self-related and isolated focus on own preferences and utility is not only inapplicable for addressing the topic of economic virtues, but a particularly unsuitable basis for the sustainable person, who essentially acts and decides as a relational, interdependent being. Also, sustainability overburdens the established economic concept of systemic rationality. Considering Pareto efficiency in the context of sustainability would require adequately representing the utility functions of global contemporaries, future generations, and non-human beings, as well as all external effects in this broad framework—which is not possible on the basis of established theory and available information.[59]

Overall, the core of the modern conceptualization of the economy is that the economic system balances the specific rational self-interests of the participating individuals in an elegant way by the systemic rationality of markets with resulting maximal overall welfare. However, if one expands the context considerably with regard to the sustainability framework, the problematic limits of this conceptualization and its underlying premises become obvious: the modern conceptualization of the economy centers on contemporaries able to participate in it and incorporate their self-interests and individual preferences. Non-human beings and future individuals cannot do so and, due to lack of capability, many contemporaries cannot either.

McCloskey's bourgeois virtues seem to be old-fashioned in the sustainability context, too.[60] They may have been important for the "Age of Commerce," but are insufficient for a new "Age of Sustainability" and a future sustainable economy. Bourgeois virtues by themselves will not support the development of a future sustainable economy; they would need to be substantially modified to become related to the broader sustainability context. For instance, justice would need to be extended to future generations and nature, which is a substantial modification of the traditional virtue of justice.[61] Ultimately, bourgeois virtues would need to be supplemented by sustainability virtues and the ideal of a sustainable person for developing a sustainable economy in the light of excellent relationships with the global community, future generations, and nature.

The Aristotelian framework has been considerably modified in my consideration of sustainability virtues and a sustainable economy, but has still been fruitful for structuring the problem and providing insights. The virtue ethics framework has been extended to capture the new normative frame and the characteristics and challenges of the modern economy. The human being is no longer understood as a social rational animal in the sense of Aristotle, but rather as a threefold relational being, as the sustainability concept suggests. The relevant community, originally conceptualized as *polis*, has been considerably expanded, now a global community including nature, non-human beings, and future generations. This constitutes the relevant expanded framework for current and future economic spheres, in which virtues and rationality must be re-oriented.

6. CONCLUSION

The relationship between virtues and economic spheres is an important topic at the intersection of ethics and economics. Thorough analysis of this subject matter can generate a better understanding of the dynamic interrelation between individual actor's virtues and economic behavior, how economic behavior is influenced by economic actors' virtues, and what economic spheres mean for the development of individual virtues, excellence and self-identity. Considering virtue ethics in economic thought can also provide a conceptual basis to reflect on the role of economic spheres in broader normative societal contexts and on possible new normative frameworks for the future economy.

This topic is a challenge for both economics and virtue ethics, challenging the perspectives and methodology of both fields and calling for the development of a new systematic framework of analysis. I have argued that the concept of rationality is crucial for such a framework. A more encompassing definition of economic rationality can provide the methodological basis for a systematic, coherent theory for the relationship between virtues and economic spheres. The systematic analysis of this relationship in an integrated way can lead to broader perspectives on, and better understanding of, the normative dimensions of the economy, and can generate new concepts and ideas to deal with current and future economic issues.

A common approach to considering recent economic crises in the U.S. and Europe is to refer to the established concept of the economy and aim to better implement it in the real world. According to this perspective, something is wrong in the real world compared to established patterns of economic thought and action, and one must better implement perfect global markets and eliminate market failures to overcome economic issues; or, in the perspective of McCloskey, we need to reaffirm the core virtues of capitalism that fostered economic success and development in the past. However, the alternative hypothesis is that there is not so much wrong with reality today, but rather something wrong with our concepts of the economy and the established economic patterns of thought and action, which simply do not fit the current economic situation and the new challenges and normative requirements of the economy going forward. A virtue ethics perspective can contribute to a critical reflection and reconsideration of the current economy and can lead to a new perspective on the economy and its normative elements and meaning. In this way, virtue ethics can stimulate a fruitful discourse about the future of the economy and its ethical orientation.

NOTES

1. Christian Becker, "Foundations of Business Ethics: Considerations on the methodology of business ethics and the roles of philosophy and economics within." *SSRN Discussion Paper*, 2011, <http://ssrn.com/abstract=1773174>, p. 9.
2. Robert C. Solomon, *Ethics and Excellence: Cooperation and Integrity in Business* (Oxford: Oxford University Press, 1992), p. 192.
3. Alasdair MacIntyre, *After Virtue. A Study in Moral Theory* (Notre Dame: University of Notre Dame Press, 1981), chapter 14. MacIntyre provides the following general definition of a virtue: "A virtue is an acquired human quality the possession and exercise of which tends to enable us to achieve those goods which are internal to practices and the lack of which effectively prevents us from achieving any such good" (ibid., 191). "Practice" here means "any coherent and complex form of socially established cooperative human activity" that aims at specific goods that are achieved by standards of excellence internal to the activity (ibid., 187).
4. See also Solomon, *Ethics and Excellence*, 107ff.

5. Ibid., 207ff.
6. Deirdre McCloskey, *The Bourgeois Virtues: Ethics for an Age of Commerce* (Chicago: University of Chicago Press, 2006), 66 and 507f.
7. Tim Kasser, *The High Price of Materialism* (Cambridge, MA: The MIT Press, 2002).
8. For example, see Taya R. Cohen, A.T. Panter, and Nazli Turan, "Guilt Proneness and Moral Character," *Current Directions in Psychological Science* 21(2012): 355–9.
9. Werner Güth, Rolf Schmittberger, and Bernd Schwarze, "An Experimental Analysis of Ultimatum Bargaining," *Journal of Economic Behavior and Organization* 3(1982): 367–88.
10. My position regarding Aristotle is in line with existing literature that also states a strong link between Aristotle's economic and ethical thought, such as Amartya Sen, *On Ethics and Economics* (Malden, MA: Blackwell, 1987), 3–4; Peter Koslowski, *Politik und Ökonomie bei Aristoteles*, 3rd ed. (Tübingen: Mohr, 1993), and *Die Ordnung der Wirtschaft* (Tübingen: Mohr, 1994), chapter 1; and Irene van Staveren, *The Values of Economics: An Aristotelian Perspective* (London: Routledge, 2001); but it is in contrast with few others who do not see a strong link, such as Scott Meikle, *Aristotle's Economic Thought* (Oxford: Oxford University Press, 1995), 108f. My contribution to this topic is the detailed demonstration of how the link between Aristotle's ethics and economic thought is established by Aristotle's specific definition of economic rationality.
11. Roger Crisp and Michael Slote (eds.), *Virtue Ethics* (Oxford: Oxford University Press, 1997); Stephen Darwall (ed.), *Virtue Ethics* (Oxford: Blackwell, 2002).
12. Bertram Schefold, "Aristoteles: Der Klassiker des antiken Wirtschaftsdenkens," in Hellmut Flashar et al., *Aristoteles und seine "Politik"* (Düsseldorf: Verlag Wirtschaft und Finanzen, 1992), 19–70; Meikle, *Aristotle's Economic Thought*, 1.
13. Aristotle, *Nicomachean Ethics*, Roger Crisp (trans. and ed.) (Cambridge: Cambridge University Press, 2000), book VI. Throughout this section, references to the *Nicomachean Ethics* will appear in the text with the designation *NE*; likewise, references to Aristotle's *Politics* (trans. Benjamin Jowett, Oxford: Oxford University Press, 1905) will be designated by *Pol.*
14. Christian Becker, "Logos und Wirtschaft bei Aristoteles: Ein dogmenhistorischer Beitrag zur Diskussion des ökonomischen Rationalitätsbegriffes," *Archives for Philosophy of Law and Social Philosophy* 95(2009): 523–39.
15. I focus in this chapter only on those aspects of Aristotle's economic thought that are crucial for my analysis of economic rationality. For further aspects of Aristotle's economic thought see, for example, Joseph A. Schumpeter, *History of Economic Analysis* (New York: Oxford University Press, 1954) and M.I. Finley, "Aristotle," in John Eatwell, Murray Milgate, and Peter Newman (eds.), *The New Palgrave: A Dictionary of Economics*, Vol. 1 (New York: Palgrave, 1987), 112–13, for interpretations from the perspective of modern economics; Meikle, *Aristotle's Economic Thought*, for a particular focus on Book V of *Nicomachean Ethics* and Aristotle's value and exchange theory; and Flashar et al., *Aristoteles und seine "Politik"* for a detailed discussion of Aristotle's *Politics*.
16. Becker, "Logos und Wirtschaft bei Aristoteles," 529–32.

17. Friederike Rese, *Praxis und Logos bei Aristoteles: Handlung, Vernunft und Rede in Nikomachischer Ethik, Rhetorik und Politik* (Tübingen: Mohr, 2003).
18. This distinguishes the concept of *practical wisdom* from the concept of *common sense. Common sense* is typically considered as a given capacity all humans have and share. In contrast, *practical wisdom* is a virtue of thought that has to be developed over time by experience, and not all may succeed in this in the same way.
19. See *Pol* 1254b and 1259b–1260a; see also Koslowski, *Politik und Ökonomie bei Aristoteles*, 51ff.
20. Koslowski, *Die Ordnung der Wirtschaft*, 39.
21. Rese, *Praxis und Logos bei Aristoteles.* This "external" element of rationality prominently reoccurs in modification in modern discourse ethics (Jürgen Habermas, *Theorie des kommunikativen Handelns*, Vol. 1 & 2, Frankfurt: Suhrkamp, 1981; *Moralbewußtsein und kommunikatives Handeln*, Frankfurt: Suhrkamp, 1983; and *Erläuterungen zur Diskursethik*, Frankfurt: Suhrkamp, 1991). It may have a more crucial role in a modern virtue ethics approach to the modern economy; see also Section 4.
22. See also *Pol* 1259a5ff. Aristotle refers here to the anecdote of *Thales the Milesian*, who made use of his wisdom to establish a monopoly in olive-presses and make a fortune with it. However, according to Aristotle, this was just to prove that philosophers could easily make money by their wisdom but due to *phronēsis*, refrain from doing so.
23. With the terms "standard economics" and "mainstream economics" I refer to neoclassical economics, which has been the dominant theoretical framework in economics from the mid-twentieth century until today. More precisely, in my methodological discussion I refer to the assumptions and characteristics of General Equilibrium Theory, as it was originally developed by Kenneth J. Arrow, "An Extension of the Basic Theorems of Classical Welfare Economics," in Jerzy Neyman (ed.), *Proceedings of the Second Berkeley Symposium on Mathematical Statistics and Probability* (Berkeley: University of California Press, 1951), 507–32; and Gérard Debreu, *Theory of Value. An Axiomatic Analysis of Economic Equilibrium* (New Haven: Yale University Press, 1959).
24. There is a large body of critical literature on *homo economicus*, particularly with regard to ethical aspects. See, for example, van Staveren, *Values of Economics*, 1–24, for an outline of main critical issues and references to the relevant research and literature. In addition, see Reiner Manstetten, *Das Menschenbild der Ökonomie. Der homo oeconomicus und die Anthropologie von Adam Smith*, (Freiburg: Alber, 2002), and Gebhard Kirchgässner, *Homo oeconomicus. Das ökonomische Modell individuellen Verhaltens und seine Anwendung in den Wirtschafts- und Sozialwissenschaften* (Tübingen: Mohr, 1991).
25. Andreu Mas-Colell, Michael Whinston, and Jerry Green, *Microeconomic Theory* (Oxford: Oxford University Press, 1995), 5–7.
26. See the references in Note 23.
27. For an overview of the field of behavioral economics, see Daniel Kahneman and Amos Tversky, *Choices, Values, and Frames* (Cambridge: Cambridge University

Press, 2000) and Colin Camerer, George Loewenstein, and Matthew Rabin (eds.), *Advances in Behavioral Economics* (Princeton: Princeton University Press, 2003); for general discussions of economic rationality concepts, see Shaun Hargreaves Heap, *Rationality in Economics* (Oxford: Oxford University Press, 1989); Kenneth Dennis (ed.), *Rationality in Economics: Alternative Perspectives* (Dordrecht: Kluwer, 1998); and Daniel M. Hausman and Michael S. McPherson, *Economic Analysis, Moral Philosophy and Public Policy*, 2nd ed. (Cambridge: Cambridge University Press, 2006).

28. Herbert A. Simon, *Administrative Behavior* (New York: Free Press, 1945), *Models of Bounded Rationality*, Vols. 1 and 2 (Cambridge, MA: The MIT Press, 1982), and *Models of Bounded Rationality, Vol. 3: Empirically Grounded Economic Reason* (Cambridge, MA: The MIT Press, 1997). See also Gerd Gigerenzer and Reinhard Selten (eds.), *Bounded Rationality: The Adaptive Toolbox* (Cambridge, MA: The MIT Press, 2001) and Matthias Klaes and Esther-Mirjam Sent, "A Conceptual History of the Emergence of Bounded Rationality," *History of Political Economy* 37(2005): 27–59.
29. Reinhard Selten, "What is Bounded Rationality?" in Gigerenzer and Selten, *Bounded Rationality*, 13–36, at 15.
30. Gerd Gigerenzer and Reinhard Selten, "Rethinking Rationality," in Gigerenzer and Selten, *Bounded Rationality*, 7.
31. Herbert A. Simon, "Rationality as Process and as Product of Thought," *American Economic Review* 68(1978): 1–16.
32. Ibid., 10.
33. Simon, *Models of Bounded Rationality*, Vol. 3, 291.
34. See also Hargreaves Heap, *Rationality in Economics.*
35. Gigerenzer and Selten, "Rethinking Rationality," 9.
36. Selten, "What is Bounded Rationality?" 24.
37. Matthew Rabin, "Incorporating Fairness into Game Theory and Economics," in Camerer, Loewenstein, and Rabin (eds.), *Advances in Behavioral Economics*, 297–325.
38. Linda Klebe Trevino and Gary R. Weaver, *Managing Ethics in Business Organizations: Social Scientific Perspectives* (Stanford, CA: Stanford University Press, 2003), 337f.
39. Ibid.
40. Milton Friedman, "The Methodology of Positive Economics," in *Essays in Positive Economics* (Chicago: University of Chicago Press, 1966), pp. 3–43.
41. Girts Racko, "On the Normative Consequences of Economic Rationality: A Case Study of a Swedish Economics School in Latvia," *European Sociological Review* 27(2011): 772–89. For an encompassing survey of the literature on the influence of economic education on individual self-identity and behavior, see Simon Niklas Hellmich, "State of the Art: Are Economists Selfish and Rational? And if so, why?" Working Paper 4, Bielefeld University, Fakultät Soziologie, Didaktik der Sozialwissenschaften, July 2012, <http://uni-bielefeld.de/soz/ag/hedtke/pdf/hellmich_state-of-the-art.pdf>.
42. Gary S. Becker, *The Economic Approach to Human Behavior* (Chicago: University of Chicago Press, 1976).

43. Reiner Manstetten, Olaf Hottinger, and Malte Faber (1998), "Zur Aktualität von Adam Smith: Homo oeconomicus und ganzheitliches Menschenbild," *Homo Oeconomicus* 15(1998): 127–68.
44. Solomon, *Ethics and Excellence.*
45. McCloskey, *Bourgeois Virtues.*
46. Kasser, *High Price of Materialism.*
47. R. Edward Freeman, *Strategic Management: A Stakeholder Approach* (Cambridge: Cambridge University Press, 2010).
48. See also Josef Wieland, *Die Ethik der Governance* (Marburg: Metropolis 1999).
49. See references in Note 23. The *invisible hand* explanation has occasionally been used by Adam Smith (see, for example, *The Wealth of Nations*, 1776, i.ii.6). Smith observed but had no explanation for the systemic rationality of the market, and seemed to assume that this is a result of a divinely well-ordered (natural and societal) world. Modern economics provides a precise technical formulation of this systemic rationality, which can be found in one of its most fundamental theorems, the first theorem of welfare economics. It states that if all individuals and firms optimize their utility and gain functions a market equilibrium is Pareto-efficient (under certain conditions); see Mas-Colell, Whinston, and Green, *Microeconomic Theory*, for more detail.
50. See, for example, Friedrich A. von Hayek, "The Results of Human Action but not of Human Design," in *Studies in Philosophy, Politics, and Economics* (Chicago: University of Chicago Press, 1967), 96–105.
51. McCloskey, *Bourgeois Virtues.*
52. See, for example, James M. Buchanan, *The Limits of Liberty: Between Anarchy and Leviathan* (Chicago: University of Chicago Press, 1975).
53. See the references to Habermas in Note 21.
54. Christian Becker, *Sustainability Ethics and Sustainability Research*, Dordrecht: Springer, 2012.
55. World Commission on Environment and Development, *Our Common Future* (Oxford: Oxford University Press, 1987); Becker, *Sustainability Ethics and Sustainability Research*, 12f.
56. I refer here to characteristics of influential traditions of modern thought that provide the underpinning of modern science, technology, and political and economic thought. In particular, I refer to the basic ideas of Francis Bacon, who considers the human being striving for independence from nature by controlling nature through rationality, and to René Descartes, who also considers humans in a certain way as autonomous rational beings.
57. Becker, *Sustainability Ethics and Sustainability Research.*
58. Ibid., 67–82.
59. For a detailed discussion of the methodological limitations of economics to refer to nature and non-human beings, see Christian Becker, "Die Mensch-Umwelt-Beziehung in den Wirtschaftswissenschaften," in Thomas Knopf (ed.), *Umweltverhalten in Geschichte und Gegenwart* (Tübingen: Narr, 2008), 212–27.
60. McCloskey, *Bourgeois Virtues.*
61. Klara Helene Stumpf, et al., "The Justice Dimension of Sustainability: A Systematic and General Conceptual Framework," *Sustainability* 7 (2015): 7438–72.

2

The Epicureans on Happiness, Wealth, and the Deviant Craft of Property Management

Tim O'Keefe

Ancient ethics concentrates on what the good life is and how to attain it. Therefore it should come as no surprise that the proper attitude towards acquiring wealth was an ethical topic, any more than it should be a surprise that, alongside virtues like courage and magnanimity, Aristotle discusses the virtue of having a proper sense of humor (*NE* IV 8).[1] The virtues we need to live well encompass both lofty and humdrum matters. And because the virtues are often conceived of as a sort of practical skill that allows us to live well and attain the good life, ancient ethicists, beginning with Plato, were also attracted to analogizing the virtues to crafts like shoe-making and medicine. So while financial planning and property management may initially seem to be mundane practical topics that do not raise ethical issues per se, it is also not surprising that ancient ethicists would be concerned with the place of the craft of financial planning or property management (*oikonomia*) in the good life.

The Epicureans stake out distinctive and plausible positions on these issues. The primary focus of this chapter will be what the later Epicurean Philodemus has to say about the craft of property management in his treatise *Peri Oikonomias*. He contends that there is indeed a craft that allows you to obtain and manage wealth skillfully, but that cultivating and exercising that craft is incompatible with being a virtuous person and obtaining happiness. Philodemus' views are an advance on the Socratic and Aristotelian positions on the craft of property management that he is reacting against—or so I will argue. Before turning to Philodemus, however, I will start by giving a thumbnail sketch of the Epicurean ethical position in general, and then summarizing what the Epicureans have to say about acquiring wealth in particular.

1. THE EPICUREANS ON WEALTH AND THE GOOD LIFE

1.1 A quick overview of Epicurean ethics

Epicurus accepts the eudaimonist ethical framework articulated by Aristotle: the highest good is *eudaimonia*, or happiness.[2] Some goods are only instrumentally valuable, for the sake of obtaining some other good, such as taking medicine for the sake of health. Other goods are intrinsically valuable: Aristotle believes there is a wide variety of intrinsic goods, such as pleasure, honor, and friendship. But these are not the highest good, as they are not valuable merely for their own sake, but also because by obtaining them we thereby help make our lives happier. Since all other goods are valuable for the sake of happiness—either as an instrumental means to happiness, such as medicine, or as a partial constituent of happiness, such as friendship—happiness is the highest good.

Epicurus disagrees with Aristotle on the content of *eudaimonia*. For Aristotle, *eudaimonia* is an *activity*, not a state of mind, and the primary constituent of *eudaimonia* is virtuous action.[3] (Nonetheless, Aristotle believes that the *eudaimôn* life will be pleasant, as the virtuous person enjoys acting virtuously; see *NE* 1099a13–21.) Epicureanism is a form of egoistic hedonism, where only one's own pleasure is intrinsically good, only one's own pain intrinsically bad (*Fin.* I 30), and the happy life is the pleasant life. But hedonism does not license reckless dissipation. While all pleasures are good and all pains bad, not all pleasures are choiceworthy, and not all pains are to be avoided. Many pleasurable activities, such as shooting up heroin or punching out people who annoy you, have bad long-term consequences, and the wise person avoids these misguided pleasures, picking and choosing among pleasures and pains in a way that makes her life, on the whole, pleasant (*Ep. Men.* 129–130).

Epicurus has an idiosyncratic understanding of pleasure, which significantly influences his recommendations on how to live your life. The absence of pain, he holds, is not merely a neutral state between pleasure and pain. Instead, absence of distress is something we rejoice at, and hence a sort of pleasure (*Fin.* I 37). In fact, the removal of all pain is the limit of pleasure (*KD* 3), and once we reach this state of "static" pleasure, our pleasure can be varied but not increased (*KD* 18). Specifically, static pleasures come in two varieties. The first is bodily static pleasure (*aponia*), not being hungry, thirsty, cold, and so forth. The second is mental static pleasure (*ataraxia*, or tranquility), not being anxious, fearful, full of regret, and so on. Both are good, but *ataraxia* is by far more important for having a pleasant life.[4]

In order to face the future free from fear and anxiety, Epicurus advocates reducing our desires. He divides desires into three classes: natural and necessary, natural and not necessary, and vain and empty (*KD* 29). Desires for food, drink, and shelter are natural in the sense that human beings congenitally have them rather than learning them, and they are necessary in that fulfilling them is needed either to live at all or to free the body from troubles (*Ep. Men.* 127). We should seek to fulfill these desires (*SV* 21) and to arrange our lives so that we will be confident that they will be fulfilled. (Having a group of trustworthy friends that help one another out in times of need is crucial for this confidence.[5]) A desire for *expensive* food in particular, though, such as filet mignon, he says is natural but not necessary, because many kinds of food can quell your hunger, and filet mignon in particular is not necessary. These desires, which typically require intense effort to fulfill, are based on "groundless opinion" (*KD* 30), that is, by thinking we need things we don't really need. Even worse are the vain and empty desires for things like fame and power. These desires have no natural limit, and pursuing them brings us into conflict with other people and leaves us vulnerable to fortune.[6]

We should sharply reject any harmful desire (*SV* 21). This is compatible with fulfilling merely natural desires when doing so does not harm us, and Epicurus says that the person who is self-sufficient and least needs extravagance is the one who enjoys it most when it happens occasionally to come along (*Ep. Men.* 130–1). So you attain tranquility by reducing your desires and living a quiet and moderately ascetic life among a group of trusted friends.

1.2 Natural wealth and the good life

Because of her reduced desires, the wise Epicurean will not need great wealth, and her recognition of the natural limits of her desires will bring her temperance and the other virtues. Seneca reports that Epicurus boasted that he could be fed for less than an obol (the most common low-denomination Greek coin, worth 1/6 of a drachma), but that his disciple Metrodorus, who hadn't made as much progress, needed an entire obol (*Letters on Ethics* 18.9).

But this still leaves open some questions. Is wealth not still instrumentally valuable, even for the wise Epicurean? And if so, wouldn't she still pursue wealth, at least insofar as she can do so in a way that does not disturb her tranquility? After all, if you have a million dollars in a trust fund, it seems initially that this money would help secure your peace of mind. Even if things go seriously wrong, you'd have that one-million-dollar backstop to obtain the meager food and shelter you need, plus any medical care you might require, as well as being able to help your friends meet their limited needs. For a wise Epicurean, there obviously will be limits on what you do to obtain wealth. Because of the anxiety associated with possibly getting caught and punished, an Epicurean would not steal a bunch of money.[7] And a high-stress occupation such as being a hedge fund manager working long hours in cutthroat competition with her co-workers for the largest annual bonus would be ruled out too. But considering the money on its own, it would still seem to be instrumentally valuable, and if so, it would seem useful for an Epicurean to have the skills needed to gain and preserve wealth well.

The suspicion that the wise Epicurean would strive to accumulate wealth is reinforced by their polemics against the Cynics, as recounted by Philodemus.[8] Although the Cynics repudiate pleasure, with the founder of the Cynic movement, Antisthenes, asserting that he would rather go mad than feel pleasure (*DL* VI 3), the Epicureans and the Cynics do share a fair amount of common ground ethically. Both find the conventional valorization of wealth and fame pernicious and assert that the wise person will instead pursue what is valuable by nature, and both agree that worrying about things like pursuing wealth is irksome. But the Cynics advocate that the wise person should heedlessly "live in utter poverty so as to be carefree,"[9] whereas the Epicureans think that you should take some care to provide for yourself. The Epicurean Metrodorus argues that, in order to achieve tranquility, you shouldn't avoid all things that involve difficulty and distress, because the absence of some of those things will cause more pain than the pain caused by striving to obtain them (*De Oec.* XIII 1–11). He gives the example of health, which "does involve some care and effort for the body but causes unspeakably more distress when absent" (*De Oec.* XIII 11–15). It may occasionally be a hassle to brush your teeth or pick up a new tube of toothpaste at the store, but the hassle is easily worth avoiding the agony of badly rotting teeth. And in this regard wealth is like health: obtaining what you need in order to satisfy your natural and necessary desires for food, drink, and shelter involves some pain, but far less than the pain you would experience if you heedlessly disregard wealth and end up on the street, hungry and disease-ridden. The Epicurean wise person "will take thought for his possessions and for the future" (*DL* X 120), and not only for his own sake: "One must philosophize and at the same time laugh and take care of one's household and use the rest of our personal goods . . . " (*SV* 41).[10]

Despite this, the Epicureans want to deny that the wise person would have a million dollar trust fund. The "natural wealth" that is needed to satisfy our natural and necessary desires is limited and easy to obtain (*KD* 15), whereas "a free life cannot acquire great wealth, because the task is not easy without slavery to the mob or those in power," and Epicurus adds that if the wise person somehow lucked into great wealth, she would give it away in order to obtain the good will of her neighbors (*SV* 67).

The Epicureans' attitude towards great wealth parallels their attitude towards political power and fame. The "natural good" of political power and fame—what is actually valuable for us that these things might provide—is security from other people. So if the lives of people with political power or fame are not secure, then pursuing these things is practically irrational (*KD* 6–7). Now, as it turns out, political power can bring us *some* security, but far better security "comes from a quiet life and withdrawal from the many" (*KD* 14), so the Epicureans recommend avoiding involvement in the business of politics (*DL* X 119; *SV* 58). Likewise, while the limited "natural wealth" needed to satisfy our natural and necessary desires is easy to obtain and worth pursuing, wealth as defined by "groundless opinion" stretches without limit (*KD* 15), and pursuing such wealth is misguided and counterproductive.

In fact, the Epicureans believe that if we build into our conception of wealth that wealth is a valuable thing that helps us obtain what is good for us, then what is commonly thought of as wealth turns out not to be wealth at all: "Poverty, if measured by the goal of nature, is great wealth; and wealth, if limits are not set for it, is great poverty" (*SV* 25). And if the wealthy person is the one who has what he needs to satisfy his desires, then, as Epicurus recommends, to make somebody wealthy you should not give him money; instead, you should reduce his desires (Stobaeus *Anthology* 3.17.23).

2. PHILODEMUS ON THE CRAFT OF PROPERTY MANAGEMENT

While the overall Epicurean position on wealth, as sketched above, is tolerably clear, it leaves several important questions open. What are the details on how one should comport oneself with regard to material goods? The Epicureans condone the pursuit of "natural wealth," but in addition to wondering about how *much* wealth one should have, a person concerned with the place of wealth in the good life should inquire into the manner in which one procures it, manages it, uses it, and disposes of it. These sorts of questions are the concern of the craft of *oikonomia*,[11] and in his treatise *Peri Oikonomias*, Philodemus asks if there is such a craft (yes), and if so, whether the wise person would learn it (no).

A small bit of historical background may be useful: Philodemus was a prominent and prolific Epicurean of the first century BCE and was well known to Cicero. However, none of his work was transmitted to us through the medieval manuscript tradition. In the mid-eighteenth century, an Epicurean library containing a large number of Philodemus' treatises was uncovered in a villa in Herculaneum, which had been destroyed (along with Pompeii) in the eruption of Mt. Vesuvius in 79 CE. The work of deciphering the badly damaged and often fragmentary papyri continues today, with the help of modern technology.[12]

Philodemus considered himself a faithful disciple of Epicurus, but Epicurus' followers disputed how to understand his teachings, and it is quite possible that Philodemus sometimes strays into inadvertent unorthodoxy.[13] So it is not guaranteed that everything Philodemus says about the craft of property management is consistent with Epicurus' ethics, but I will leave aside questions of this sort.

Oikonomia is the etymological ancestor of "economics," and there are also conceptual links between the two, but it differs significantly from contemporary economics. *Oikonomia* concerns the management of one's *oikos*, or household. So a decent translation would be "household management," or—because *oikonomia* is often concerned more narrowly with the management of one's household *goods*, rather than everything that goes into being a good member of a household—"property management." Both *oikonomia* and economics are bodies of knowledge about wealth. But "an inquiry into the nature and causes of the wealth of nations" and related topics, like trade imbalances and inflation, would have been considered not a part of *oikonomia*, but of *politikê*, the study of how to manage the *polis*, or city-state. *Oikonomia* overlaps more with some parts of microeconomics, such as opportunity costs, but it is important to keep in mind that *oikonomia* is supposed to be primarily a kind of *practical* knowledge, a skill about how to use your own property successfully. So it would be most akin to advice books on personal finance, budgeting, and money management, albeit with its advice (sometimes) rooted in theorizing about human nature and human happiness. I will follow Tsouna in translating *oikonomia* as "property management," but not in the sense of what property management companies do (administering residential, commercial, or industrial real estate on somebody else's behalf).

I will start by giving some background on *technê* (craft) and the dispute between Gorgias and Socrates as to what counts as a genuine *technê* in Plato's dialog *Gorgias*. I'll then lay out the positions of Xenophon and Theophrastus on the craft of property management, as Philodemus builds his own position in reaction to theirs, before closing with Philodemus' criticisms of Socrates, Xenophon, and Theophrastus and his reasons for asserting that the craft of property management is pernicious.

2.1 What is a genuine *technê?*

Although Socrates would disapprove of the method, I'll start by enumerating some examples of crafts: shoe-making, medicine, bridle-making, horsemanship, and military strategy. Crafts aim at some end; they have a product, which can be more or less tangible, such as shoes, bodily health, bridles, skillful riding, or military victory. This end is the good of the craft, and the craft is organized around producing that end well. A craft is a skill, a kind of practical knowledge that can be learned and taught.

The *Gorgias* opens with Socrates asking Gorgias to define his supposed area of expertise, rhetoric. Rhetoric, says Gorgias, is the art of persuasive speaking, of getting people to believe what you want them to believe and do what you want them to do. It is a *morally neutral* skill, which can be used for good or for ill. But this does not show that there is anything wrong with rhetoric or teachers of rhetoric, any more than it is a problem for boxing or boxing instructors that boxers can use their skill either to defend the innocent or to pummel small children for fun. Socrates presses Gorgias on how rhetoric differs from other crafts that allow you to speak persuasively—for instance, the way a doctor can persuade a sick patient to take a drug by explaining to him the reasons why doing so is a good idea—and Gorgias concedes that rhetoric is persuasion in the absence of knowledge, but is no less useful or effective as persuasion for that (*Gorgias* 456a–459c).

In response, Socrates proposes two constraints that an ability must satisfy to count as a genuine craft. If a *technê* is a kind of practical *knowledge* that brings about some *good*, we should accept the *theoretical sophistication constraint*, that it is based on a knowledge of the nature of its subject, and the *normative constraint*, that it brings about some genuine good. Medicine would be a paradigm craft for Socrates.[14] It aims at producing health, the genuine *good* of the body, and hence satisfies the normative constraint; and the craft's prescriptions are based upon a *knowledge* of the nature of the body, and hence meets the theoretical sophistication constraint. The two constraints are distinct, but not entirely unrelated: it is a grasp of something's nature that allows a craftsman to understand what its good is and how to promote it effectively. Any purported "craft" that fails to meet these criteria is merely an *empeiria*, an empirical "knack." Pastry-baking, for instance, is given by Socrates as a knack, the counterpart to the craft of medicine. The baker of Krispy Kreme doughnuts does not aim at producing what's genuinely good for the body, but merely at gratifying a person's appetites for what is yummy and pleasant. And the practices of pastry-baking are not based on an understanding of the body's nature; instead, through empirical guesswork and trial and error, bakers have discovered *what* works without understanding *why* it does (*Gorgias* 462b–465e).[15]

2.2 Xenophon and Theophrastus on the craft of property management

The surviving portions of Philodemus' *On Property Management* open with a recapitulation of the views of Theophrastus and Xenophon, before going on to criticize their views and offering his own account. Fortunately, we do not have to rely on Philodemus' (often fragmentary) summary, as both treatises survive independently.[16]

Although the two treatises differ considerably in their particulars, their overall positions are consistent. Both try to preserve an important place for the craft of property management, conceived of as aiming at maximizing your wealth, within the Socratic and Aristotelian ethical tradition that puts virtue and virtuous activity at the center of the happy life. Xenophon was one of the young men who followed Socrates around, and many of his treatises feature Socrates as a speaker. Xenophon's *Oikonomikos* has Socrates speaking with Critoboulos, a wealthy Athenian living beyond his means. Theophrastus was a student of Aristotle and assumed the headship of the Lyceum after Aristotle's death.

Both Xenophon and Theophrastus accept Socrates' normative condition on a genuine craft, which must aim at the genuine good. Xenophon has Socrates claim that the good property manager knows how to use things so as to derive benefit from them (*Oec.* I 15), and Critoboulos and Socrates agree that, on the assumption that wealth is a good thing, only that which a person can derive benefits from is wealth. It follows that the same thing can be wealth for the person who knows how to use it well, and not be wealth for the one who does not (*Oec.* I 7–13). Later, in a passage strongly reminiscent of what Epicurus says about natural wealth and poverty, Socrates claims that he is rich while Critoboulos is poor, even though his possessions are less than a hundredth of Critoboulos', because he has enough to provide himself with what he needs, whereas Critoboulos does not (*Oec.* II 2–10). Theophrastus does not engage in this sort of linguistic revisionism, but he does open the *Oikonomika* by comparing household management to politics, where politics concerns the right constitution and use of the city-state as a whole for the sake of attaining the good life, whereas the function of household management is to found and make right use of a household for the sake of the good life (*Oik.* I 1).[17]

On Xenophon's account, it may seem to follow that Socrates is himself the expert property manager, as he knows how to use things so as to benefit himself. But Socrates denies this, saying that because he has never had many possessions, he has never had the opportunity to learn how to manage estates well, just like a person who has never owned or borrowed flutes would not develop the talent for playing them well (*Oec.* II 12–13). So in the latter part of the dialogue, the humdrum everyday advice about matters like how to choose an effective foreman, or when to sow grain, is not given by Socrates himself. Instead, he recounts what he was told by Ischomachus, a virtuous gentleman who has had the relevant experience. Both Xenophon and Theophrastus accept the traditional view of property management as an autonomous discipline with its own distinctive norms and aims, just as is true with other crafts, such as shoe-making or flute-playing, rather than collapsing it into being merely one application of practical wisdom writ large.

Neither Xenophon nor Theophrastus thinks that there is a tension between the autonomy of the craft of property management and the normative constraint that genuine crafts aim at what is genuinely good. Theophrastus maintains that the habits needed to manage your property well also help you develop the virtues (*Oik.* 1345a13–14), while Xenophon says that the expert property manager pursues and maintains possessions only by fair and honorable means (*Oec.* VII 15). As noted above, Xenophon believes that genuine wealth must be beneficial for the person possessing it. And on the further assumption that only the virtuous person knows how to use things well so that they are beneficial for them, virtue is necessary to be a skilled property manager, even if property management has additional skills peculiar to it. And because Theophrastus situates the narrower skills of managing your property well within the wider context of managing your household well, which would include having developed the proper sorts of character traits regarding interacting with your wife, children, and slaves, it is reasonable to suppose that only the virtuous person has fully realized the craft of property management, even though learning how to manage property well is a specialized skill distinct from developing virtuous character traits.[18]

Both Xenophon and Theophrastus combine their general account of property management with everyday advice about the practices of the skilled property manager, concerning matters like regulating your monthly expenses, what sort of food and drink to give to your slaves, and how to select a suitable overseer for your household. For instance, Xenophon recommends arranging things in the house so as to find them easily (*Oec.* VII 37–45), while Theophrastus says the household manager and his wife should arise before the servants and retire after them and should never leave the house unguarded, so they sometimes will need to get up in the middle of the night to check on things (*Oik.* 1345a12–18).

The upshot, then, is that the skilled property manager has, over time and with practice, developed a set of skills related to maximizing his income and preserving his property, albeit in a way that is directed by his virtue and constrained by his ethical commitments to what is noble, and the exercise of this skill allows him to obtain wealth in a way that facilitates a happy life.

2.3 Philodemus against Socrates, Xenophon, and Theophrastus

Philodemus' explicit foils are Xenophon and Theophrastus, but he also implicitly rejects Socrates' constraints in the *Gorgias* on what counts as a genuine *technê*. He rejects the normative constraint—that crafts aim at what is genuinely good—as going against our usual linguistic practices. This is part and parcel of Philodemus more generally objecting to building in normative constraints where they do not belong. To call a rich person like Critobolous poor and a poor person like Socrates rich is not "in accordance with ordinary usage" but merely "a matter of opinion" (*De Oec.* V 1–4). Likewise, he objects to Socrates (in Xenophon) calling the vicious masters of a household "slaves" to their vices as a violation of ordinary language (*De Oec.* IV 1–16).

Critobolous has lots of goodies and Socrates few, so Critobolous is the rich guy and Socrates the poor one, even if we think that Socrates is living well and Critobolous badly. Rather than confusingly saying that Socrates is "genuinely rich" and Critobolous "genuinely poor," it would be better to say that Socrates is poor but happy, and Critobolous rich but miserable.

Philodemus' criticisms of Socrates here would seem also to apply to much of what Epicurus says, for example, that you make a person wealthy by reducing his desires. But as Tsouna notes, Philodemus should not be understood as flat-footedly objecting to all metaphorical usages of terms; instead, he is objecting to Socrates' particular linguistic revisionism.[19] When used literally, "possessions" and "wealth" refer to your stuff like your shoes, house, and gold, without prejudging whether or not that stuff is good for you, and *oikonomia* is the craft aimed at the acquisition and preservation of that sort of stuff. To stipulate that this craft must produce what is genuinely good for you is misguided.

Philodemus' description of *oikonomia* also implicitly rejects Socrates' theoretical sophistication constraint. Recall that Socrates contrasts a *technê*, a skill that is based upon a grasp of the nature of its subject, with an *empeiria*, a mere empirical knack whose practices are based on guesswork without an understanding of why they work. Rather than contrasting *technê* and *empeiria*, Philodemus runs them together. He calls *oikonomia* a craft (*technê*), an empirical practice (*empeiria*), and an empirical practice involving expertise (*empeirias entechnou*). He allows for there to be empirical expertise even in practices like making bread.[20] Philodemus says that a craft arises from the observation of what is common in particular cases, and it allows a person to accomplish things in a way that cannot be accomplished by those who have not learned it.[21]

Philodemus' characterization of a craft does not preclude crafts, like Socrates' (idealized) vision of the craft of medicine, whose practices proceed from a grasp of their subjects' natures. But neither does it require such a grasp. Instead, it allows for a continuum of crafts that are more or less theoretically informed, but all of which can be contrasted with mere guesswork.

At this point, it may seem that Philodemus should endorse Gorgias' position. Property management, like rhetoric, is an empirically based, morally neutral skill that can be used for good or for ill, depending on the character of the craftsman. But insofar as wealth, like persuasive speaking, is often useful—and the Epicureans admit that it is—then it looks like the Epicureans should admit that having this skill is worthwhile, at least for the wise person who knows how to deploy it appropriately. But Philodemus rejects Gorgias' position, saying that the wise person will not acquire or exercise the skill of property management (*De Oec.* XVII 6–14).

Philodemus has practical objections to the advice regarding property management given by Xenophon and Theophrastus, but more fundamentally he believes that becoming an expert property manager involves adopting a destructive set of attitudes. For instance, targeting Theophrastus, Philodemus writes that it is "wretched and unfitting for the philosopher" to wake up before the servants and go to sleep after them, and that getting into the habit of waking up in the middle of the night is bothersome and probably bad for your health and for studying philosophy (*De Oec.* XI 30–41).[22] It is important to note that Philodemus does not dispute that developing these habits would be an effective means of preserving your wealth—in fact, given what he says elsewhere about the craft of property management, he would probably concede that they are effective. His objection, instead, is that doing things like waking up in the middle of the night to check on your property is a real drag, and the possible financial gain is not worth the trouble. Being willing to do such things and developing such habits show that you are a money-lover (*philochrêmatos*, *De Oec.* XVII 13), and having such an anxious attitude is destructive. Eagerly watching over your possessions at all times is troubling and "is accompanied by bitter worry" (*De Oec.* XIX 10–16), and wanting to increase your property as much as possible makes you agonize over your losses (*De Oec.* XIV 30–37).

2.4 The expert manager of property versus the Epicurean sage

At this point, it seems like Xenophon and Theophrastus would have an obvious response to Philodemus' objections against the craft of property management. They would agree that the anxious, money-grubbing craftsman of property that Philodemus depicts would live a horrible life. But they would deny that there is any reason to suppose that the person who acquires the skill of managing his property expertly need acquire the destructive attitudes that Philodemus describes. Instead, the virtuous person who acquires this skill would understand the appropriate place of property within the happy life, and its relative importance compared to other goods like the welfare of one's friends, and justice, so that his acquisition and preservation of property would not interfere with his overall pursuit of happiness.

Philodemus distinguishes between the expert property manager and the Epicurean sage, and this distinction allows him to parry this response.[23] As noted above, a craft is a skill whose practices and norms are organized around producing some end. Philodemus takes the end of property management to be maximizing your wealth. Philodemus repeatedly refers to the expert property manager as concerned with the "more and less," that is, with measuring how much wealth he has and with doing what he can to maximize his gains and minimize his losses. Philodemus is willing to concede to Xenophon and Theophrastus that the expert property manager will pursue the accumulation and preservation of his wealth only within the bounds of what is lawful and not shameful (*De Oec.* XX 22–32), so that he will not do things like embezzle money or break his promises to his friends in order to make more money. Nonetheless, in devoting himself to becoming as skillful as he can in accumulating property, the expert property manager will acquire habits and attitudes that distort his personality and disturb his peace of mind.

On Philodemus' behalf, we may draw an analogy to Aristotle on the virtues of character, such as generosity. A virtue of character is not just a developed disposition to do the right thing, such as helping out your friends financially in an appropriate manner, but also to have the right sorts of feelings, such as wanting to help them when they need it, and finding it pleasurable to help them (*NE* II 3). This is true in part because inappropriate feelings are themselves indicative of a character flaw: if I hate parting with my money in order to help my sick friend, there is something morally wrong with me, even if I manage to overcome this inappropriate feeling. But also, having the right sorts of feelings helps you realize the mean in action and perform virtuous action in a smooth, savvy, unimpeded manner. Likewise, crafts have ends—and therefore goods—internal to them. And being a skilled craftsman involves, in part, having the proper set of attitudes, taking pleasures and pains in the right sorts of things, in order to perform well *qua* craftsman. Philodemus, however, thinks that the attitudes that make you better *qua* property manager make you worse *qua* human being. As Epicurus puts it, "it is impious to love money unjustly, and shameful to do so justly; for it is unfitting to be sordidly stingy even if one is just" (*SV* 43).

Philodemus contrasts the attitudes of the expert property manager with those of the Epicurean sage. The sage realizes that she needs little to live well, and that even if hard times befall her, she can count on her friends to come to her aid. So she will not have an obsessive zeal concerning the more and the less, and she will not feel distressed about what she loses (*De Oec.* XIV 23–30). The sage is not bound by her wealth in a way where she will be willing to endure great toils to preserve it, and she has no heavy cares about preserving it (*De Oec.* XV 31–45).

Philodemus admits that the sage will be worse *qua oikonomikos*: she cannot acquire a very large quantity of money in a short time (*De Oec.* XIX 4–10), and even if she does, it will not be easy for her to keep it (*De Oec.* XVIII 37–9). But unlike the heedless Cynic, she is not a *bad* property manager. She does not waste her property rather than keep it. This "good enough" know-how is neither hard to attain nor pernicious (*De Oec.* XVI 21 ff.), but rather the "common experience that is adequate for the management of one's possessions, though not for excessive moneymaking" (*De Oec.* XVI 35–39).[24]

Philodemus stakes out a distinctive position on craft knowledge. A craft like property management does have an internal "good," and it does display genuine skill, so Socrates is wrong to dismiss it as a mere pseudo-craft. At the same time, Gorgias is wrong to think that crafts are morally neutral skills that can be used for good or ill. We cannot detach the skills we cultivate from the sort of person we become. Developing these skills takes time and effort; these skills have goals internal to themselves that the person acquiring them will tend to accept; and acquiring the skills involves cultivating a set of attitudes that can be beneficial or harmful.

So Philodemus would also dissent from the picture of the crafts that Aristotle sketches in the *Nicomachean Ethics.* Aristotle himself, rightly, thinks that craft knowledge, while a genuine form of human intellectual excellence (*NE* VI 4), does not require that the craftsman be a virtuous person; a person can be both a skilled saddle maker and a cowardly jerk. But when discussing the crafts, he posits a hierarchy of goods such that all forms of craft knowledge can be subsumed and coordinated towards the achievement of the highest good, *eudaimonia.* Saddle making is subordinate to horsemanship, which is subordinate to military strategy, which is subordinate to politics. And politics coordinates all other skills and bodies of knowledge for the sake of having the members of the community achieve happiness (*NE* I 1–2). Philodemus challenges this optimistic assumption. Because we live in a sick society with widespread false beliefs about the place of wealth in the good life, we have developed deviant crafts like property management that embody these false beliefs. These deviant crafts cannot be subsumed and coordinated towards the achievement of happiness, because they aim at ends, or aim at them in such a way, that detracts from the good.[25]

3. CONCLUSION

When it comes to wealth, then, the Epicurean sage is a satisficer and not a maximizer: she will not spend a lot of time worrying about finding the option that gets her the best financial return, but will go ahead and act once she has found an option that is good enough. And given the Epicurean conception of what we need in order to satisfy our natural and necessary desires, "good enough" is easy to achieve. We should be satisficers because worrying a lot about material goods and trying to maximize them, and acquiring the craft expertise and associated attitudes to do extremely well with regard to financial gain, leads to unhappiness.[26] Having many choices and worrying about them generally leads to anxiety and unhappiness, but especially when it comes to wealth.[27]

NOTES

1. Henceforward, references to these and other texts will be made according to the following conventions: Aristotle, *Nicomachean Ethics* = *NE*; Cicero, *De Finibus* (On Goals) = *Fin.*; Diogenes Laertius, *Lives of the Philosophers* = *DL*; Epicurus, *Kuriai*

Doxai (Principle Doctrines) = *KD*; Epicurus, *Sententiae Vaticanae* (Vatican Sayings) = *SV*; Epicurus, Letter to Menoeceus = *Ep. Men.*; Philodemus, *On Property Management* = *De Oec.*; pseudo-Aristotle/Theophrastus, *Economics* = *Oik.*; Xenophon, *Oeconomicus* = *Oec.* Translations of Philodemus are from Voula Tsouna, (ed. and trans.), *Philodemus, On Property Management* (Atlanta: Society of Biblical Literature, 2012), and of other Epicurean texts are from Brad Inwood and L. P. Gerson (eds. and trans.), *The Epicurus Reader* (Indianapolis: Hackett, 1994). My English paraphrases of other ancient texts use common renderings not drawn from any particular source.

2. "Happiness" is the customary and probably best translation of *eudaimonia*, but it is far from perfect, because *eudaimonia* applies to one's life as a whole and need not be a state of mind; for example, Aristotle thinks *eudaimonia* is a kind of activity. See Julia Annas, *The Morality of Happiness* (Oxford: Oxford University Press, 1993), chapter 1, for more on these issues.
3. At *NE* I 7, Aristotle's definition of *eudaimonia* seems to make virtuous activity its sole constituent, but other passages appear to include other goods, such as good health or a good reputation, as partial constituents as well. For more on this issue and a defense of virtuous activity as the sole constituent of *eudaimonia*, see Eric Brown, "Wishing for Fortune, Choosing Activity: Aristotle on External Goods and Happiness," *Proceedings of the Boston Area Colloquium in Ancient Philosophy* 22(2006): 221–56.
4. In a letter dictated while he was dying and in physical agony, Epicurus claims that he is still supremely happy, in part because of the joy he derives from the memory of his past philosophical conversations (*DL* X 22).
5. For a good discussion of the place of friendship in the Epicurean life, see Matt Evans, "Can Epicureans Be Friends?" *Ancient Philosophy* 24(2004): 407–24.
6. It is worth noting that, in order to eliminate anxiety, this practical wisdom about the natural limits of your desires is not sufficient. To remove the fears of death and of the gods, you must also have correct beliefs about the nature of things, so that you are confident that death is annihilation and that gods have nothing to do with the workings of the world.
7. The Epicureans hold that it is never prudent to act unjustly, because of the fear of getting caught and punished, although hostile critics like Cicero found this implausible (see *KD* 34 and *Fin.* II 58–9). For more on the Epicureans' justification for acting justly and their replies to folks like Cicero, see Tim O'Keefe, "Would a Community of Wise Epicureans Be Just?" *Ancient Philosophy* 21(2001): 133–46, and John Thrasher, "Reconciling Justice and Pleasure in Epicurean Contractarianism," *Ethical Theory and Moral Practice* 16(2013): 423–36.
8. My understanding of Philodemus on *oikonomia* is deeply indebted to Tsouna's edition of *On Property Management* and chapter 8 of Tsouna, *The Ethics of Philodemus* (Oxford: Oxford University Press, 2007).
9. Tsouna, *Ethics of Philodemus*, 177.
10. The Epicureans say that the wise person cares for her friends as much as for herself (*Fin.* I 65–70). See Evans, "Can Epicureans Be Friends?" for an argument that such concern can be squared with the Epicureans' egoism.
11. Tsouna, *Philodemus, On Property Management*, xiii ff.

12. A good introduction to Philodemus and other Epicureans of the period is David Sedley, "Epicureanism in the Roman Republic," in James Warren (ed.), *The Cambridge Companion to Epicureanism* (Cambridge: Cambridge University Press, 2009), 29–45.
13. For Epicurean reverence of the master, see David Sedley, "Philosophical Allegiance in the Greco-Roman World," in Miriam Griffin and Jonathan Barnes (eds.), *Philosophia Togata: Essays on Philosophy and Roman Society* (Oxford: Oxford University Press, 1989), 97–119. My own view is that Philodemus does shade Epicurean views in the direction of making them less out of touch with contemporary Roman views, sometimes with the result of making them inconsistent with overall Epicurean doctrine, but this is controversial. For possible unorthodoxy with regard to friendship, see Tsouna, *Ethics of Philodemus*, 27–31, and with regard to death, see Tim O'Keefe, "Review of *Philodemus, On Death*, ed. and trans. W. Benjamin Henry," *Notre Dame Philosophical Reviews*, July 21, 2011, <http://ndpr.nd.edu/review.cfm?id=24309>.
14. For understanding Socrates' position, it does not matter whether medicine as actually practiced in his day met (or would have been thought to meet) Socrates' standards.
15. Socrates uses these standards to condemn rhetoric as a mere knack. Although he condemns knacks both for being mere empirical guesswork and for aiming at what's merely apparently good, it is not difficult to think of practices that meet one of his criteria but not the other. (For instance, Ignaz Semmelweis instituted the practice of having medical students wash their hands between visiting the autopsy room and the delivery rooms prior to the development of germ theory, conjecturing that the medical students carried some unknown "cadaverous particles" on their hands, and one can imagine advertising techniques that aim to persuade people to buy harmful things that they find pleasing, where these techniques are based on a sophisticated psychology.)
16. Xenophon, *Oikonomikos*, and Theophrastus, *Oikonomika*. The identification of Theophrastus as the author of the *Oikonomika* is uncertain, but I will follow Philodemus here.
17. Compare with Aristotle's discussion of politics as the master-craft of the good in *NE* I 2.
18. See also *NE* 1140b7–11: people with practical wisdom know what is good for them and for others, which allows them to manage households or states.
19. Tsouna, *Ethics of Philodemus*, 170n18.
20. *De Oec.* XVII 2–40. I follow Tsouna's translation: although *empeiria* is most commonly rendered as "knack" in translations of the *Gorgias*, given that Philodemus' estimation of *empeiria* is higher than Socrates', "empirical practice" is more suitable here.
21. *Rhet.* 2a, *PHerc.* 1674.xxxviii.2–18, text in Francesca Longo Auricchio "Edition of Philodemus *Rhetorica I and II*," in *Ricerche sui papiri ercolanesi*, vol. III, edited by Francesco Sbordone (Naples: Giannini, 1977), 132. For further discussion of this passage and of Philodemus' understanding of *technê*, see David Blank, "Philodemus on the Technicity of Rhetoric," in Dirk Obbink (ed.), *Philodemus and Poetry* (Oxford: Oxford University Press, 1995), 178–88.

22. See chapter 8 of Tsouna, *Ethics of Philodemus*, for some further examples of disagreements, for instance, about the proper profession of a philosopher and the proper treatment of slaves.
23. To be clear, Philodemus himself does not present this distinction as a reply to such an objection, and he does not explicitly raise the above objection. And below I present Aristotle's doctrine about what feelings the virtuous person would have as a way of helping to justify Philodemus' contentions regarding the attitudes the expert property manager would have; Philodemus himself does not do so. All of this is my attempt to understand Philodemus' position and assess its strength.
24. Philodemus thinks that the wise person will not become an expert property manager, but she may be willing to take advantage of the financial acumen of the poor sap who is an expert (*De Oec.* XIX 23–32).
25. This label of "deviant crafts" is my own, not Philodemus', although I believe it is faithful to Philodemus. It is worth noting that nothing in Aristotle's overall ethical position should preclude him from granting Philodemus' revision to his claim concerning the crafts. In fact, Aristotle says that the politician will ordain which sciences should be studied in a state and to what extent (*NE* 1094a28–30), suggesting that the wise politician could exclude some crafts as pernicious. (I thank Jennifer Daigle for pointing this out.)
26. See Michael Slote, *Beyond Optimizing* (Cambridge, MA: Harvard University Press, 1989) for an in-depth discussion of issues related to maximizing vs. satisficing and a defense of the rationality of satisficing, and Barry Schwartz, *The Paradox of Choice: Why More Is Less* (New York: HarperCollins, 2004) for evidence that satisficing is a hedonically superior strategy to maximizing.
27. I'd like to thank Jennifer Baker, Jennifer Daigle, Anne Farrell, Hal Thorsrud, Mark White, and the colloquium audience at UT-Knoxville for their thoughtful feedback on this chapter.

3

Economic Good as Indifferent

The Stoics' Radical Approach

Jennifer A. Baker

> Man, according to the Stoics, ought to regard himself, not as something separated and detached, but as a citizen of the world, a member of the vast commonwealth of nature.
>
> —Adam Smith[1]

In *The Bourgeois Virtues: Ethics in an Age of Commerce*, Deirdre McCloskey argues that the "American bourgeoisie . . . moralizes its riches as just rewards for cowboy courage, or as a gospel of philanthropy of the Carnegie/Mellon type, or as democratic creed of opportunity seized." She describes market society as one of "contract and guilt" rather than "status and shame," and she thinks the prime bourgeois virtue is "honesty." In today's bourgeois society, we hold up the "courage, justice, and faith to be reliable in making a deal."[2] Jane Jacobs, just a bit earlier, suggested a similar list of the morality of the trader, including "collaborate easily with strangers," "be efficient," "come to voluntary agreements," and "dissent for the sake of the task."[3] And philosophers of economics, such as Elizabeth Anderson, read off of markets the values they project, such as use values, freedom, and exit.[4]

None of these descriptions amount to the same thing as "virtue"—not virtue on the traditional, practical-rationality-based account anyway, a psychological condition that only particular agents have. If markets can be found to have salubrious social impacts, to make us more "ethically complete" or to open up "moral space," this still does not refer us back to the psychological account to which virtue has traditionally referred.[5]

Scholars know this, of course. McCloskey writes, "virtue in each person is strictly speaking neither necessary nor sufficient for the virtue of and certainly not the survival of the whole community."[6] "Social observers" are aware that accounts of moral psychology are part of well-developed theories of virtue, both ancient and modern; they simply are not speaking strictly when they refer to the social impacts of commercial society as "vices" or "virtues."[7] These descriptions are made at a very general level, or they might refer to ethical stories held up by a culture.

There are several reasons why those most interested in social conditions, and this includes economists and philosophers alike, are more comfortable working without reference to any psychological account of virtue. Perhaps using "virtue" to refer to perceived strengths of a culture is a way to refocus our attention on more regular matters. Virtue ethics is, after all, still of mainly academic interest. But even theorists who do not invoke actual ethical theory themselves can acknowledge that the justification of markets requires it, at some point. McCloskey, for example, argues that a specified ethical theory ("an ethical theory worthy of the name," as she puts it) would be necessary to back up the ethical claims made at the level of maximum generality. She goes even further, suggesting that the ethical theory will have to include a depiction of "a conscientious moral agent, a virtuous person."[8]

Bringing all ethical claims back to the impact it can be expected to have on a person is a way to fill out the details on why virtue matters. Any analysis of the ethical dimensions of markets (and calculations concerning them) depends on some explanation of why ethics matters. Until an answer is provided, we are working without detail, specifically detail that would expose disagreements or unfinished work. Unsettled disagreement about how markets relate to our values is just elided. Put simply: it is important to be as clear and specific as we can be about ethics, revealing even the moral psychology we take to be necessary to it.

And yet, most often the details of moral psychology that are associated with accounts of virtue are just pointed to, not put to *use*. We still tend to argue on behalf of virtue ethics being potentially useful. Once we move from this stage, and virtue ethics is used to wage actual arguments, this will be done only by invoking of a particular account of moral psychology.[9] A virtue ethic attached to an account of moral psychology brings some benefits, even if in the form of reminders. For example, it reminds us that virtue has to reside in a person. Persons face options and could not be guided by market norms alone even if they wished for that. General market norms cannot answer all of the questions agents face, not even while at work in a business justified by market norms. Also, any account of virtue with an attached account of moral psychology reminds us that we may follow good norms for unimpressive reasons. Much "good" behavior is instrumentally justified, but to fail to acknowledge the difference between acting for benefit and acting out of moral concern is to fail to acknowledge the experience of facing this type of choice. Even if we, as theorists, might be able to suggest that ethical behavior is just one preference, this is certainly failing to acknowledge how the option of losing expediency for ethics *feels*. And finally, without some account of moral psychology, ethics is done only broadly, at most settling upon a set of very general norms.

General ethical norms are, of course, crucial to our understanding of the various domains in which we operate. (We may even need them first, to test against accounts of virtue to see if they are compatible.) But any ethics meant to be practical—and virtue ethics is certainly meant to be practical—requires us to eventually meet agents where they are. Providing the rest of the story about why and how ethics matters is a way to do this. Simply citing general norms, even the right ones or the applicable ones, is not. To be practical we need to recognize the perspective of agents in the market and describe the problems as they see them. And I want to suggest that agents do not get faced with the need to discover market norms, or with a lack of arguments as to whether to honor them. Agents get saddled with settling conflicts between "market norms" and other norms of behavior, and are faced with decisions about when market norms get overridden or are inapplicable.

This is to say that arguing on the basis of moral psychology is not enough, not when it comes to markets. In this chapter I am going to suggest that we need, in addition to an account of virtue, a tool for considering on a case-by-case, agent-by-agent basis the role markets play in our lives—and only the Stoics provide us with the right kind of theoretical tool in their virtue ethic.

1. WHAT IS STOICISM?

Stoicism was founded by Zeno of Citium in the fourth century BC, after who came Cleanthes and Chrysippus in the third century BC. We only have fragments left of these three original Stoics, but they are enough to see that they had markedly different styles. For example, Zeno wrote a Republic to rival Plato's; all we have left from Cleanthes is a poetic hymn to Zeus; and Chrysippus was highly argumentative and rigorous. We know about these three founders of Stoicism from Diogenes Laertius's *Lives of Eminent Philosophers* and Arius Didymus' *Epitome of Stoic Ethics*.[10] Although the Stoics divided philosophy into three parts, logic, physics, and ethics, it is Stoic ethics that authors such as Seneca and Cicero applied and popularized. Epictetus in the first century AD and Emperor Marcus Aurelius in the second used Stoic theory to exhort others to live well, using examples from the choices we still face in daily life today.[11]

Stoicism is a version of ancient eudaimonist theory, which tells us how our lives ought to be organized. Julia Annas deserves credit for emphasizing the shared commitments between the various ancient virtue theories.[12] Each school of eudaimonist thought maintains that we can develop a second nature if we aim to be ethical. This second nature will have us taking pleasure in more than what our first nature found enjoyable: it allows us to enjoy ethical behavior itself. The process by which we get there is one of focusing intensely on the reasons and goals behind our behavior. The suggestion is that we pursue our interests more consistently than we would otherwise, were we not interested in being ethical. When we are not motivated to do what we think is right, we are supposed to challenge ourselves to either become motivated or to revise a potentially unworkable notion of "what is right" by considering if it clashes with other ethical claims we (or others) endorse. The thinking is not supposed to be abstract; both Aristotle and the Stoics would have us focus on commonplace norms of behavior. Following these norms, when appropriate and for the right reasons, is what will develop our virtue. This is a voluntary process and one that most of us never bother to take up. Yet, it is only if we begin to prioritize acting ethically that we have a chance of reaching satisfaction or true happiness in our lives.[13]

If an ancient description of our nature seems implausible, it can be helpful to see it reflected back in the work of contemporary behavioral scientists and others working on the neuromechanics of choice.[14] They have found some of what the ancient eudaimonists emphasized: that we all regularly experience *akrasia* or the inability to do what we think is right. Some approaches that have been used to supplement ethics, such as rational choice theory, fail to problematize motivation enough to acknowledge how often we are akratic. Identifying the appeal or "inconsistent propositions" involved in akrasia is the same focus that traditional virtue ethics has always had.

Behavioral scientists are also pointing out that it is "our brains" that generate rewards, and not rewards themselves that provoke some regular response.[15] Traditional virtue ethics has always insisted this was the case. (And as we shall see, the Stoics put the idea to a very specific use as they discuss economic value.) If we fail to recognize that we so often "appoint" rather than "discover" value, we could assume that an agent would choose in the same way over time until she got some new information. But neither animals nor humans do this. Instead, as the psychiatrist and behavioral scientist George Ainslie writes that while making a choice, we "try out scenes before entering them." In doing so, "a scenario competes for our engagement against alternatives such as preparing coffee, taking a nap, or imagining something else."[16] We entertain self-determined and *prospective* rewards—dessert before or feeling self-controlled later—just as the ancients described.

The ancient eudaimonists also depict us as internalizing personal rules. If we violate these rules, we we're said to experience negative psychological feedback: "those who do not attend to the disturbances in their own soul" are "inevitably in a state of unhappiness."[17] The idea that there are psychological consequences to violating a personal rule is something scientists report. They are attempting to determine how we decide which choices we've made constitute lapses of personal rules. If you catch yourself lying to a client, you may never get caught, but there may be a psychic cost and an impact on your agency in the form of a loss of self-trust. As Ainslie puts it, we succeed at following our own rules only if we convince ourselves we "can't get away with cheating" and that our "current compliance" gives us "enough reason not to cheat subsequently." The more doubtful we become of maintaining our personal rules, the more likely we are to violate them. "Personal rules," Ainslie explains, "are a recursive mechanism; they continually take their own pulse, and if they feel it falter, that very fact will cause further faltering."[18] This will sound familiar to students of the ancients. The age-old suggestion concerning how important it is that we follow the ethical standards we set for ourselves has found much modern support, even if virtue itself has not yet been "found" in a lab.

Actual completed virtue is, for the Stoics, just an ideal. The Stoics write that it is "as rare the Phoenix," but they develop a term "progressors" to describe the benefits that come to those of us who at least attempt to order our lives.[19] What is involved in this is described well by the contemporary Stoic Lawrence Becker; as he puts it, "living virtuously is the process of creating a single, spatio-temporal object—a life."[20] With only modern commitments, Becker argues that the way we develop coherent life plans is to recognize the Stoic claim that virtue is the one value to which no others can be compared.

How can virtue be said to play this role? We have to turn to their theory of value to get an answer. Again, it is more than psychological detail that is necessary to the morality of markets. A virtue ethics that helps with markets has to have an explanation for, at least, how to determine the market's role in virtue.

2. THE STOICS ON ECONOMIC VALUE

Aristotle and modern Aristotelian approaches to economics (of which there are many) attempt to explain the market's role in virtue by looking to markets as moral entities. They argue that we should *moralize* markets and market norms. If markets are not yet ethical, Aristotelian-styled proposals have suggestions. The Aristotelian line is that wealth has a positive ethical value but is subject to ethical constraints. To be "ethically positive," it "should be neither too much nor too little: ethics determines the measure of wealth is right."[21] This requires either the idealization of the market or an attempt to limit markets or market participation in a way that suggests a sort of bifurcation between economic and ethical values.

The Stoics do what Carlo Natali calls "the opposite," a move that involves a complex sort of concatenation of ethical and economic value. Natali terms this a "radical" turn from the suppositions of Aristotle. Where Aristotle takes goods "external" to virtue to be necessary requirements for virtue and a good society, the Stoics flip this around so that virtue *operates on* external goods. External goods, such as our bodies, our loved ones, and our commodities, are the *material* on which virtue operates. Markets are this same type of material for human agency. We do not need markets for acting virtuously—we act virtuously *with* them. The Stoics will not task us with transforming markets into something more palatably ethical. (They do not do this with other external goods, either, often talking about how to care for a bad friend, for example.)

Instead of moralizing markets and market norms the Stoics regard markets as *natural*, as a part of nature. For them even the term "economics" (the Greek *oikonomia*) applies to not just markets but to management of persons and material in general; everything from a recipe to a community's political affairs is thought of as requiring a similar approach.[22] Their commitment to seeing markets as such a natural part of our environment, I will argue, enables the Stoics to be clear-eyed about markets. (Later I will soon suggest several features of markets as an example.) It enables them to recognize the full moral relevance of markets *as they are*.

It was no accident that the Stoics developed the unique approach to economic value that they did. Over hundreds of years they worked on the puzzles that Aristotle's approach to economics could not resolve. It is no real surprise, either, that a Stoic approach to economics is so rarely invoked today. Those studying ancient philosophy have not been particularly focused on this aspect of Stoic work; the last debate between scholars on the issue seems to be from the nineteenth century.[23] Even the most recent scholarship on Stoic economics remains untranslated from the Italian. Carlo Natali provides new translations of, and comments on, historical corrections to earlier translations of the Stoics, gathering the extant passages in order to indicate the general outline of the Stoic approach.[24] We are left with more ancient titles than ancient Stoic texts, and yet the titles indicate to us that internal debates between Stoics debating economics continued for centuries.[25] Cicero is a useful chronicler of Stoic economic views, but our main extant source of Stoic economics is Arius Didymus's *Epitome of Stoic Ethics*. Let's now turn to what makes the Stoic approach so uniquely helpful.

What may be most difficult about the notorious account of the Stoics on external goods—that is, any goods external to virtue—may be the term Stoics give them: *indifferents*, which Annas calls an "odd term."[26] Cicero tells us that the indifferents form "the subject-matter, the *given material* with which wisdom deals."[27] This means that virtue is the true good, vice is an evil, and all manner of things, including "life, health, pleasure, beauty, physical strength, wealth, fame, and good birth as well as their opposites, death, disease, pain, ugliness, weakness, poverty, disgrace, low birth, and the like" are to be described as indifferent.[28] We are not meant to be or said to be apathetic towards indifferents, for we could not survive without them.[29] We could not even survive without being motivated in regard to them. The Stoics describe our interest in and motivation for indifferents as natural. They take our interest in wealth as a natural one, not even just properly instrumental or for the sake of something else.[30] But natural motivations have their limits: the Stoics recognize that you can successfully pursue desirable external goods and still not have virtue.

They are certain that it is not the achievement of a goal that matters for happiness, but the manner of pursuing it. The Stoics tell us that the bad person will be unhappy "whether he has material or not."[31] Annas describes the Stoic depicting life as like an archer aiming at a target. The goal is to hit the target but also to display one's skill. No true archer is pleased to see an arrow placed in the target as a replacement for her effort.[32] The Stoics are worried about our current vocabulary in that we have no way to refer to ends that would be good only if achieved with virtue. Lottery winners do not always fare well after their wins, and the Stoic emphasized the relevance of these types of examples so that we would focus on how only virtue itself serves as an all-encompassing (and therefore satisfying) goal. They coined the term indifferents for this same reason, but it serves one more purpose, allowing Stoics to maintain their beliefs regarding virtue but still refer to the "kinds of things the majority believe to be good," even if the majority gives no real thought to virtue at all.[33]

When a course of action or object is referred to as an indifferent, it is best to think of it this way: the speaker is saying nothing about the absolute value of the good. The word indifferent is to serve as a constant reminder of how crucial the *use* of such things is to their normative evaluation. The speaker is specifying which of two scales of value (moral and non-moral) is being invoked. Some Stoics offered more vocabulary for this still, suggesting we could say we "choose" virtue but only "select" any good that is actually external to virtue.[34] The point is to make us practiced in recognizing the higher value of virtue.[35]

There is a joke about an economist at a cocktail party who is told by a fellow partygoer that he always wanted to learn Italian, to which the economist replies, "Apparently not." We could write a similar joke for the Stoics about the plausibility of their account of external goods representing a different type of value than virtue. A mother could say she would do anything for her children, and the Stoic could reply by showing her the headline of the mother who hired a hitman to take out her daughter's cheerleading rival. We speak casually about what our priorities are, and we find it shocking to hear that our children are not most important. But our good behavior indicates that we maintain our ethical commitments and filter our love for our children through these. To explain that we do this, we would need a theory like that offered by the Stoics.

A.A. Long explains that morality is "indifferent" to the "favorable circumstances that any normal person, including Stoics, would in principle prefer for themselves."[36] This does not mean that we do not love our daughters, and it is fine to want our daughter to be cheerleading captain. It does mean, however, that we stop ourselves from killing (or lying or cheating) to achieve this end of making her better off. The Stoics knew the term "indifferent" would shock their ancient audience, but they were aiming to get us to think clearly about the role of ethics in our decision-making. Indifferent goods are still, indeed, *goods.*

Orthodox Stoics (there were always disagreements over these matters) might refer to wealth as a "preferred indifferent," a good external to virtue that was so regularly worth choosing that we could note that by referring to it as "preferred." But no ethical analysis, the Stoics thought, could come through consideration of indifferents alone. The interplay between considerations of indifferents and ethical decisions keeps the Stoic view from being akin to "may justice be done even if the heavens fall." While the Stoics certainly recognize the potential for us to sacrifice our lives for a cause, this is something an agent determines is appropriate for her. The value of indifferents or "favorable circumstances" counts in ethical decisions. If they were not considered, the decision would not then be ethical.

Let me give an ancient example. Cicero records a number of cases of ancient Stoic debates over standard market behavior. In one, the "Famine at Rhodes," he describes two Stoics arguing over what it would be best to do if trying to sell grain to a famine-torn island. One side of the debate is represented by Antipater, and the other by his teacher Diogenes. Antipater argues that, given the famine, any information the grain seller has about ships behind him must be disclosed to the residents of the island. According to Diogenes, a good person selling grain need only follow the "common law of the land," which includes the expectation that a seller not actively deceive, but if "has goods to sell, he may try to sell them to the best possible advantage, provided he is guilty of no misrepresentation."

Antipater responds:

> it is your duty to consider the interests of your fellow-men and to serve society; you were brought into the world under these conditions and have these inborn principles which you are in duty bound to obey and follow, that your interest shall be the interest of the community and conversely that the interest of the community shall be your interest as well.

Diogenes then explains that the seller can follow standard business norms without ever forgetting "the bonds of fellowship forged by Nature and existing between man and man."[37] Cicero notes how extraordinary it is that the Stoics may disagree but need never refer to what is expedient as being worth pursuing if it is morally wrong. This example shows how indifferents play a role in model ethical decision-making. To Diogenes and Antipater, the value of the grain remains relevant—but it cannot solve the ethical dilemma.

For the Stoics, no general social good functions as the criterion to determine the moral value and the amount of wealth that is ethically appropriate (as they do in Aristotle's account). This orientation of the Stoics justifies (though does not require) a value-free approach in economics. Goods external to virtue, no matter how valuable, can be assessed through virtue *or* assessed "independent of the moral sphere." If economists look to value in the latter manner, the Stoics will merely recognize that they are studying what they call indifferents. They do not require us to consult virtue in doing something like this.[38] It is useful information, to be sure, even if not related to ethics. The Stoic account of virtue, along with its account of indifferents, enables strong, strident, ethical claims alongside ethics-neutral approaches to determining the value of measurable outputs or gains.[39]

3. ARISTOTELIAN ECONOMICS

There is no denying that the term indifferents can still seem unpalatable, and certainly is not catchy, but as is often the case, the appeal of the Stoic approach might be best seen in comparison to alternatives. To that end, let us move to consider the far more common Aristotelian approach to economic value. Aristotelian approaches to economics regard descriptive insights into general human nature and actual humans' situations as fundamental to the development of sciences that concern human behavior. This, I imagine, is not a controversial contribution. Much of the work by philosophers of economics is in this vein; also, when philosophers such as Elizabeth Anderson, Debra Satz, or Michael Sandel discuss the ethics of various commodities being sold, they are working in the Aristotelian tradition.[40] So, I would argue, is work that emphasizes the positive social outcomes of market-based societies (such as that of Deirdre McCloskey).[41] I also see attempts to compliment the virtues of entrepreneurs (discussed below) as Aristotelian.

Aristotle himself, of course, offers a very particular account of moral psychology in his ethics—he just does not make use of it in his approach to economics. In his ethical theory he painstakingly makes distinctions between different varieties of pleasure. When he is speaking in terms of ethics and personal agency, Aristotle makes it clear that the good man experiences a wholly superior type of pleasure and worries about how pleasure tempts many of us away from virtue. Here are Aristotle's *merely* ethical reasons for defending, provisionally, a type of private property:

> The exhibition of two virtues, besides, is visibly annihilated in such a state (a communist state): first, temperance towards women (for it is an honorable action to abstain from another's wife for temperance's sake); secondly, liberality in the matter of property. No one, when men have all things in common, will any longer set an example of liberality or do any liberal action; for liberality consists in the use which is made of property.[42]

This defense is dependent on an account of moral psychology and a ranking of value that applies to the agent. As an argument, it suffers terribly; we can imagine easily being temperate and generous even without private property. We also wonder why we would want to engage in temperance or generosity. The argument needs the rest of his ethical theory to be complete.

Aristotle simply decides not to burden the *Politics* with these types of puzzles or any of those concerning pleasure that he lays out in his *Nicomachean Ethics*. This is because Aristotle is considering the matter of what is good for cities as a political theorist, not an ethical theorist. When Aristotle discusses communism in his *Politics*, he talks about some social goods it might not encourage. He rejects a policy that solely permits communal property (including wives, which is his focus) because, in what may be the first articulation of the tragedy of the commons problem, goods held in common are not cared for in the way that private goods are. Holding wives in common would, he predicts, "water down" family relations. Next he suggests that communal property would result in our experiencing less pleasure because it denies us pride in ownership. In using these reasons to reject the proposal that property be held in common, he is endorsing the following specification as to what is to be valued: the preservation of property, strong family relations, and pleasure.

Holding up some certain values and assessing market behaviors against these is the same methodology used by Irene van Staveren and Elizabeth Anderson. Both of these authors agree that paid surrogacy violates the ethical limits of markets. If pay were involved in the having of a child, this would, van Staveren writes, "not be a meaningful transfer of the values of the domain of care to the domain of freedom." Permitting surrogacy "would undermine our caring for our children if it were done instrumentally for purposes that reside outside the domain of care and the children would notice this and feel uncared for."[43] This analysis is not designed to match how surrogacy appears to interested agents, and it is not invoking ethical theory. Interested agents will be focused on indifferents, either the child (I know, the term is "odd" here) or the compensation possible. How are we to imagine one of these agents to borrow or relate to the reasoning of the philosophers of economics? It is difficult to imagine the process. The analysis given these theorists is not designed to be adopted by agents themselves.

When developing a moralized conception of rationality it is tempting to assume that we can describe people as generally rational and as generally moral. But the degree of morality people embrace should not, for an ethical approach that invokes standards for ethics, be a non-issue or considered unproblematic. There are very few grounds for assuming that people's morality is developed to some extent, or that their reactions to various domains will be predictable or uniform. I want to argue that working at a level of such generality hides the way options in the market appear to us as agents. We often see that we will lose goods if we choose to do the right thing, and we are often not motivated to do the right thing. We also, as the example from Cicero shows, can be genuinely puzzled as to which option is the ethical choice. It is the Stoics, with their theoretical devise of indifferents, that reminds us that we are not under the sway of any one scale of value at any time. This reflects the flexibility we actually feel and have.

The Stoic alternative does not apply ethical considerations to general economic transactions. The Stoics have no expectation of uniform commitments to ethics in others and they do not see market norms as something that shape us, but rather things we can opt out of following. The theoretical category of the indifferents frees economics from the notion of *ethical limits* (such as surrogacy being wrong) imposed by an Aristotelian notion of "the right size." Because surrogacy is not obviously egregious (in which case they could condemn it generally in a sort of shorthand for having exhaustively reviewed cases which all turn out the same with no exception), the Stoics would remain open to the idea that those engaging in surrogacy may be blameless. The Stoics generally avoid trying to attach outcomes or situations in life to ethics. As Natali writes, "the Stoic position implies that a virtuous person can practice virtue in all manner of contexts: even a mogul could be a virtuous person, and today, instead of going racing in Panticapaeum, the virtuous could play the New York Stock Exchange, and remain good: in fact what matters is the attitude, not the amount of external goods one obtains."[44]

It may be that philosophers of economics do not delve into personal ethics because they would see that as too much of an affront on others' personal decision-making. But as we see with the Stoics, an approach to the market based on ethical theory can address our entire set of norms and the whole of our behavior without bringing pre-set answers to questions that depend so much on psychology and circumstance.

4. THREE FEATURES OF MARKETS "AS THEY ARE"

We now conclude by looking to three features of markets that seem to be more easily accommodated by a Stoic approach than by any other.

4.1 Social assistance in markets

James Surowiecki, in his book *The Wisdom of Crowds*, highlights many examples and studies that find us making better numerical, ranking-based, or comparative judgments when we can view the estimates others have made.[45] We judge poorly if we are guessing alone, but if you can see the estimates a few dozen other people have made about how many jellybeans are in a jar, for example, you can be guided to an answer that is "surprising good." Vernon Smith writes that much of his book *Rationality in Economics* can be thought of in terms of the wisdom of crowds. He thinks features of markets enable crowds to be wise rather than very unwise, and writes that

> We have already seen a host of examples in which collectives in markets are getting things "right" in the sense of efficiency without the individual participants being aware that they are achieving a rule-governed emergent order: equilibrium in multiple market supply and demand, the hub and spoke airline service network, equilibrium adjustment of price and quality in some asymmetric information markets.[46]

His list goes on until he gets to racetrack betting, markets which, he explains, are often found to be "surprisingly" efficient. But we should not be so surprised: the discovery that racetrack betting is efficient is only "surprising" to "behavioral economists whose methodology is restricted to deviations from the standard model."[47] But as is emphasized in his research, even markets that arise in experimental environments are "rational in the sense that they economize on information, understanding, the number of agents, and consciously rational individual mental effort and action."[48] Racetracks are no different. Racetrack betting markets also represent a form of "intelligence embodied in the rules, norms, and institutions of our cultural and biological heritage that are created from human interactions but not by deliberate human design."[49] Smith stresses that we need not articulate the rules or customs we follow to efficient ends. Agents do not need to be aware of the way that they get better returns on their bets because so many other people are estimating the most efficient bets for them. This point is intuitive. If we reflect on the choices we make ourselves, in the grocery or any other market, we are pulled along and benefited by observing what others are willing to pay. If by ourselves we had to figure out the true value of some commodity, or even its relative value to us, with some type of consistency, it would sap our energies. Markets are by their nature social, our choices in markets are by their nature social, and our communities guide us to efficient choices through signals we may not even feel ourselves perceiving. This is the first desideratum for a clear-eyed description of markets.

The Stoics give us a way to put this aspect of the market in a context, and would also consider Smith's work evidence of markets being natural, just as they insisted. A naturalized market is not one that requires we examine each market norm for its source. The Stoics take market norms to be justified not just by long-term benefits to a community but also by how they arise. If there are some gaps in our ability to understand what we are doing in markets, the Stoic account, which assesses as ethical your aims and intentions, is humble. Stoicism can readily accommodate the idea that we are not always conscious of what leads us to efficiency.

An Aristotelian approach, in contrast, is not looking to long-term efficiency to justify market norms; surrogacy may be wrong due to the nature of love or parenthood. It seems possible for an Aristotelian approach to somehow accommodate insights like Vernon Smith's "wisdom of crowds," but it will not be an easy fit. Aristotelian economics requires markets conform to our ethical nature, and if the workings of markets are more complex and mysterious than even our own psychologies, how markets will be related back to claims about social good is left very unclear.

4.2 The various roles we have in markets

I mentioned Jane Jacobs at the start, as she identified some of the norms of those who participate in markets. But she presents them alongside the norms of those, living in the same market society, whom she terms "guardians"; their norms say to "shun trading," "exert prowess," "respect hierarchy," "be exclusive," and "treasure honor."[50] There is not one role that people play in commercial society. We do have judges, police, and military, all of them adhere to these "guardian" norms, even though we would be likely to forget this if we only read the conventional criticisms and compliments of market societies.

In describing the distinct roles we may play, Jacobs reminds us of another point that ought to be accommodated in a justification of the ethics of markets: some of us must resist the impulse to trade and barter.[51] We teachers should not be offering "A" grades for sale. Others must ensure "justice is lopped and bound."[52] We do not want police taking bribes or responding to the requests of the person who can pay them a tip.[53] The ethics of many careers are at odds with those that require the pursuit of profit. Any ethical justification of the market ought to accommodate the roles that resist the benefits of ongoing transactions and trade. This is a second desideratum for a realistic approach to the ethical justification of markets.

Aristotelian approaches to the economy fail to meet these desiderata due to the very generality of their analyses. To be Aristotelian about economics is to take a "one size fits all" approach. The norms that Aristotelian-styled approaches recommend as necessary to ethical markets are not relativized to particular agents. For example, Joseph Heath has recently recommended these as the right market norms: (a) do not exploit market failure, (b) do not cheat, (c) do not game the system, and (d) refuse to lobby against regulations designed to correct market imperfections.[54] They nicely transcend some of the distinctions Jacobs points out, but agents themselves will be working from within a role and will have other norms than these to contend with—which the Stoics acknowledge.

The Stoics would never presume that we are all engaged in one and the same manner with markets. The multiplicity of our roles is something built into the original Stoic approach. Stoicism certainly has no difficulty speaking to guardians of our society, people who see their duty to resist trade, at the same time that it also speaks, in a different way, to market traders.[55] The Stoics can readily recognize the market norms that economists and philosophers have articulated and use them in defense of standard business behavior, but they are not prescriptive to us all in some general way. Furthermore, to be Stoic about market norms is to never fail to remember that direct contributions such as charity or other service is always an option before *any* agent at *any* moment. You may always give the company to your employees, no matter how many bourgeois values that violates.[56]

4.3 The values associated with success in markets

It is easy to lionize entrepreneurs or others who have been successful in markets. In one recent example, the Kellogg family (of cereal fame)

> cultivated the habits of hard work, accurate research methods with record-keeping, and even "liberality." They did not overspend, and were in fact quite thrifty in their habits. But once they hit upon a successful recipe, they went all in, investing in expansion and inventing a series of mechanical improvements to the production processes.[57]

And another, more general:

> A person's actions are motivated from within . . . Whatever his incentives, he must be committed to action, reality, and the need to transform ideas into concrete form. An entrepreneur obtains wealth and his other objectives by providing people with goods and services that further flourishing on earth. Entrepreneurs are specialists in prudence—the virtue of rationally applying one's talents to the goal of living well.[58]

But let us leaven these descriptions with what those in business, working alongside these entrepreneurs, want recognized: that they do not have to be ethical to achieve success in the market. Marc Pincus, the founder of Zynga, has been helpfully frank about this; he describes his early success as involving some dubious "products":

> I knew that I wanted to control my destiny, so I knew I needed revenues, right, now. Like I needed revenues now. So I funded the company myself but I did every horrible thing in the book to, just to get revenues right away. I mean we gave our users poker chips if they downloaded this zwinky toolbar which was like, I don't know, I downloaded it once and couldn't get rid of it. We did anything possible just to just get revenues so that we could grow and be a real business . . . So control your destiny. So that was a big lesson, controlling your business. So by the time we raised money we were profitable.[59]

Ethics can be related to markets while acknowledging the likelihood of successful trajectories like that of Pincus. Yet an Aristotelian approach to economics is designed to prevent this; it is part of what imposing ethical limits on markets is to do. The idea that an unethical person can succeed is a form of challenge to that approach. The Stoics, in contrast, are prepared for this possibility and consider it likely. It is even extremely important to recognize. We would confuse ethical good with mere economic good if virtue and wealth always coincided. And so the Stoics, better than Aristotelians, better meet this third desiderata concerning markets.

To underscore how the distinction between virtue and economic good is supposed to work, we can think of the wealthy Stoic. Natali explains that the wealthy Stoic is depicted not unlike later Protestant ideals: they may work hard to acquire profit or wealth, but do not hold it as equal to ethical concerns. The wealthy Stoic would be able to shake off their wealth like a light cloak if called to. As the Stoics write, to lose a great fortune to a good person should be like "the loss of a drachma."[60] This ideal, at least, is what we are afforded, if we see wealth as a natural good but an ethical indifferent.

5. CONCLUSION

Attempting to relate the good of markets to conventional thoughts about ethics is a challenge. We must honor skill in production and trade alongside sharing, giving, and direct contributions to others. But there are also puzzles for those of us already committed to participating in markets. Our ethical choices in the market are made somewhat simpler by the fact that markets can increase general affluence over time.[61] Market norms that contribute to the affluence can be justified in terms of concern for the human community, just as Diogenes expected. But we never, not even if we are exemplars of bourgeois virtue, lose the perspective of our more general judgment.

It is only the Stoics, I want to conclude, who recognize that agents are the ones balancing market norms against greater material gain, their other rules, and their personal ideals. If the Stoics did not give us an account of virtue, we would not be able to describe or address the options agents face, such as: Should I follow a market norm or quit? How should I value my time? Should I hand this child the toy for free rather than sell it? Should I share credit with a colleague or not? With the Stoic account of indifferents, we don't settle ethical questions once and for all, but rather we are provided the theoretical tool that allows us to ask why, even when we are in the market, we should not question whether profiting for one's self is the best thing you can do for others.[62] Is there any better compliment to a theory than recognizing that it lets us see what we already must have known through experience but could not before put into words?

NOTES

1. Adam Smith, *The Theory of Moral Sentiments*, D.D. Raphael and A.L. Mackie (eds.) (Indianapolis: Liberty Fund, 1759/1982), III.iii.11.
2. Deirdre McCloskey, *The Bourgeois Virtues: Ethics for an Age of Commerce* (Chicago: University of Chicago Press, 2007), 84, 297.
3. Jane Jacobs, *Systems of Survival: A Dialogue on the Moral Foundations of Commerce and Politics* (New York: Random House, 1992), 23.
4. Elizabeth Anderson, *Value in Economics and Ethics* (Cambridge, MA: Harvard University Press, 1995), 159.
5. For more on markets as "moral spaces," see Virgil Storr, "Why the Market? Markets as Moral and Social Spaces," *Journal of Markets & Morality* 12 (Fall 2009): 277–96, as well as the chapter by Choi and Storr in this volume.
6. McCloskey, *Bourgeois Virtues*, 247.
7. Ibid.
8. Deirdre McCloskey, "Giving a Damn: The Missing Ethics in Political Philosophy," *Bleeding Heart Libertarians*, June 11, 2012, <http://bleedingheartlibertarians.com/2012/06/giving-a-damn-the-missing-ethics-in-political-philosophy>.
9. See Jennifer Baker, "Virtue Ethics and Practical Guidance," *Social Philosophy and Policy* 30(2013): 297–313.
10. Diogenes Laertius, *Lives of Eminent Philosophers*, 2 vols., trans. R.D. Hicks (Cambridge, MA: Harvard University Press, 1925); Arthur Pomeroy (ed.), *Arius Didymus. Epitome of Stoic Ethics. Texts and Translations 44; Graeco-Roman 14* (Atlanta, GA: Society of Biblical Literature, 1999).
11. Julia Annas, "Ethics in Stoic Philosophy," *Phronesis* 52(2007): 58–87; A.A. Long and David Sedley, *The Hellenistic Philosophers*, 2 vols. (Cambridge: Cambridge University Press, 1987); Brad Inwood and Lloyd Gerson, *Hellenistic Philosophy*, 2nd ed. Indianapolis: Hackett Publishing, 1997).
12. Julia Annas, *The Morality of Happiness* (Oxford: Oxford University Press, 1993).
13. Julia Annas, *Intelligent Virtue* (Oxford: Oxford University Press, 2011).
14. Paul W. Glimcher, "Choice: Towards a Standard Back-Pocket Model," in Paul W. Glimcher et al. (eds.), *Neuroeconomics: Decision Making and the Brain* (Amsterdam: Elsevier, 2009), 501–19.
15. In his recent work, George Ainslie has been drawing on the implications of behavioral scientists having come to agree on the basic neural mechanics of choice. Multiple studies of monkeys entertaining choices in their intraparietal cortex indicate they are engaging in "vicarious trial and error." When we, too, do this, we are not just considering the route to greater rewards; we "bring up a memory so as to relive a scene, or a plan so as to anticipate one, or another person's experience so as to model one, and may stay engaged with any of them for a considerable time without necessarily being moved to any actual behavior" (Ainslie, "Money as MacGuffin: A Factor in Gambling and Other Process Addictions," in Neil Levy (ed.), *Addiction and Self-Control: Perspectives from Philosophy, Psychology, and Neuroscience*, Oxford: Oxford University Press, 2013, 16–37, at 25–6).
16. Ibid., 26.

17. Marcus Aurelius, *The Meditations*, trans. G.M.A. Grube (Indianapolis: Hackett Publishing, 1983), 13.
18. George Ainslie, "Précis of Breakdown of the Will," *Behavioral and Brain Sciences* 28(2005): 635–73, at 642.
19. Not even Chryssipus described himself as a sage; see R.W. Sharples, *Stoics, Epicureans and Sceptics: An Introduction to Hellenistic Philosophy* (East Sussex, UK: Psychology Press, 1996), 106.
20. Lawrence Becker, *A New Stoicism* (Princeton, NJ: Princeton University Press, 1998), 20.
21. Carlo Natali, "L'oikonomikos nella tradizione stoica," in Carlos Lévy et al. (eds.), *Art et ratio. Sciences, arts et métiers dans la philosophie hellénistique et romaine* (Paris-Bruxelles: Latomus, 2003), 75–88, at 78 (translation mine).
22. Carlo Natali, "*Oikonomia* in Hellenistic Political Thought," in André Laks and Malcolm Schofield (eds.), *Justice and Generosity: Studies in Hellenistic Social and Political Philosophy* (Cambridge: Cambridge University Press, 1995): 95–128.
23. Natali, "L'oikonomikos," 77.
24. See Notes 21 and 22.
25. Some titles we have without associated texts: Chrysippus, *On Ways of Living*; Dionysius of Heraclea, et al., *On the Wealth*; Hemisphere, *On Wealth*.
26. Annas, *Morality of Happiness*, 167.
27. Marcus Tullius Cicero, *On Final Ends*, trans. H. Rackham (Cambridge, MA: Harvard University Press, 1931), 281.
28. Diogenes Laertius, *Lives of the Eminent Philosophers*, Book VII, chapter 1, quoted by Tad Brennan, *The Stoic Life: Emotions, Duties, and Fate* (Oxford: Oxford University Press, 2005), 119. Diogenes continues, "This Hecato affirms in his *De fine*, book vii., and also Apollodorus in his *Ethics* and Chrysippus. For, say they, such things (as life, health, and pleasure) are not in themselves goods, but are morally indifferent, though falling under the species or subdivision 'things preferred'" (Diogenes Laertius, *Lives of the Eminent Philosophers*, Book VII, chapter 1).
29. Julia Annas is helpful on this point which earlier interpreters had sometimes missed (in *Morality of Happiness*).
30. "Of those some are acceptable according to nature itself, others for more efficiency . . . They are the ones who are able to elicit an impulse for inference turned to other things and not to themselves, such as wealth" (Stobaeus II 82.22–83, 6, available at <https://archive.org/stream/ioannisstobaeiec00stobuoft#page/n15/mode/2up>).
31. *Pseudo-Archytas, On Moral Education, 40.22*, available at <https://archive.org/stream/ioannisstobaeiec00stobuoft#page/n15/mode/2up>, cited in Julia Annas, *Platonic Ethics: Old and New* (Ithaca, NY: Cornell University Press, 1999), 43, n40.
32. Annas, *Morality of Happiness*, 402.
33. Aurelius, *Meditations*, 41.
34. Annas, *Morality of Happiness*, 167.
35. John Sellars, *Stoicism* (Berkeley, CA: University of California Press, 2006), 110–14.
36. A.A. Long, *Epictetus: A Stoic and Socratic Guide to Life* (Oxford: Oxford University Press, 2002), 196.

37. Cicero, *Selected Works*, Michael Grant (ed.) (London: Penguin, 1971), 177–80.
38. If economists with no real interest in ethics come close to modeling common decision-making, the Stoics would be pleased. They just know this is not the whole of the story.
39. They even prepare us to insert consideration of rights into discussion of economic goods. For more on this, see Jennifer Baker, "Don't Let the Best Be the Enemy of the Good: A Stoic Defense of the Market," in Mark D. White (ed.), *Accepting the Invisible Hand: Market-Based Approaches to Social-Economic Problems* (New York: Palgrave Macmillan Press, 2010).
40. Anderson, *Value in Ethics and Economics*; Debra Satz, *Why Some Things Should Not Be for Sale: The Moral Limits of Markets* (Oxford: Oxford University Press, 2010); Michael J. Sandel, *The Moral Limits of Markets* (New York: Macmillan, 2012).
41. McCloskey, *Bourgeois Virtues.*
42. Aristotle, *Politics*, trans. Benjamin Jowett, 1263b24–29, available at <http://classics.mit.edu/Aristotle/politics.2.two.html>.
43. Irene van Staveren, *The Values of Economics: An Aristotelian Perspective* (London: Routledge, 2001), 160.
44. Natali, "L'oikonomikos," 83.
45. James Surowiecki, *The Wisdom of Crowds: Why the Many Are Smarter Than the Few and How Collective Wisdom Shapes Business, Economies, Societies and Nations* (New York: Doubleday, 2004), cited by Vernon Smith, *Rationality in Economics* (Cambridge: Cambridge University Press, 2008), 182.
46. Smith, *Rationality in Economics*, 182.
47. Ibid., 69.
48. Ibid., 70.
49. Ibid., 37. See also Vernon Smith, "Constructivist and Ecological Rationality in Economics," *American Economic Review* 93(2003): 465–508.
50. Jacobs, *Systems of Survival*, 24.
51. Ibid., 186.
52. Bernard Mandeville, *The Fable of the Bees* (London: J. Tonson, 1724).
53. The non-trader instinct seems to be honored by Adam Smith in *The Theory of Moral Sentiments* when he describes prudence: "Wise and judicious conduct, when directed to greater and nobler purposes than the care of the health, the fortune, the rank and reputation of the individual, is frequently and very properly called prudence. We talk of the prudence of the great general, of the great statesman, of the great legislator. Prudence is, in all these cases, combined with many greater and more splendid virtues, with valor, with extensive and strong benevolence, with a sacred regard to the rules of justice, and all these supported by a proper degree of self-command" (VI.i.16). He continues, "the most extensive public benevolence which can commonly be exerted with any considerable effect, is that of the statesmen" (VI.ii.31).
54. Joseph Heath, *Morality, Competition, and the Firm: The Market Failures Approach to Business Ethics* (Oxford: Oxford University Press, 2014), 113.
55. In fact, Stoicism has been of interest to those in the military for some time. See Nancy Sherman, *Stoic Warriors: The Ancient Philosophy behind the Military Mind* (Oxford: Oxford University Press, 2007).

56. Dana Tims, "On 81st Birthday, Oregon Man Gives Company to Employees," *Seattle Times*, February 17, 2010, <http://seattletimes.com/business/on-81st-birthday-oregon-man-gives-company-to-employees/>.
57. Juan Pablo Couyoumdjian Netle and Michael C. Munger, "The 'Character' of Profit and Loss: Entrepreneurial Virtues," Duke PPE Working Paper 13.0306, February 24, 2013, <http://polisci.duke.edu/uploads/media_items/entrep-virtues-paper-version.original.docx>.
58. Edward W. Younkins, *Capitalism and Commerce: Conceptual Foundations of Free Enterprise* (Lanham, MD: Lexington, 2002), 113, quoted in Benjamin Powell and Rosolino Candela, "Markets as Processes of Moral Discovery," *Studies in Emergent Order* 7(2014): 258–72, at 269.
59. Michael Arrington, "Zynga CEO Mark Pincus: 'I Did Every Horrible Thing In The Book Just To Get Revenues,'" *TechCrunch*, November 6, 2009, <http://techcrunch.com/2009/11/06/zynga-scamville-mark-pinkus-faceboo/>.
60. Natali, "L'oikonomikos," 94.
61. This is the type of guidance that Chryssipus is referencing when we read "Where am I to begin, and what am I to take as the starting points of due action and the material for virtue if I pass over nature and the material for nature?" (quoted in Annas, *Morality of Happiness*, 168).
62. We might ask why Smith was not a Stoic when he borrowed heavily from aspects of their view? Here is, as best I can tell, his reasoning. Morality, he was certain, could only be represented by an account with at least the psychological complexity of the Stoic one. His own account added more still, of course. He writes that the Stoics had one element of our psychology described properly, but that we have limits that the Stoics did not recognize. We are capable, he writes, of evaluating only our local situations, the "little department" over which we have "some management and direction." As Charles Griswold writes, Smith takes us to only be able to think of ethics "with an eye to how we are placed in this part of the whole, here and now" (*Adam Smith and the Virtues of Enlightenment*, Cambridge: Cambridge University Press, 1999, 322). Smith concludes that "the plan and system which Nature has sketched out for our conduct seems to be altogether different from that of the Stoical philosophy" (*Theory of Moral Sentiments*, VII.ii.43). The issue can be put simply: when it came to the Stoics, Smith recognized only Antipater and not Diogenes.

4

Adam Smith on Virtue, Prosperity, and Justice

James R. Otteson

The reception of Adam Smith's political economy has undergone a sea change. For almost two centuries, Smith was hailed as the founding father of capitalism, with his 1776 *Inquiry into the Nature and Causes of the Wealth of Nations* seen as the definitive case for free trade and free markets.[1] Since the 1970s, however, a succession of commentators has claimed that Smith was not a classical liberal after all but more like a progressive liberal: his concerns for the poor, his worries about the damage that excessive division of labor can do to workers, his criticisms of merchants and monopoly corporations, and his apparent support for progressive taxation all taken as evidence that he was no supporter of laissez-faire.[2] Indeed, some have gone so far as to claim that Smith was a proto-Marxist.[3] So who is the real Adam Smith?

The problem is exacerbated by the fact that Smith wrote only two books: his *Theory of Moral Sentiments*, first published in 1759, and then *Wealth of Nations*, first published in 1776. The former focused its analysis on what Smith called our natural desire for "mutual sympathy" of sentiments (*TMS* I.i.2),[4] while the latter focused its analysis on what Smith claimed was our "desire of bettering our condition," which, Smith continued, was a desire that "comes with us from the womb, and never leaves us till we go into the grave" (*WN* II.iii.28). Several prominent German scholars in the nineteenth century thought that the two books thus offered conflicting conceptions of human nature and human motivation, assuming sympathy to be an other-regarding motivation and the desire of bettering one's own condition to be a self-interested motivation. The German scholars gave it the grave name "Das Adam Smith Problem." Although their formulation was in important respects misguided—more on this in a moment—nevertheless it signaled an important question that remains with us today, namely, "How do markets and morality mix?" Smith's answer to that question might thus help us understand how we should construct a system of what Smith called "political economy" that can integrate economics and virtue.

In what follows, I begin with an overview of Smith's account of virtue. I then turn to his conception of justice, and after spelling it out, I raise an objection to it, drawing on recent criticism that might fall under the heading of "social justice." I suggest what I think would be three "Smithian" responses to the objection, and then conclude by considering a connection between Smithian justice and equality that might underlie a broader claim about a Smithian connection between economics and virtue.

1. SMITH'S ACCOUNT OF MORALITY AND VIRTUE

Smith argues that moral standards arise as a result of an interactive social process.[5] Since human beings live in different times and places, the systems of commonly shared moral standards vary in their details; but since human beings also share, in some specific respects, a common human nature, their moral systems also enjoy significant overlap. The element of human nature most crucial for Smith's account is what he calls the *desire for mutual sympathy of sentiments.* Smith's usage of "sympathy" is broader than mere pity: "Pity and compassion are words appropriated to signify our fellow-feeling with the sorrow of others. Sympathy, though its meaning was, perhaps, originally the same, may now, however, without much impropriety, be made use of to denote our fellow-feeling with any passion whatever" (*TMS* I.i.1.5). The desire for the mutual sympathy of sentiments is, according to Smith, the desire to see our own sentiments, whatever they are, reflected in others: "nothing pleases us more than to observe in other men a fellow-feeling with all the emotions of our own breast; nor are we ever so much shocked as by the appearance of the contrary" (*TMS* I.i.2.1).

This desire is the *sine qua non* of Smith's theory. Smith believes it is what drives us into society, what motivates much of our conversation and conduct, what leads us to moderate our sentiments and behavior so that they more closely accord with what others would expect, and what ultimately gives rise to the habits and rules of moral judgment that come to constitute commonly shared morality. Smith provides many examples that he believes show that we not only feel, to varying degrees, the "sentiments" of others but that we also receive pleasure from realizing or imagining that our sentiments correspond with theirs.[6] Though this is a descriptive claim for Smith, he nevertheless believes it serves as the mechanism that generates what we regard as "moral" sentiments.

Here is how Smith thinks the process works. We are born, he thinks, with no morality whatsoever. A baby knows only its own wants, with no notion of a proper (or improper) thing to ask for, of a proper (or improper) way to ask for it, or of shame or remorse for having asked for something it should not have asked for. The baby attempts to have its wants satisfied simply by alarming its caregiver with howls and cries. According to Smith, it is not until the baby begins interacting with other children that it has jolting experiences leading it to realize that it is not the center of everyone's life. This is the child's introduction into the "great school of self-command" (*TMS* III.3.22): the experience of being negatively judged by others generates in the child the displeasure associated with not sharing a mutual sympathy of sentiments (MSS).[7] When one becomes aware that others do not share one's sentiments, one feels embarrassed, chagrined, isolated. The degree of one's displeasure depends on the particulars of the situation, but it is always unpleasant. When the child is spurned by his playmates, it causes the child to cast about for a way to relieve the displeasure. Eventually the child comes to modify his behavior to more closely match the expectations of his playmates.[8] When he does so, a new pleasure is experienced, that of the mutual sympathy of sentiments (MSS), and a new and permanent desire for that pleasure has been aroused. From that point on, according to Smith, the child regularly engages in trial-and-error investigation into what behaviors will achieve this sympathy and thus satisfy this desire.

This investigation encourages the individual to discover and then adopt rules of behavior and judgment that increase the chance of achieving mutual sympathy. By the time the individual becomes an adult, he has adopted, often unconsciously or only implicitly, a wide range of principles of behavior and judgment. Because everyone else is similarly engaging in the same investigation,[9] our desire for mutual sympathy of sentiments thereby generates, via an invisible-hand mechanism, commonly shared standards of behavior and judgment and even a shared system of morality.[10] It is an *invisible* hand because the agents in question do not intend to create a shared system of morality—they intend only to achieve mutual sympathy here, now, with this person. In so doing, however, they (unintentionally) establish the precedents and behavioral habits that will generate, constitute, and maintain a shared system of expectations and sentiments.

For Smith, then, the principles informing moral judgments are generalizations arrived at inductively on the basis of past experience. The experience in this case is of our own approvals and disapprovals of our own and others' conduct, as well as of our observations of others' approvals and disapprovals. Frequently repeated patterns of judgment can come to have the appearance of moral duties or even commandments from on high, while patterns that recur with less frequency will enjoy commensurately less confidence.

That is Smith's basic account. Let me now elaborate on three of its elements: "sympathy," moral objectivity, and utility.

1.1 Sympathy

Though there is more to the "Adam Smith Problem" than many contemporary scholars allow,[11] nevertheless its early versions rested on a crucial mistake. Smithian "sympathy" is not a motive to action at all. It is, rather, the "concord" or "harmony" between agents' sentiments. It is generated, moreover, not by mere observance of another's sentiments,[12] but, rather, by a comparison of a person's sentiments against what one imagines would be the sentiments generated in either oneself or in an impartial observer in the same situation as the "person principally concerned" (PPC).

Whether a sympathy of sentiments is achieved in any given case is dependent, for Smith, on the degree to which we can "bring home to our own breast the situation of those principally concerned" (*TMS* II.i.5.3 and passim). And this, in turn, is dependent on several factors: our knowledge of the PPC and of the PPC's situation; our willingness to "enter into" the PPC's situation imaginatively; our skill at imaginatively fleshing out another's situation; what our experiences have been with the PPC, with people like the PPC, and with situations like the PPC's; and so on. This means that the process of seeking sympathy of sentiments is complicated and delicate, and it frequently, despite our mutual desires, fails. Some have argued that Smith's description of the process of passing a moral judgment is indeed too complicated to be an accurate portrayal of what we do.[13] But the process is not obviously more complicated than, for example, driving a car in traffic, and if, as Smith suggests, it involves skills, then, as with driving, practice can lead to better, or at least more routine and less deliberate, performance.

Smith believes that the level of propriety of most sentiments lies "in a certain mediocrity," by which he means that the "pitch" of one's passions must not be too high or too low (*TMS* I.ii.intro.1). This is the natural result of the interactions Smith believes go on between the PPC, who wants others to enter into his sentiment, and the spectators, who are not as inclined to enter into them: they settle on a level somewhere in the middle. As these negotiations are executed over and over again, patterns emerge that become the equilibrium default settings. Deploying "self-command" to keep one's behavior close to those levels typically results in MSS, while straying too far from them results in a lack of sympathy or even an antipathy unless special circumstances obtain.

Although Smith's analysis might not qualify as a proper moral injunction, it does indicate that there are incentives at work leading us in mutually beneficial ways. Given that you desire MSS, and given that your chances of achieving it increase with the delicacy of your imagination and the accuracy of your judgments,[14] you should strive to hone your skills of imagining others' situations. If you do so, you will thereby increase the chances of satisfying your own desire for MSS, while simultaneously—if unintentionally—providing others with the MSS they also desire. Though Smith does not use the phrase "invisible hand" here, I suggest that this is an invisible-hand argument nonetheless. Language from WN applies here, *mutatis mutandis*: as each of us strives to satisfy his own desire for MSS, each of us is encouraged to behave in ways that enable others to satisfy his desires for MSS, thereby leading to behavior that "is most advantageous to the society" (see also *WN* IV.ii.4); thus each of us "is in this, as in many other cases, led by an invisible hand to promote an end that was no part of his intention" (*WN* IV.ii.9).

1.2 Moral objectivity

In a striking thought experiment, Smith asks what sort of moral judgments a person would make, and what sort of moral sentiments he would have, if he grew up entirely alone: "Were it possible that a human creature could grow up to manhood in some solitary place, without any communication with his own species, he could no more think of his own character, of the propriety or demerit of his own sentiments and conduct, of the beauty or deformity of his own mind, than of the beauty or deformity of his own face" (*TMS* III.1.3). He might have a sense of which things in his environment conduced to his ends and which did not—whether things "pleased or hurt him" (ibid.)—but he would have no sense of propriety or impropriety of his own behavior. The reason is suggested by Smith's continuation of the thought experiment: "Bring him into society, and he is immediately provided with the mirror which he wanted before" (ibid.). What the solitary man lacked while in isolation is experience of the judgment of others, which makes him confront his own behavior: this is the social "mirror" to which Smith refers. Once in "society" with other humans he experiences their (sometimes negative) judgments, and his formerly latent desire for mutual sympathy of sentiments is triggered, initiating the process of gradually developing moral sentiments.

This thought experiment provides two key elements indicating the moral objectivity Smith thinks our moral judgments enjoy: (1) moral judgments are the products of rules that develop historically and are not eternally fixed or handed down from on high; (2) they originate from and depend upon human "society" and interaction. Smith repeatedly describes the sentiments of morality as unfolding according to a process of negative and positive feedback dependent upon whether people achieve or fail to achieve MSS. Smith writes of the solitary man:

> Bring him into society, and all his own passions will immediately become the cause of new passions. He will observe that mankind approve of some of them, and are disgusted by others. He will be elevated in the one case, and cast down in the other; his desires and aversions, his joys and sorrows, will now often become

> the cause of new desires and new aversions, new joys and new sorrows: they will now, therefore, interest him deeply, and often call upon his most attentive consideration. (*TMS* III.1.3)

Smith here recapitulates the process through which he believes all humans normally go when they transition from infants with no sense of moral propriety to adults with a sophisticated sense of it. The moment in that process described here—when the solitary man is brought "into society"—is analogous to the moment Smith elsewhere describes as normally occurring to children when they first play with their mates and thus enter "the great school of self-command" (*TMS* III.3.22).[15]

The mutual adjustment of sentiments and behavior that begin upon this first experience of being judged by others leads to the development of habits and conventions of behavior, and then gradually, Smith thinks, to "general rules of morality": "It is thus that the general rules of morality are formed. They are ultimately founded upon experience of what, in particular instances, our moral faculties, our natural sense of merit and propriety, approve, or disapprove of.... The general rule... is formed, by finding from experience, that all actions of a certain kind, or circumstanced in a certain manner, are approved or disapproved of" (*TMS* III.4.8). Note the repeated emphasis on experience: Smith's argument is apparently that there is no way to form moral judgments other than by relying on one's experience of what oneself and others approve or disapprove. This act of generalizing from one's past experience is also what generates the perspective of the "impartial spectator" by which we judge ourselves. When judging our own conduct, we engage in a kind of moral triangulation. When we behave in a certain way towards another person, we have not two but three perspectives to consider: "We must view [our sentiments], neither from our own place nor yet from his [that is, the object of our actions], but from the place and with the eyes of a third person, who has no particular connexion with either, and who judges with impartiality between us" (*TMS* III.3.3). In practice, Smith thinks we accomplish this feat of triangulation often unconsciously: "habit and experience have taught us to do this so easily and so readily, that we are scarce sensible that we do it" (ibid.). Our moral standards thus arise from "habit and experience," not from apprehension of first principles, and they are pragmatically oriented towards the actual purposes and experiences people have.

But are they *right?* If the standards of morality are merely the coalescence of our inductively arrived-at generalizations based on our past contingent experiences, then are they not simply a creature of the particular place and time in which one lives? And how could Smith's account provide any normative reason, beyond strategic prudence, to follow them?

In the process of passing judgment, what one does, according to Smith, is consult the relevant general rules, ask whether the sentiment or behavior one is judging comports with those rules, and thereby deduce whether it should be approved. Such a deduction might approximate the following form:

Step 1: Observe that a "stranger passes by us in the street with all the marks of the deepest affliction" (*TMS* I.i.3.4).
Step 2: Apply the general rule that, unless there are special circumstances, a person should not behave like that in public.
Step 3: Realize that there are no special circumstances in this case.
Step 4: Therefore disapprove of his behavior.

The disapproval is caused by our realization that the stranger's behavior is inconsistent with the general rule. But the rule has no special authority of its own; it is merely our shorthand heuristic representing what an imagined "impartial spectator" (*TMS* I.i.5.4 and passim), whose perspective is formed by induction from our past experiences, would hold in the present case.

Suppose, however, "we are immediately told that he [the stranger] has just received the news of the death of his father" (*TMS* I.1.3.4). Now the deduction changes:

Step 1′: Same as Step 1.
Step 2′: Same as Step 2.
Step 3′: Realizing that this is a special circumstance, apply a new rule based on the nature of the special circumstance in question: People who recently learned of the death of a close relative are given far more latitude to express their emotions, even publicly.
Step 4′: Realize that this stranger's public display falls within the proper scope.
Step 5′: Conclude that it is now "impossible that, in this case, we should not approve of his grief" (*TMS* I.i.3.4).

Moral standards that arise in the way Smith describes are thus what John Searle calls "institutional facts," which "are portions of the real world, objective facts in the world, that are facts only by human agreement."[16] They are, using Searle's terminology, *ontologically subjective*, meaning that their existence depends on the beliefs and attitudes of particular agents; on the other hand, they are *epistemically objective*, meaning that it is not simply a matter of any single person's opinion whether they exist or not or what their basic features are. Their existence and nature are rather a matter of objectively ascertainable fact. I call this a "middle-way" objectivity, not directly dependent on any transcendent sanction—like God, pure reason, or natural law—and yet neither arbitrary nor dependent on any person's individual opinion.[17] They are objective facts of our social reality. This objectivity arises because they are the result of the invisible-hand process of local (micro) behaviors creating general (macro) patterns of order. It also arises because the shared standards rely on and develop in consequence of certain features of our common human nature, in particular our desire for MSS. A community's moral standards will, Smith says, vary along less important themes—conventions of dress, forms of greeting and address, and so on[18]—so the complete description of any given community's shared system of morality will be itself both unique and changing, at least at the margins. Nonetheless, because of our shared humanity and the overlapping commonalities of the human condition, certain rules will almost invariably obtain—in particular, what Smith calls the "rules of justice," to which we return momentarily.

1.3 Utility

Smith's account suggests that moral systems can be judged by utility. He did not envision an exact mathematical calculation or a summation of individual utility functions, but he does seem to believe that an empirical judgment can be formed about whether a given set of rules conduces to people's well-being.[19] His expectation is that the systems of order produced will tend overall and in the long run to be beneficial rather than harmful. Because each person is always acting to better his own condition, the rules of behavior and judgment that the community develops tend to be conducive to everyone's benefit.[20]

The role Smith ascribes to utility in morality is more complicated, however, than this description would suggest. Early in TMS, Smith writes, "Philosophers have, of late years"—he is thinking of Hume—"considered chiefly the tendency of affections, and have given little attention to the relation which they stand in to the cause which excites them. In common life, however, when we judge of any person's conduct, and of the sentiments which directed it, we constantly consider them under both these aspects" (*TMS* I.i.3.8). Smith continues, "The utility of those qualities [viz., the intellectual virtues], it may be thought, is what first recommends them to us; and, no doubt, the consideration of this, when we come to attend to it, gives them a new value. Originally, however, we approve of another man's judgment, not as something useful, but as right, as accurate, as agreeable to truth and reality" (*TMS* I.i.4.4). These passages contain not one but two levels of explanation for a moral judgment.[21] The first is the deduction from the applicable general moral rule of approval or disapproval, as described earlier. This is the level that Smith here describes as what one does "originally," and a sentiment's or behavior's comportment with the relevant rules is, I suggest, what he describes here "as right, as accurate, as agreeable to truth and reality."

The second level of explanation, however, pertains to the origin of the general rules themselves: to the winnowing and culling market-like process by which rules of morality are selected according to whether they conduce to MSS. When Smith writes that the "idea of the utility of all qualities of this kind, is plainly an after-thought, and not what first recommends them to our approbation" (*TMS* I.i.4.4), he means that the first level of explanation—the deduction—takes place without any conscious reference to utility. He does not mean to suggest, however, that utility is irrelevant to the entire process; utility's role comes in the second level of explanation.

Utility often does not, then, immediately inform the judgment people make about sentiments or behaviors: instead it is the sentiment's or behavior's adherence to the applicable general rule. Similarly, it is initially a sentiment's or behavior's comportment with the relevant general rule that prompts the moral judgment. Awareness of a sentiment's or behavior's conduciveness towards utility can amplify or diminish the initial judgment but it does not constitute the judgment. On the other hand, a sentiment or behavior that leads to an increase in utility tends to reinforce the sentiment or behavior and may ultimately establish a rule that will inform future judgments. When, therefore, Smith writes, "But still I affirm, that it is not the view of this utility or hurtfulness which is either the first or principal source of our approbation and disapprobation" (*TMS* IV.2.3), he is referring to the first level of moral judgment noted above. The rules applied at this level are themselves based in utility, though we often, perhaps usually, do not realize it.

2. SMITH ON JUSTICE

Smith offered what he called a "negative" conception of justice, one that can be fully realized merely by refraining from certain kinds of actions rather than positively engaging in any actions. As Smith writes, "Mere justice is, upon most occasions, but a negative virtue, and only hinders us from hurting our neighbor" (*TMS* II.ii.1.9). Yet this conception of justice seems to exclude many kinds of positive actions required by other conceptions, such as justice as fairness, justice as capability, or some conceptions of social justice.[22] What reasons does Smith offer in support of his conception of justice, and can it withstand scrutiny?

Smith draws a sharp distinction between what he calls *justice* and what he calls *beneficence.* He argues that "because the mere want of beneficence tends to do no real positive evil," it follows that (1) beneficence therefore "cannot be extorted by force" and (2) "the mere want of it exposes to no punishment" (*TMS* II.ii.1.3). According to Smith, acting with justice towards you leaves neither you nor anyone else worse off than you already were, though it may not by itself leave you or anyone else better off. For this reason, Smith calls it "a negative virtue" (*TMS* II.ii.1.9), claiming, remarkably, "We may often fulfil all the rules of justice by sitting still and doing nothing" (ibid.). The person sitting still and doing nothing is not acting with *positive* virtue—that is, is not generating any benefit—"but," Smith contends, "still he does no positive hurt to anybody. He only does not do that good which in propriety he ought to have done" (*TMS* II.ii.1.3).

So failing in proper beneficence—a category that for Smith includes things like charity, compassion, generosity, and "humanity"—might give us reason to disapprove of and be reasonably disappointed by another's behavior, but it does not license coercive punishment like retribution, jailing, or fines.[23] If I do not do you the good office you hoped or expected I would, you may be disappointed, even justifiably so; but you are no worse off than you were before. Because I have done you no "positive hurt," meaning I have not worsened your *ex ante* position, you may not take positive action to punish me. By contrast, if I fail to act with justice towards you, that means I did indeed do "positive hurt" to you; I left you worse off than you were before, which engenders the justified resentment that Smith believes licenses punishment (*TMS* II.ii.1–2).

According to Smith, there are only three rules of justice: "the laws which guard the life and person of our neighbor," "those which guard his property and possessions; and last of all come those which guard what are called his personal rights, or what is due to him from the promises of others" (*TMS* II.ii.2.2). We act justly, then, according to Smith, when (1) we do not kill or molest others, (2) we do not steal from or defraud others, and (3) we do not break our voluntary contracts or promises. By contrast with justice, Smith argues that beneficence involves making at least one person better off, while—assuming justice was also respected—no one was made worse off. If, however, that improvement was not required of me by law, by contract, by promise, or by any other specific obligation, you cannot have had an enforceable expectation of improvement.

This is a rather thin conception of justice: do not kill, steal from, or defraud others. What about charity, or helping others who need it, especially when we are in a position to help? Smith argues that beneficence is indeed frequently morally required, but since it is positive, not negative, it is not part of justice, and therefore not a proper object of state or other third-party imposition.[24]

Smith offers several reasons for supporting his thin conception of negative justice. The first is Smith's empirical claim that no society can subsist unless its members respect these rules of conduct. Even a society of "robbers and murderers," Smith says, must at least "abstain from robbing and murdering one another" (II.ii.3.3). On the other hand, a society can subsist if its members respect these rules of justice but do not act with beneficence towards each other. Because beneficence "is less essential to the existence of society than justice," Smith concludes, "society may subsist, though not in the most comfortable state, without beneficence; but the prevalence of injustice must utterly destroy it" (ibid.). Justice, therefore, "is the main pillar that upholds the whole edifice" of society, while beneficence "is the ornament which embellishes, not the foundation which supports the building"; for that reason, Smith argues, it is "sufficient to recommend, but by no means necessary to impose" beneficence (*TMS* II.ii.3.4). Thus justice is both necessary and sufficient for the existence of society, while beneficence is neither necessary nor sufficient. That means that they enjoy a lexical priority—justice first, beneficence only thereafter—and, if we assume that the state is justified in providing only what is necessary for human society, then it follows that it is justified in providing only justice.

A second reason Smith supports this "thin" conception of justice is its relative ease of administration in terms of (1) capturing its essence in simple rules, (2) detecting infractions of it, and (3) remedying infractions. By contrast, beneficence is far more difficult to describe in rules, far more difficult to detect in its absence, and far more difficult to remedy.[25] Unlike infractions of justice, improper beneficence can be detected and adjudicated only on the basis of detailed, context-specific knowledge of the situation and persons involved in particular cases. We might all agree, for example, that we should be generous and that generosity is a virtue; nevertheless, it would be very difficult to generate a set of precise rules that will allow us to determine what generosity requires of me, here, now. In practice, we have to rely on practical judgment, which Smith, like Aristotle, believes does not operate by mechanical execution of general rules.

Thus Smith believes that his negative conception of justice allows for a proper sensitivity to individual circumstances. What counts as being sufficiently generous depends on the particular circumstances of the case in question: the history and situation of the people involved, their available means and tradeoffs and opportunity costs, and even their goals and ambitions are all material considerations. There is also typically a *range* of behaviors or actions that might qualify as properly beneficent, which means that no single course of action will be required to satisfy one's obligations. Therefore, beneficence cannot plausibly be incorporated into the definition of justice, which, because it can license coercion, requires predictable and relatively precise application of clear rules. Smith's thin concept of justice restricts it, therefore, to those few areas of conduct that it can plausibly and effectively address, and leaves to localized judgment the determination of what positive beneficence requires in light of particular circumstances.

3. A SOCIAL-JUSTICE OBJECTION TO SMITH

Those are some of Smith's reasons for his conception of justice, but what are some reasons to object to it? To start, it fails to rectify, or even address, material inequality. It does presume a formal equality insofar as it holds all people equally subject to its conception of justice, but it would not deem material inequality per se as injustice. It would also run afoul of a luck–egalitarian conception of justice that requires inequalities due to things other than deliberate choice (properly defined) to be reduced to the extent possible or feasible.[26]

But let me raise a social-justice objection that can be adapted from an argument John Tomasi has given recently in defense of what he calls "market democracy."[27] Tomasi argues that social justice, which pays attention not only to the rules regarding acquisition and transfer of property but also the resulting patterns of holdings, should be a robust concern of all political theorists, including those espousing market economies. Tomasi finds wanting the argument that holds that the free market is justified because it adheres to proper principles of acquisition and transfer, but holds that its (allegedly) beneficial effects for the poor are merely a happy consequence. Instead, Tomasi argues that concern for proper distribution of holdings, which focuses in particular on the holdings of the poor, should be a central aspect of both the analysis and putative judgment in favor of market economies. Tomasi laments "Traditional classical liberals and libertarians oppose social justice so strongly that their reaction seems almost biological," adding that their resistance is "a malady that I shall call *social justicitis*."[28] Tomasi's argument is that the Rawlsian "justice as fairness" argument should (1) be taken seriously even by (classical) liberals like Adam Smith and (2) that the market's relative ability to realize the social justice implied by "justice as fairness" should be an integral component in the evaluation of market economies: "In a just society, institutions and rules should be crafted so that whatever broad patterns of inequality emerge reflect our commitment to respecting all citizens as valued members of a cooperative whole."[29] Even more recently, Thomas Piketty took a similar position when he argued, "social inequalities are acceptable only if they are in the interest of all and in particular of the most disadvantaged social groups."[30]

This objection to Smith relies on a conception of justice that requires us to take positive action to remedy at least some kinds of inequalities that, as both Tomasi and Piketty put it, are inconsistent with social justice.[31] Although "social justice" is defined differently by different people, one common feature is what I call the Incorporation Doctrine, or the incorporation into negative justice of at least some positive moral obligations—typically a positive requirement to help the poor, the powerless, and perhaps the undeservedly unlucky. The social justice argument suggests that the Smithian conception of justice, including the limitations it places on justified state action, is too narrow because (1) it disallows too many important vehicles for the alleviation of misery and suffering, (2) it fails to acknowledge any corporate or public obligation towards those less fortunate, and (3) it seems unduly to privilege its negative conception of individual freedom over, for example, welfare or equality.[32]

3.1 First argument defending Smith's conception: Knowledge

Let me now propose three considerations that I think a "Smithian" would marshal in defense of Smith's thin conception of justice.

The first is based on what I call Smith's *Local Knowledge Argument* (LKA): given that everyone has unique knowledge of his own "local" situation, including his goals, desires, and opportunities, each individual is therefore typically the person best positioned to make decisions about what courses of action he should take to achieve his goals.[33] That does not mean that people are infallible in judging their own situations, but rather that individuals have a better chance of knowing how best to use their own resources and what courses of actions to take to achieve their own goals than do third parties because they are more likely to possess the knowledge required to make such determinations reliably. Because third parties do not know your schedule of value, your opportunity costs and tradeoffs, or your tastes and preferences, the LKA implies that they are unlikely to be able to make reliable judgments about how you should allocate your scarce resources and energies.

A challenge to the LKA comes, however, from recent neo-behaviorist work informing public policy—as found, for example, in Thaler and Sunstein's *Nudge*, which argues that experts should arrange the way options appear so that people are more inclined to choose things they should.[34] An example will illustrate both the challenge and the Smithian position. Suppose the mayor of your city has banned soft drinks over sixteen ounces out of concerns for the growing incidence of obesity. But you like a big soda with your pastrami sandwich, so because of the ban you decide not to go to a particular deli for lunch today. Perhaps you were not dead-set on going to this deli anyway, so something as seemingly trivial as this was enough to tip you in a different direction. The Smithian argues that it cannot be known by the mayor of your city, or by any centralized authority (however expert), whether you were better off going somewhere else because of that large soda ban. It is possible that you would be better off, even if only marginally, but *possible* does not mean *probable.* To justify such a ban on the grounds that it would benefit people, one would have to demonstrate, not merely presume, that it would in fact benefit people—or at least that it is *likely* to benefit people. But this cannot be shown for you, or, probably, for any other single person because such a demonstration would require knowledge of all those crucial facts about individuals and their peculiar circumstances that are unknown, and perhaps unknowable, to centralized experts or policy-makers. The policy imposes costs—on soda drinkers, delis, soda manufacturers, and so forth—but we cannot know whether it is helping anyone because we cannot know (1) what the right amount of soda is for any given person in any particular circumstance, (2) what the opportunities and tradeoffs any individual faces are, or (3) how any given individual will alter his behavior in light of the ban. So the ban imposes certain costs in the hope of uncertain gain.

This Smithian response counts against the Incorporation Doctrine in two ways. First, it claims that mayors, legislators, or other third parties would know neither what exactly to incorporate nor how to do so effectively. The second is a two-step argument: because justice implicates state duties and thus coercion, it claims that a higher threshold of certainty should be met when proposing to incorporate duties into "justice" than into other virtues, and the implication of the LKA regarding the absence of this certainty constitutes a reason to oppose incorporating such positive duties into justice.

3.2 Second argument: Trust

Market-based societies generate material prosperity, yet they seem to require a background ethic that may not be produced by the market order itself. This ethic includes things like keeping one's word, honest dealing, industriousness, and so on—what Deirdre McCloskey calls the "bourgeois virtues."[35] But there is another requirement that, while not a virtue, is still crucially important: trust.

Numerous studies have shown the high correlation between a country's prosperity and the relative level of trust its citizens have for one another.[36] The higher their background implicit trust, the more prosperity; the lower the trust, the less prosperity. One can see why: if people do not trust one another to keep their promises and not to steal, even if confronted with what Robert Frank calls "golden opportunities,"[37] then there is significant incentive not to enter into cooperative agreements in the first place, thereby negatively affecting the production of prosperity. The question is: how do we create, and then maintain, a high-trust society? I do not believe anyone has quite figured that out yet.[38] But what we can show is one principal *threat* to trust: namely, the Incorporation Doctrine.

Social justice requires that we ask ourselves, when contemplating action, what the likely consequences might be, and then act on whatever it seems would lead to the best overall consequences.[39] This position implies that there are no specific actions that must always be followed or avoided; instead, we determine, on a case-by-case basis, what potential action we might take that we judge would lead to increasing utility (or perhaps to achieving social justice) and that judgment determines what we do. Thus in my associations with you, although my default might be to keep my promise to you, nevertheless I deliberate about what I should do *this* time, and I will do so every time

I make a promise to you; similarly, I will deliberate about whether I should steal from you or not, every time I am faced with an opportunity to do so; and so on. You will do the same.

Put aside for the moment whether the intent or even the ultimate result of the actions I take as a result of these deliberations is beneficial. Consider instead merely the effects of the uncertainty that is generated when you do not know whether I will steal from you or keep my promise to you. Perhaps you have run your own calculation and determined that, all things considered, I should keep my word and not steal, and this initially inclines you to cooperate with or trust me; but then you realize that you cannot know whether my own calculations will run the same way—and nothing I can tell you will give you dispositive evidence one way or another, because my statements will also be subject to my calculations. You thus realize you can have little confidence in your ability to predict what I will do, which means you cannot know whether I will defraud or steal from you *this* time. But since you know that fraud or theft will leave you worse off, your uncertainty about what I will do generates a disincentive for you to cooperate with me. Thus whatever gains we might have achieved from our associations with one another are foregone. As this process is repeated across society—meaning, as more and more people employ a social-justice ethic to guide their actions—more and more potentially mutually beneficial gains are foregone, leading to real, if perhaps unseen, losses.[40]

By contrast, if the people in a society have a background ethic that includes following Smithian rules of justice no matter what, then trust, and hence cooperation, is encouraged. Because Smithian justice debars the central threats to mutually beneficial cooperation—namely assault, theft, and fraud—it is relatively easy to predict what it will require and thus relatively easy to rely on. It can thus conciliate trust in society, which is a necessary element for generating prosperous cooperation.

3.3 Third argument: Failure to launch

Finally, a third argument a Smithian would marshal in defense of his thin conception of justice is this: being both undeservedly unlucky and suffering reasonable disappointment does not necessarily justify rectification.

An example will illustrate. Suppose Jack and Jill have been dating for some time; they are in love, and Jack is preparing to ask Jill to marry him. His expectation is that she will say yes, and Jill, for her part, not only expects Jack to ask but also plans to accept. Right before Jack asks Jill to marry him, however, Jill unexpectedly meets Joe. Jill and Joe fall madly in love, and they decide to elope. Jack, of course, is devastated. He has invested a lot of time, energy, and emotion into his relationship with Jill; he developed reasonable expectations that their relationship would continue indefinitely into the future; and his disappointment at this sudden, unforeseen, and unlucky change of fortune is both understandable and lamentable. We feel for Jack (and no doubt Jill does as well). But should we do something about it? What? Prevent Jill from marrying Joe? Prevent people like Joe from meeting or courting people like Jill? Should we allow Jack to sue for damages or demand compensation? The answer to all these is, it seems obvious, no. Jack's disappointment at this undeserved bad luck is entirely reasonable, but he has no *right* to be with Jill. He has no right to Jill's affections or to her company; he has no right to prevent Joe from associating with her if he and she so choose; and he has no right to punish either of them, or anyone else, if they choose differently from what he wishes they would.

The same applies to firms that go out of business in market economies. Suppose I have been frequenting Coffee Shop A for some time, and the owner has come to expect that I will continue to do so; indeed, I expect I will continue to do so. Then Coffee Shop B opens, and I am surprised to discover that I like its offerings better; I therefore stop going to Coffee Shop A. Does the owner of Coffee Shop A have any rights against me? No, for the same reasons Jack has none against Jill: bad luck and reasonable disappointment do not justify a demand for punishment or compensation. If enough people turn out to prefer Coffee Shop B that Coffee Shop A can no longer remain in operation, Coffee Shop A still has no claim to press; people are entitled to patronize whatever coffee shop they wish. The losses that Coffee Shop A may come to suffer are real, but they generate no justifiable limitation on others' choices or on others' behaviors. We can lament the losses, we can provide our own help to Coffee Shop A's owner or employees, and we can try to convince people not to patronize Coffee Shop B but to patronize Coffee Shop A instead. But we may not force people to patronize Coffee Shop A who do not wish to, and we have no more justification in imposing costs on people who choose not to patronize Coffee Shop A than Jack does in imposing costs on people who choose not to marry him.

In both of these cases, we have undeserved back luck and reasonable expectations that went unfulfilled. Smithian justice denies that you may seek reparation or compensation unless you were done "positive hurt" in your person, your property, or your expectations generated by voluntary promises; since none of those obtain in either of these cases, neither Jack nor the owner of Coffee Shop A can generate a claim of injustice and thus neither of them can justifiably call on state or other third-party coercive intervention.

By contrast, the social justice position holds that justice can require compensation either because of (undeserved) bad luck or because your legitimate expectations were not fulfilled—and especially if both those obtain.[41] But I think that these examples indicate that the Smithian conception is more plausible. Bad luck and real disappointment are regrettable, and in specific circumstances they may require us to offer help; but they do not by themselves constitute injustice entitling reparations because we must respect other people's moral agency too.

4. CONCLUSION: SMITH ON VIRTUE, PROSPERITY, AND JUSTICE

Smith's account of virtue holds it to be, like the market, an evolutionary and developmental phenomenon of creative destruction in which the particular application of "propriety" changes dynamically over time. Even the rules of justice, which Smith claims should be honored and enforced in all communities, were discovered in this historical, trial-and-error fashion and maintain their importance only because of the central role they continue to play in sustaining human communities. Thus Smith's account holds virtue to develop in the way that prices, property relations, contracts, and economic development do in market-based economies. For this reason I have described Smith's explanatory model elsewhere as a "marketplace of life."[42] And we can thus see how Smithian political economy offers an integrated account of both virtue and prosperity.

Although Smith's account of justice, then, is admittedly "thin," I have argued that a social justice objection does not yet defeat it. Let me now close by offering an independent reason to think that Smith might have been on to something important in his discussion of justice.

In both Smith's account of the development of morality and in his discussion of wealth creation in economic markets, there is an important aspect of *equality*. The commonly shared sentiments that come to constitute a community's system of moral judgments arise from the interactions of all people. Though no single person creates, changes, or destroys this system, and though no (or few) people intend to create any such system, nevertheless every single person's judgments, sentiments, and behaviors contribute to the dynamic and living signature of moral sentiments that constitutes a community's moral character. Everyone counts, and no one's sentiments are excluded.

Moreover, near the beginning of *The Wealth of Nations*, Smith argues for a rough equality of human persons: "The difference between the most dissimilar characters, between a philosopher and a common street porter, for example, seems to arise not so much from nature, as from habit, custom, and education" (*WN* I.ii.4). This was a radical claim to make in the eighteenth century, but for Smith it is connected with the implication of his argument that the principles of political economy he presents apply equally to all peoples, regardless of location, race, or creed. When Smith famously writes that "it is not from the benevolence of the butcher, the brewer, or the baker, that we expect our dinner, but from their regard to their own interest" (*WN* I.ii.2), some see this as an admission of the fundamental selfishness that motivates market-based economies. For Smith, however, it is a profession of respect. If the rules of justice preclude my commanding your obedience or mandating that you trade or exchange or labor in only the way I want, then the sole means left at my disposal to cooperate with you is by focusing on your needs and desires, and treating them as equally important to mine. As long as you retain the right to say "no, thank you" and go elsewhere, I am disciplined to respect you, your desires, and your wishes, and to treat them as equal in importance to my own. Otherwise you will indeed go elsewhere. For Smith, then, mutually voluntary market transactions presume a profound equality of moral authority.

Thus while Smithian political economy does not forbid inequality in material outcomes, it does require an equality of respect for moral agency. Smith's conception of justice applies equally to all people: we must respect the person, property, and promises of every person, regardless of station. The prospects of growing prosperity that his political economy promises are possible only if we act on a mutual respect for all parties. If, however, a fully virtuous life also requires numerous, context-specific acts of positive beneficence—which Smith argues it does—then such obligations fall not on the state or other third parties but on us as individuals. The Smithian requirements of virtue, then, are perhaps more demanding than one might have suspected: justice towards all, beneficence towards those whom we credibly believe we can actually help. Constraining the state to the enforcement of the rules of justice would not exhaust virtue, but on Smith's argument it would enable the prosperity required for us as individuals to effectuate the remaining positive aspects of virtue. Smith's conception of justice, then, though "thin," is for him the deep connection between economics and virtue: it is the first, necessary step towards enabling not only a prosperous society but also a fully virtuous life, both for ourselves and for others. For these reasons, I suggest it warrants consideration both from proponents of classical-liberal negative liberty and from progressive and liberal proponents of social justice.

NOTES

1. See, for example, James M. Buchanan, *The Limits of Liberty* (Indianapolis: Liberty Fund, 1975/2000), and Friedrich A. Hayek, *The Constitution of Liberty* (Chicago: University of Chicago Press, 1960/2011).
2. See, for example, Samuel Fleischacker, *A Third Concept of Liberty: Judgment and Freedom in Kant and Adam Smith* (Princeton: Princeton University Press, 1999), *On Adam Smith's "Wealth of Nations": A Philosophical Companion* (Princeton: Princeton University Press, 2004), and *A Short History of Distributive Justice*

(Cambridge, MA: Harvard University Press, 2004); and Emma Rothschild, "Adam Smith and Conservative Economics," *Economic History Review* 45(1992): 74–96, and *Economic Sentiments: Adam Smith, Condorcet, and the Enlightenment* (Cambridge, MA: Harvard University Press, 2001). For discussion, see James Otteson, "Adam Smith and the Right," in Ryan Patrick Hanley (ed.), *Adam Smith: A Princeton Guide* (Princeton: Princeton University Press, 2016); and Craig Smith, *Adam Smith's Political Philosophy: The Invisible Hand and Spontaneous Order* (New York: Routledge, 2006) and "Adam Smith: Left or Right?" *Political Studies* 61(2013): 784–98.

3. See, for example, Ronald L. Meek, "Smith, Turgot, and the 'Four Stages' Theory," *History of Political Economy* 3(1971): 9–27, and Murray Rothbard, *An Austrian Perspective on the History of Economic Thought*, 2 vols. (Northampton, MA: Edward Elgar, 1995).
4. Adam Smith, *The Theory of Moral Sentiments*, I.i.2. Here and throughout, I use the Glasgow Edition of the Works and Correspondence of Adam Smith, published by Liberty Fund (Indianapolis) in 1982: *The Theory of Moral Sentiments* (1759), D.D. Raphael and A.L. Mackie (eds.); *The Wealth of Nations* (1776), R.H. Campbell and A.S. Skinner (eds.); and *Essays on Philosophical Subjects* (1982), W.P.D. Wightman, J.C. Bryce, and I.S. Ross (eds.). I also use the now standard notation in referring to both *The Theory of Moral Sentiments* (*TMS*) and to *The Wealth of Nations* (*WN*): "*TMS* I.i.2" means *Theory of Moral Sentiments*, part one, section one, chapter two.
5. The following account of Smith's moral theory draws on James R. Otteson, "Adam Smith," in Roger Crisp (ed.), *The Oxford Handbook of the History of Ethics* (New York: Oxford University Press, 2013), 421–42.
6. Here are three of Smith's examples: we agonize when we see "our brother" "upon the rack" even when we ourselves are not threatened (*TMS* I.i.1.2); we "naturally shrink and draw back our own leg" when "we see a stroke aimed and just ready to fall upon the leg or arm of another"; and the "mob, when they are gazing at a dancer on the slack rope, naturally writhe and twist their own bodies, as they see him do" (*TMS* I.i.1.3).
7. And displeasure it is. A small but, for Smith, telling example: "A man is mortified when, after having endeavoured to divert the company, he looks round and sees that nobody laughs at his jests but himself" (*TMS* I.i.2.1).
8. Smith's audience for the lectures on which *TMS* was based was all male, a fact reflected in various references retained in *TMS* to "our" sex as opposed to the "fair" one, and so forth. For this reason, and not to beg any questions, I retain Smith's use of the masculine pronouns throughout.
9. See *TMS* I.i.2.6.
10. The phrase "invisible hand" appears three times in Smith's extant works: first in his essay "History of Astronomy" (published posthumously in 1795, included in *Essays on Philosophical Subjects*), then once in *TMS* (IV.i.11), and then again, most famously, in *WN* (IV.ii.9). Discussion of the significance of this phrase is legion. For a selection from a range of perspectives, see William D. Grampp, "What Did Adam Smith Mean by the Invisible Hand?" *Journal of Political Economy* 108 (2000): 441–65; Gavin Kennedy, *Adam Smith* (New York: Palgrave Macmillan,

2008); Leonidas Montes, *Adam Smith in Context: A Critical Reassessment of Some Central Components of His Thought* (New York: Palgrave Macmillan, 2004); James Otteson, *Adam Smith's Marketplace of Life* (Cambridge: Cambridge University Press, 2002); and Rothschild, *Economic Sentiments*.

11. I make this case in James Otteson, "The Recurring 'Adam Smith Problem,'" *History of Philosophy Quarterly* 17(2000): 51–74, and *Adam Smith's Marketplace of Life*. For other discussions of the "Adam Smith Problem," see the editors' introduction to *TMS*; Laurence Dickey, "Historicizing the 'Adam Smith Problem': Conceptual, Historiographical, and Textual Issues," *Journal of Modern History* 58 (1986): 579–609; Dogan Göçmen, *The Adam Smith Problem: Reconciling Human Nature and Society in "The Theory of Moral Sentiments" and "Wealth of Nations"* (London: Taurus Academic Studies, 2007); Montes, *Adam Smith in Context*; and Jack Russell Weinstein, *Adam Smith's Pluralism: Rationality, Education, and the Moral Sentiments* (New Haven: Yale University Press, 2013).
12. This is one difference between Smith's conception of "sympathy" and that of Hume; see Alexander Broadie, "Sympathy and the Impartial Spectator," in Knud Haakonssen (ed.) *The Cambridge Companion to Adam Smith* (Cambridge: Cambridge University Press, 2006), 158–88.
13. See D.D. Raphael, *Adam Smith* (New York: Oxford University Press, 1985).
14. Also required is what Smith calls "self-command," from which Smith says "all the other virtues seem to derive their principal lustre" (*TMS* VI.iii.11).
15. Smith summarizes this process in an abbreviated but arguably clearer way in a crucial letter to Gilbert Elliot dated October 10, 1759 (in *The Correspondence of Adam Smith*, Ernest Campbell Mossner and Ian Simpson Ross (eds.), 2nd ed. (Oxford: Oxford University Press, 1987), 48–57; see especially 54–5).
16. John Searle, *The Construction of Social Reality* (New York: Free Press, 1997), 1.
17. See James Otteson, *Adam Smith* (London: Bloomsbury, 2013), chapter 4.
18. See *TMS* V.2.1 and V.2.7–8.
19. Fleischacker interprets Smith quite differently; see Fleischacker, *On Adam Smith's "Wealth of Nations."*
20. Scholars disagree about whether Smith was ultimately an optimist or a pessimist about such "natural" systems of order. See James E. Alvey, *Adam Smith: Optimist or Pessimist? A New Problem Concerning the Teleological Basis of Commercial Society* (Burlington: Ashgate, 2003); Lauren Brubaker, "Why Adam Smith Is Neither a Conservative nor a Libertarian," *The Adam Smith Review* 2(2006): 197–202; and Craig Smith, *Adam Smith's Political Philosophy*.
21. Failure to distinguish these two levels leads some commentators to find Smith's position on utility "puzzling"; see Robert Shaver, "Virtues, Utility, and Rules," in Haakonssen, *The Cambridge Companion to Adam Smith*, 189–213.
22. On justice as fairness, see John Rawls, *A Theory of Justice* (Cambridge, MA: Harvard University Press, 1971); on justice as capability, see Martha Nussbaum, *Creating Capabilities: The Human Development Approach* (Cambridge: Harvard University Press, 2011) and Amartya Sen, *The Idea of Justice* (Cambridge, MA: Harvard University Press, 2009); and on justice as social justice, see Cass Sunstein, *Free Markets and Social Justice* (New York: Oxford University Press, 1997), and Pope Francis, *Evangelii Gaudium* (2013), chapter 2, <http://w2.vatican.va/

content/francesco/en/apost_exhortations/documents/papa-francesco_esortazione-ap_20131124_evangelii-gaudium.html>.

23. Smith distinguishes beneficence from benevolence: by beneficence Smith means taking positive action to do good for another, and by benevolence Smith means merely wishing another well.
24. Though see *TMS* II.ii.1.8, where Smith writes, "A superior may, indeed, sometimes, with universal approbation, oblige those under his jurisdiction to behave, in this respect, with a certain degree of propriety to one another." For an interpretation of Smith's conception of justice that differs from mine, see Fleischacker, *On Adam Smith's "Wealth of Nations"* chapter 2, and *Short History of Distributive Justice*, chapters 8 and 10.
25. Smith offers an analogy illustrating the differences: "The rules of justice may be compared to the rules of grammar; the rules of the other virtues, to the rules which critics lay down for the attainment of what is sublime and elegant in composition. The one, are precise, accurate, and indispensable. The other, are loose, vague, and indeterminate" (*TMS* III.6.11). Smith also claims that although there are "general rules of almost all the virtues," nevertheless, regarding the rules of beneficence, "to affect, however, a very strict and literal adherence to them would evidently be the most absurd and ridiculous pedantry" (*TMS* III.6.8).
26. See, for example, Richard Arneson, "Luck Egalitarianism and Prioritarianism," *Ethics* 110(2000): 339–49, and "Luck Egalitarianism: An Interpretation and Defense," *Philosophical Topics* 32(2004): 1–20.
27. See John Tomasi, *Free Market Fairness* (Princeton: Princeton University Press, 2012).
28. Ibid., 124.
29. Ibid., 89.
30. Thomas Piketty, *Capital in the Twenty-First Century* (Cambridge: Harvard Belknap, 2014), 480.
31. See Tomasi, *Free Market Fairness*, chapter 5; and Piketty, *Capital in the Twenty-First Century*, 20–1, chapter 13, and 575–7.
32. See, for example, Kasper Lippert-Rasmussen, "Luck Egalitarianism and Group Responsibility," in Carl Knight and Zofia Stemplowska (eds.), *Responsibility and Distributive Justice* (New York: Oxford University Press, 2011), 98–114.
33. The argument in Smith's words: "What is the species of domestick industry which his capital can employ, and of which the produce is likely to be of the greatest value, every individual, it is evident, can, in his local situation, judge much better than any statesman or lawgiver can do for him" (*WN* IV.ii.10).
34. Richard Thaler and Cass Sunstein, *Nudge: Improving Decisions about Health, Wealth, and Happiness*, rev. and exp. ed. (New York: Penguin, 2009). See also Peter Ubel, *Free Market Madness: Why Human Nature Is at Odds with Economics—and Why It Matters.* (Cambridge, MA: Harvard Business School, 2009) and Sarah Conly, *Against Autonomy: Justifying Coercive Paternalism* (New York: Cambridge University Press, 2012).
35. See Deirdre McCloskey, *The Bourgeois Virtues: Ethics for an Age of Commerce* (Chicago: University of Chicago Press, 2006).

36. See David Rose, *The Moral Foundation of Economic Behavior* (New York: Oxford University Press, 2011) for a compilation and discussion.
37. See Robert Frank, *Passions within Reason: The Strategic Role of the Emotions* (New York: Norton, 1988).
38. But see Deirdre McCloskey, *Bourgeois Dignity: Why Economics Can't Explain the Modern World* (Chicago: University of Chicago Press, 2011).
39. We need not spend time defining "best": assume it means something relatively uncontroversial, like producing the most overall good, reducing the most misery, or perhaps Rawls's maximin principle of redounding most to the benefit of the least advantaged in society.
40. Smith writes: "The moment he thinks of departing from the most staunch and positive adherence to what those inviolable precepts [of justice] prescribe to him, he is no longer to be trusted, and no man can say what degree of guilt he may not arrive at. The thief imagines he does no evil, when he steals from the rich, what he supposes they may easily want, and what possibly they may never know has been stolen from them. The adulterer imagines he does no evil, when he corrupts the wife of his friend, provided he covers his intrigue from the suspicion of the husband, and does not disturb the peace of his family. When once we begin to give way to such refinements, there is no enormity so gross of which we may not be capable" (*TMS* III.6.10).
41. See Elizabeth Anderson, "What Is the Point of Equality?" *Ethics* 109(1999): 287–337, especially 299.
42. See Otteson, *Adam Smith's Marketplace of Life.*

5

The Virtues of a Kantian Economics

Mark D. White

For a field that traces its modern form back to the work of a moral philosopher from Scotland, economics has struggled to reconcile itself with ethics. Since the marginalist revolution in the late nineteenth century and the widespread adoption of the constrained preference-satisfaction framework in the twentieth century, economists have focused on exploring how a rational economic agent allocates fixed resources towards maximizing his or her self-interested utility in a deterministic fashion. When ethical motivations are considered, they are normally included as "tastes" for altruism or fairness, constraints on proscribed action, or alternative types of utility or reward. These techniques are all valuable contributions to economics, allowing ethical decision-making to be modeled alongside self-interested choice using the same recipe with slightly different ingredients. For the most part, however, the outcome is still predetermined by its inputs, which belies the true nature of ethical reasoning that requires adaptability and practical judgment.

Given the algorithmic nature of the economic model of choice, ethical systems based on consequences (such as utilitarianism) or ideals (such as deontology) are the natural candidates when an element of ethics is required. However, the simple rules of these systems provide only guidelines for moral deliberation, not hard and fast prescriptions for action, and therefore are insufficient to accurately represent true moral judgment in models of decision-making. Models are by necessity abstractions, of course, but it may be the case that ethical decision-making is too imprecise and qualitative to model mathematically and deterministically, as is the norm in economics.

This critique suggests an alternative ethical framework, such as an ethics of virtue. As most commonly presented, virtue ethics takes the focus away from actions and places it instead on the person performing them. Rather than prescribe right or best actions, philosophers working in the virtue tradition emphasize the character traits that render a person good (or virtuous) and thereby lead to moral action. This type of ethical system does not endorse simple rules to guide moral action, but rather dispositions that people should cultivate, which then influence choice and action. Consider lying, for instance: a deontologist would say lying is wrong because it violates duty, right, or dignity, while a utilitarian would say that it is bad because it usually leads to adverse results on the whole. Either may make exceptions—when lying prevents a worse wrong, or when a specific lie will lead to better outcomes—but these are clearly delineated as exceptions to general rules. Virtue ethics, in contrast, eschews general rules entirely, and instead encourages a disposition to be honest that would result in truthful behavior *when* the person judges it appropriate in a particular circumstance. The resulting behavior may be the same under all three systems, but the thought process behind each is different, and virtue ethics dispenses with the pretense that a general rule is at all useful.

As this example suggests, judgment is a necessary component of ethical decision-making in the context of virtue—in a sense, sound judgment may be considered the most important virtue of all. Agents must assess all the morally relevant features of choice situations, weighing them to determine their relative importance and ultimately issuing a decision to act accordingly. Judgment plays an important yet under-recognized role in deontological and utilitarian ethics as well, being necessary to apply simple rules to actual choice situations, but it is widely recognized as the central method of decision-making in virtue ethics. Most accounts of virtue deny any value to rules in the deliberative process, which also aligns closely with the criticisms of standard economics models when applied to ethical decisions.

Critics point to this lack of simple rules as a shortcoming of virtue ethics. One can believe in the value of truthfulness as well as the other virtues, but these do not provide as much assistance to the process of judgment as do utilitarianism and deontology, both of which provide more "raw material" to ethical decision-making. For this reason, it may be preferable to supplement an ethics of virtue with a more explicit value system drawn from utilitarianism or deontology. Such a hybrid system, I maintain, is found in the ethics of Immanuel Kant, who is normally regarded as the pre-eminent deontologist. Beneath his immediate focus on duty, however, is a richer emphasis on character, virtue, and will, as well as support for the importance of judgment for ethical decision-making.

In this chapter, I will argue that an economic model of choice that incorporates Kantian duty and judgment can provide the emphasis on character that makes virtue ethics attractive, as well as a sound foundation in principle, both of which can enhance the descriptive and predictive power of economics. The first half of the chapter will highlight the aspects of virtue ethics that Kant shares, specifically a concern for motivation in moral action, an emphasis on agents rather than acts, and a disdain for rules. The second part will present a Kantian-economic model of decision-making augmented by a conception of judgment based on the jurisprudence of Ronald Dworkin, which shares an emphasis on character and integrity with both Kant and virtue ethics. I will also suggest several examples of economic problems drawn from individual choice, firm behavior, and policy-making, which illustrate the widespread importance of judgment to economic decision-making and the appeal of a model that emphasizes the moral character of the individual or institution when balancing various principles.

1. KANT AND VIRTUE

1.1 Kantian ethics and the critiques from virtue

The basic presentation of Immanuel Kant's moral philosophy begins with *autonomy*, the capacity of persons to act morally despite contrary influence from external factors such as authority and peers as well as internal factors such as preferences and inclinations. This capacity for autonomous choice grants all persons *dignity*, an intrinsic, incalculable, and incomparable worth that separates persons from things and implies that they must be treated as valuable ends. Based on the respect and reciprocity demanded by the equal dignity of persons, Kant derived the *categorical imperative*, a set of related formulae which agents use to judge plans of action, or *maxims*, for consistency with the moral law. If a maxim fails the categorical imperative test, it results in a duty not to engage in that behavior.[1]

While all duties are negative in the sense that they are derived from rejected maxims, they can be divided into two types based on whether they prohibit action or inaction. *Perfect duties* prohibit particular actions, such as "do not lie" and "do not kill," and are also called *strict duties* because they do not admit of any exceptions based on desire or inclination: for example, lying is prohibited no matter how much it might benefit the liar (or others he might be considering). *Imperfect duties*, on the other hand, prohibit inaction, such as ignoring the suffering of others or letting one's natural talents atrophy, which, when flipped to positive form, become duties of beneficence and developing one's talents (respectively). These are also called *wide duties* because they do not mandate any particular action, but rather ends that must be adopted and acted upon when appropriate. We are not required to help all in need, but if we can help someone without compromising our other duties and responsibilities (including to ourselves), we should, although there is no strict requirement regarding where or when.[2]

Based on the emphasis given to these duties—especially the perfect or strict ones—many regard Kant to be a demanding moralist, imposing a list of rules that must be followed, regardless of any reasons to the contrary, in order to be a moral person. Furthermore, these duties not only must be followed but must be followed for the right reason, namely, for the sake of duty itself, rather than honors, rewards, or satisfaction. This only enhances the perception of Kant's ethics as cold, seeming to imply that the person who helps the poor out of natural inclination is less moral than the person who does it out of a strong sense of duty but begrudgingly so. Finally, because the categorical imperative is based solely on logic, it applies equally to autonomous beings everywhere, whether in Jamestown, Jakarta, or Jupiter, which suggests that, at its core, Kantian ethics are insensitive to the realities of human nature and the moral importance of context, culture, and circumstance.

This less-than-flattering picture of Kant's rich and nuanced moral philosophy can be attributed, in all fairness, to the brief and relatively sterile treatment given in the *Groundwork for the Metaphysics of Morals*, the paucity of English translations of Kant's later work until recently, and some of Kant's own ill-considered rhetoric. All the same, when virtue ethics was revived in the second half of the twentieth century, it was presented in opposition to Kant along these very lines. In the paper often credited with the rise of virtue ethics in the 1950s, G.E.M. Anscombe described Kant as simplistic and dogmatic:

> His own rigoristic convictions on the subject of lying were so intense that it never occurred to him that a lie could be relevantly described as anything but just a lie (for example as "a lie in such-and-such circumstances"). His rule about universalizable maxims is useless without stipulations as to what shall count as a relevant description of an action with a view to constructing a maxim about it.[3]

Alasdair MacIntyre agreed with Anscombe regarding the empty formality of Kant's ethics, adding that

> Practical reason, according to Kant, employs no criterion external to itself. It appeals to no content derived from experience... It is of the essence of reason that it lays down principles which are universal, categorical and internally consistent. Hence a rational morality will lay down principles which both can and ought to be held by *all* men, independent of circumstances and conditions, and which could consistently be obeyed by every rational agent on every occasion.[4]

MacIntyre also criticized the focus on duties and rules in Kant's ethics, writing that in Kant "we have reached a point at which the notion that morality is anything other than obedience to rules has almost, if not quite, disappeared from view."[5] Finally, other philosophers criticized the lack of feeling or emotion in Kant's ethics, such as Michael Stocker's famous characterization of modern deontology (and utilitarianism) as necessitating "a schizophrenia between reason and motive," and as a result leaving persons themselves out of accounts of what they should do.[6]

As opposed to Kant, whom they regard as offering a rigorous, dispassionate ethics that elevates rules over the persons who are bound to follow them, critics such as Anscombe and MacIntyre argue for a return to the character-based virtue ethics of the ancient Greeks and Romans, primarily Aristotle and, to a lesser extent, the Stoics. In response, Kantian philosophers have defended his ethics against this characterization, arguing that Kant's moral philosophy incorporates many of the features of virtue ethics that critics find lacking, resulting in a growing consensus among many philosophers that Kant and the virtue ethicists are not so far apart after all.

1.2 Finding the virtue in Kant

In this section, I provide an overview of the virtue-related aspects of Kant's ethics, relying on Robert Louden's three distinctions between virtue ethics and Kantian deontology, which reflect the critiques cited above.[7] First, and perhaps most basic, virtue ethics focuses on persons rather than actions, regarding an agent's virtues (in particular) and character (in general) to be primary in ethical terms. Second, more specifically, virtue ethics eschews the formality of rules or principles in favor of general dispositions guided by practical judgment, referring back to the moral character of the agent in making choices in alignment with both virtue as well as specific context and circumstances. Finally, whereas Kant's ethics are regarded as purely rational and even opposed to sympathetic feeling, advocates of virtue in ethics emphasize the role of desires and emotions in moral character and behavior, in general focusing on the motivation behind action as much as the action itself.

1.2.1 Motivation

While the nature and source of motivation differs between Kant and the early virtue ethicists, motivation in general is critically important to both. For Kant, as described above, performing one's duty for the sake of duty is integral to being a moral person, as opposed to simply acting in accordance with duty but for other reasons. Virtue ethicists acknowledge this focus on motivation in Kant but nonetheless bemoan the absence of human feeling in it, as typified by Kant's infamous passage in the *Groundwork* about charitable dispositions being of no moral value.[8] They argue that a virtuous character trait must be an integral part of a person's character so that it issues in action naturally and, ideally, accompanied by positive emotion because the person wants and likes to act in that way.

It is true that emotion does not play such a direct role for Kant in motivating moral action, but it is not, as critics claim, antithetical to it, and in fact Kant's language regarding emotion reflects a general orientation in virtue. Louden acknowledges the standard claims regarding Kant on this issue but argues "Kant explicitly asserts that the emotions have a necessary and positive role to play in moral motivation in his later writings."[9] This is better understood in light of Kant's recognition that human beings are by their nature morally imperfect, and therefore any reinforcement of morality is appreciated, even if it would not be necessary for a perfect moral being. For example, in the *Metaphysics of Morals* he sounds a pragmatic note when he writes that "what is not done with pleasure but merely as compulsory service has no inner worth for one who attends to his duty in this way and such service is not loved by him; instead, he shirks as much as possible occasions for practicing virtue."[10]

After quoting this passage, Louden notes that "here and elsewhere Kant addresses the need to cultivate an 'habitually cheerful heart,' in order that the feeling of joy accompanies (but does not constitute or determine) our virtue."[11] He also quotes from Kant's *Religion*, including an indictment of the person driven by cold duty alone, whose "slavish frame of mind can never be found without a hidden hatred of the law, whereas a heart which is joyous in the compliance with its duty (not just complacency in the recognition of it) is the sign of genuineness in virtuous disposition," an explicit nod to the language of virtue.[12] Nancy Sherman calls attention also to the need for moral sensitivities to alert us to when duty needs to be practiced, acting as "modes of attention that help us track what is morally salient in our circumstances, and thus locate possible moments for morally permissible and required actions."[13] She quotes Kant from the *Metaphysics of Morals*, in which he writes that it is

> an indirect duty to cultivate the compassionate natural (aesthetic) feelings in us, and to make use of them as so many means to sympathy based on moral principles and the feeling appropriate to them.... For this is still one of the impulses that nature has implanted in us to do what the representation of duty might not accomplish.[14]

In Kant's ethics, the role of emotion in motivating ethical action may not be as direct as in most accounts of virtue, but it plays an important role nonetheless, and serves to bring Kant one step closer to an ethics of virtue.[15]

1.2.2 Agents and acts

As explained above, both deontology and consequentialism focus on determining the right action in a given situation. Virtue ethics, on the other hand, focuses on the person having and cultivating the character traits or dispositions that lead to moral action. However, much of Kant's work abstracts away from duties and actions to encompass the person behind them, bringing him closer to an ethics of virtue. Furthermore, the combination of character as well as duty (or principle), some argue, renders his position superior to that of virtue ethicists, who lack a firm basis in principle or rules.[16]

The first example of this appears famously in the very first line of the *Groundwork*: "There is no possibility of thinking of anything at all in the world, or even out of it, which can be regarded as good without qualification, except a *good will*."[17] It would be simple to interpret this statement as implying that, above individual acts performed in accordance with (and for the sake of) duty, the most important ethical aspect of a good person is her overall moral character, that which determines how often and to what extent she reasons and acts out of respect for the moral law. But the fact that the "good will" is based on something higher—namely, the moral law—means that the good will itself is not primary, as virtues are normally regarded. The basic issue here is whether duty or virtue is primary: does acting in accordance with (and for the sake of) duty make one virtuous, or does the virtuous person act in accordance with duty? In virtue ethics, a person's possession of virtues leads to that person performing virtuous acts, but if Kant's good will is based on a person acting out of respect for the moral law, then the moral law is primary. As Louden writes, "since human virtue is defined in terms of conformity to law and the categorical imperative, it appears now that what is primary in Kantian ethics is not virtue for virtue's sake but obedience to rules."[18]

Nonetheless, the good will can be considered an analog of character and virtue despite its being secondary to the moral law and its corresponding duties and rules. As Louden continues,

> Kantian virtue therefore is subordinate to the moral law, and this makes him look more like an obedience-to-rules theorist. However, it is obedience to rules not in the narrow-minded pharisaic manner for which rule ethics is usually chastised by virtue theorists, but in the broader, classical sense of living a life according to reason. The two perspectives of agent and rule are thus both clearly present in Kant's account of the good will.[19]

Jeanine Grenberg provides a similar take, writing that "a further Kantian constraint on virtue is that virtuous action must be autonomous action," and to choose to live according to the moral law "is the ultimate expression of an agent's autonomous and virtuous self."[20] This depicts virtuous acts as deriving from an autonomous will out of respect for the moral law rather than from specific virtues or dispositions, but with the same grounding in the character of the person that virtue ethics emphasizes. We see this in Louden's description of the duty of self-perfection, which "includes as its most important component the obligation to cultivate one's will 'to the purest attitude of virtue'" and "is the linchpin of Kant's entire system of duties."[21]

Kant did write of virtue more explicitly than in the case of the "good will," although not usually in the sense of virtues as specific character traits, about which he was dismissively critical (despite their commendation by "the ancients"):

> Some qualities are even conducive to this good will itself and can facilitate its work. Nevertheless, they have no intrinsic unconditional worth; but they always presuppose, rather, a good will, which restricts the high esteem in which they are otherwise rightly held, and does not permit them to be regarded as absolutely good.[22]

His most common use of the word "virtue" was in the sense of strength, self-constraint, or "fortitude in relation to the forces opposing a moral attitude of will in us."[23] Because human beings are imperfect, even a person with a good will cannot have absolute moral strength; as Hill writes, "a good will is a fundamental commitment to doing what is right, despite obstacles, but a good will may be weak. A virtuous person has a will that is both good and strong."[24] However, this strength must be developed and maintained: "For while the capacity to overcome all opposing sensible impulses can and must be simply *presupposed* in man on account of his freedom, yet this capacity as *strength* is something he must acquire."[25] This is done through practice, both mental and practical: "the way to acquire [strength] is to enhance the moral *incentive* (the thought of the law), both by contemplating the dignity of the pure rational law in us and by *practicing* virtue."[26] If this is not done, however, strength atrophies: "if it is not rising, [it] is unavoidably sinking."[27]

While Kant's notion of moral strength is not a specific virtue in the traditional sense, it does serve in his ethics as an *executive virtue*, enabling the agent to more reliably act in accordance with duty in the face of temptations to the contrary. As Louden acknowledges, in this sense the virtue of strength or self-constraint precedes all other duties, and provides an example of virtue serving a primary purpose in Kant's ethics: "for Kant, virtue's role is thoroughgoing: human morality cannot get under way without it."[28] However, even in light of these various emphases on different elements of virtue, Onora O'Neill stops short of arguing that Kant's ethics are agent-centered, claiming merely that his position "can allow for agent-centered ways of thinking" but that "its basic framework is not specifically agent-centered."[29]

A final aspect of virtue in Kant appears in his imperfect duties, requiring that an attitude (such as beneficence) be held and the corresponding end be pursued when possible, given the requirements of other duties. Appropriately, Kant also referred to these as "duties of virtue" (which are described at length in *The Doctrine of Virtue*, the second half of *The Metaphysics of Morals*). Given their wide nature, the fact that they endorse positive action, the importance of judgment in executing them, and the inner strength required to adhere to them in the absence of external sanction, this is perhaps Kant's most obvious overlap in substantive terms with virtue (again, in the form of principle).[30] However, even perfect duties, those strict prohibitions of acts such as lying and stealing, do not require specific positive actions; one must not lie but one need not be completely forthright either, and may in fact be evasive as long as it does not involve deception. In this sense, both imperfect and perfect duties are "wide" with respect to what *can* be done, and both require the use of judgment to guide action in the same way that virtues do. As Marcia Baron writes, incorporating the role of emotion described above, the duty of beneficence

> entails transforming ourselves (as needed) so that we are disposed to help others and, moreover, disposed to do so in a generous and cheerful frame of mind, maintaining our cheerful resolution to help them even if because of some petty grudge, or because we are preoccupied with some personal matter, we don't feel like helping. In sum, the duty of beneficence calls for us to be beneficent: to have, or at least strive to have, the virtue of beneficence.[31]

She goes on to say, "it is hard to imagine how the imperfect duties could be understood or articulated without the notion of a virtue."[32] One critical difference, however, noted by Philip Stratton-Lake, is that virtues must issue in action, whereas duties need not.[33] Nonetheless, recognizing the latitude for positive action under all of Kant's duties belies the accusation of demandingness in his moral system, and shows it instead to be flexible and, more important, useless in practice without judgment.

1.2.3 Rules and character

Related to the issue of whether acts or agents are the focus of Kantian ethics is the way moral decisions are made, either according to duties or rules or resulting from virtues as processed by practical judgment. We have already seen that Kant's emphasis on duties and rules is overstated and that there is much more flexibility in his ethics than is normally understood, flexibility that requires the same use of judgment upon which virtue ethics relies for decision-making.

In her work on Kant and virtue, Onora O'Neill downplays the role of duties and rules in Kantian ethics, and instead emphasizes the principles they embody and which represent "guidelines for living," echoing the language of virtues and the good life. According to O'Neill, "the core of morality would lie in having appropriate underlying principles rather than in conforming one's actions to specific standards."[34] Hill echoes this, writing that the principles Kant presents

> are a philosopher's attempt to articulate reasonable answers to recurrent moral questions that human beings face despite many differences in their circumstances. The principles are offered, with supporting arguments, in order to convince a reflective, critical audience that *doing what these principles prescribe* is necessary for a morally good life.[35]

He goes on to say that Kant "proposes the principles as considerations that anyone would need to respect as grounds for their decisions in order to be fully virtuous."[36] O'Neill originally argued that Kant proposed an "ethic of virtue rather than of rules," but based on this emphasis on principles—which will play an essential role in our discussion of judgment to follow—she later revised this statement to "an ethic of principles, rather than one specifically of virtues."[37]

Some argue that the dichotomy between principles and virtues maintained by many virtue ethicists is mistaken.[38] For instance, Grenberg argues that principle is essential to virtue:

> Principle should not be thought to be something entirely distinct from virtue, a mere appendage to the virtues, something added on to them as a supplement. It is, rather, something integral to virtue itself, and indeed, that thing that defines a virtue as a virtue. For, without appeal to principle, that is, to some guiding value of the person, we can't understand what is virtuous—good or valuable—about the state of character under consideration. . . . To affirm that principle is the ultimate realm of moral evaluation thus does not undermine virtue theory; rather, it affirms the moral centrality of just that thing which makes a virtue a virtue at all.[39]

Robert Audi agrees, writing that "moral virtue seems best construed as a kind of internalization of moral values or perhaps moral principles or other standards of moral conduct."[40] In general, this reiterates the convergence described above between virtue or character and the moral law and the claim that neither one must be considered primary to the other.

In fact, this convergence can be taken to suggest that the explicit combination of a "principled virtue" (to use Grenberg's term), as represented by the virtue-oriented portrayal of Kant offered here, is superior to either alone, due to its focus on character and persons while being grounded in principle derived from respect of the dignity of those same persons. (This will be the position I take in my support of the Kantian-economic model later in this chapter.) In his seminal contribution to this literature, Louden asserts from the start that Kant serves as a bridge between virtue and deontology *simpliciter*: "The real Kant lies somewhere in between these two extremes. He sought to build an ethical theory which could assess both the life plans of moral agents and their discrete acts. This is to his credit, for an adequate moral theory needs to do both."[41] Hill elaborates, writing that "Kant's basic idea" is that "*to be virtuous*—and properly beneficent, grateful, honest, just, and so forth—*just is* in part to know and respect the *prior* reasons for acting rightly. And to respect those independent reasons is ultimately just to acknowledge fully the value of humanity in each person."[42]

Shifting the emphasis of Kantian ethics from duties and rules to character (based on principles) invokes the need for judgment, which is emphasized in much of Kant's work (even the *Groundwork*). Kant was well aware that the categorical imperative alone did not issue duties precise enough to be applied to specific moral dilemmas, and stressed the need for "a power of judgment sharpened by experience, partly in order to distinguish in what cases they are applicable, and partly to gain for them access to the human will as well as influence for putting them into practice."[43] Contrary to those who accuse him of being obsessed with rules, he ridiculed those who followed them blindly: "Dogmas and formulas, those mechanical instruments for rational use (or rather misuse) of [man's] natural endowments, are the ball and chain of his permanent immaturity."[44] As O'Neill recognized, "Discussions of judgment . . . are ubiquitous in Kant's writings. He never assumes agents can move from principles of duty, or from other principles of action, to selecting a highly specific act in particular circumstances without any process of judgment. He is as firm as any devotee of Aristotelian *phronēsis* in maintaining that principles of action are not algorithms and do not entail their own applications."[45]

At the same time that he stressed the need for judgment to transform general negative duties into specific action, Kant was just as emphatic that there was no formula or algorithm that could represent it: "though understanding is capable of being instructed . . . judgment is a peculiar talent which can be practiced only, and cannot be taught. It is the specific quality of so-called mother-wit; and its lack no school can make good."[46] As O'Neill put it, Kant's description of judgment is "a rejection of purely calculative conceptions of practical reasoning."[47] Roger Sullivan fleshes out Kant's idea when he writes,

> Through simply living, facing ordinary moral problems day by day, we all accumulate a store of moral experience to help us judge how to act; we all develop some sensitivity to the features to which we should attend. Moreover, most of the situations in which we find ourselves are familiar ones, and we do not need to deliberate over how to act. We simply act on maxims that reflect our long-standing commitments and values.[48]

At the same time, because judgment for Kant is based on basic moral principles derived from the categorical imperative and ultimately from dignity and autonomy, it rests on a firmer foundation than does traditional virtue ethics, as discussed above in the context of principle and virtue. As Hill wrote, "Kant insisted, as in fact Aristotle did also, that judgments of practical reason are also essential; but Kant goes farther than Aristotle apparently did in claiming that the grounds on which practical judgment relies can be reliably and usefully articulated."[49]

Furthermore, Kantian judgment also incorporates specific contextual factors that are stressed by virtue ethicists. While his ethics are often regarded as formal, it is only the categorical imperative itself that Kant argues applies in any society at any time.[50] The duties that result from the categorical imperative, however, require knowledge of context, circumstances, and human nature to determine how they are both derived from the categorical imperative and, more important, applied to specific decision-making situations. As Kant wrote, "all morals . . . require anthropology in order to be applied to humans," and later, "a metaphysics of morals cannot dispense with principles of application, and we shall often have to take as our object the particular *nature* of human beings, which is cognized only by experience, in order to *show* in it what can be inferred from universal moral principles."[51] As Sherman recognizes,

> it has not been adequately appreciated that Kant develops a complex anthropology of morals—a tailoring of morality to the contingent features of the human case—which at times brings him into surprising alliance with Aristotle and his project of limning an account of human excellence.[52]

In summary, Kantian ethics has many elements in common with virtue ethics, especially its focus on character and judgment, which are most important to the economic analysis to follow and will be detailed further then. I will conclude this section with Louden's summary statement on the topic of Kant and virtue:

> As I see it, character *is* the central concern of Kant's ethics, and thus, at this basic level, we are entitled to say that he develops not just a *theory* of virtue (which of course nearly all serious moral philosophers have done) but a *virtue-based* ethics. At the same time . . . it has also become increasingly evident to me that Kant's understanding of character and virtue differs substantially from that of nearly all of the contributors to this literature who regard themselves as virtue ethicists. Those of us who defend the centrality of character and virtue within Kant's ethics need to be careful not to collapse Kant's position into theirs.[53]

My claim here is somewhat milder: I am not arguing that Kant is a virtue ethicist or that he has an ethics of virtue. To coin a term, I think of Kant's ethics as "virtue-ous," that it has enough elements of virtue theory to combine the act-focused and agent-focused sides of ethics, and to supply the important elements of character and judgment, based on principles, to economic modeling.

2. KANTIAN ETHICS, ECONOMICS, AND THE ROLE OF JUDGMENT AND CHARACTER

2.1 Kantian economics and the need for judgment

Having argued that Kant's ethics, as opposed to consequentialism and "simple" deontology, incorporates substantial elements of what is important to virtue ethicists, I will now suggest an economic model of decision-making that incorporates Kantian ethics.[54] I will argue not only that Kantian ethics contributes to the explanatory power of economic models, but that it does so in a way that incorporates essential concepts commonly associated with virtue ethics, specifically character and judgment, with the firm grounding in principle supplied by Kant's focus on autonomy and dignity.

One way that Kantian duty can be included in economic conceptions of choice is by exploring the parallels between Kant's categories of perfect and imperfect duties and the constraints and preferences that comprise the standard economic model. In this model, the agent has a preference ranking over options, from which she chooses the most preferred one attainable with her resources and given market prices, which represent her constraints. Her preferences (and the "utility" index that represents the degree of their satisfaction) are devoid of psychological content; they do not necessarily reflect desires, as might be supposed, but can result from any source, including altruism, and are usually understood (heuristically) to be fixed. The agent's constraints, such as limitations on wealth, credit, or time, are usually understood to be fixed as well (although monetary constraints are to some extent a function of previous market choices).

The two types of Kantian duty correspond in function to the two parts of the traditional economic model of choice. Given their function as limits on the pursuit of inclination (or preference), perfect duties fit among the agent's constraints. Likewise, given their status as ends that admit of trade-offs with other ends (including inclination), imperfect duties fit among the agent's preferences (which may include "moral preferences" to begin with). Assuming the agent has included perfect and imperfect duties among her constraints and preferences as described, her choice problem is formally the same: select the most preferred option (including those based on imperfect duties) achievable within her constraints (including perfect duties). Furthermore, the agent must incorporate these duties into her decision-making for their own sake rather than her own interests (whether selfish or altruistic). This implies that the agent consciously and deliberately adopts her duty-based preferences and constraints, whereas in the standard model, preferences and constraints are assumed to be exogenously "given" to the agent, and also rules out models of altruism and moral duty that rely on variants of utility.[55] Ideally, this incorporation of perfect and imperfect duties into the standard economic model of decision-making allows the agent to maximize "utility" as usual, while satisfying the basic demands of Kantian ethics.[56]

But the inclusion of perfect and imperfect duties among the agent's constraints and preferences is not as straightforward as it sounds. Even if we assume that the agent adopts duty-based preferences and constraints for the sake of duty, this does not address the thornier problem of *how* these duties are determined or weighted against preferences and other duties. Because all duties, perfect and imperfect, are essentially negative—such as "do not steal" and "do not be indifferent to the suffering of others"—they are silent on exactly what the agent *should* do. As we saw earlier, Kant was emphatic that general duties alone could not determine right action in specific choice situations—judgment is necessary to bridge the gap, judgment which represents the more virtue-oriented nature of Kantian ethics.

There are two obvious and common cases where the need for judgment arises: when imperfect duties are ranked among non-duty-based preferences, and when duties conflict. Given that trade-offs are permitted by the wide nature of imperfect duty, the agent is free in some circumstances to rank preferences, even those based on pure self-interest, above duties such as beneficence. But this has to be done within a moral context; the agent cannot simply rationalize naked selfishness by ranking her own preferences above duty. She must take the basis of her imperfect duty seriously and weigh them against her own preferences in some principled way. Yet there is no formulaic way to do this; it requires judgment, to be discussed in the next section.

Some interpreters of Kant favor a stricter reading of wide duties and thereby insist on ranking them above most if not all self-interested preferences.[57] Were we to agree with them, we would still need to confront the issue of conflicts between duties themselves (or, to be precise, conflicts between obligations). Conflicts between imperfect duties represent a problem similar to the ranking of imperfect duties among preferences: wide duties can be satisfied in many ways, implying significant flexibility between them that can only be managed using judgment. Conflicts between perfect duties are less common because normally it is not difficult to manage more than one constraint at the same time; for example, most people have no problem abstaining from lying *and* stealing as they go about their lives. In this sense, perfect duties can be seen as narrowing the option space available to an agent, and as long as some option space remains, there would be little problem. Nonetheless, this remaining option space may block the pursuit of other principles, in which case a conflict would result; for example, one may feel the need to lie to either one friend or another to preserve a relationship (which embodies the principle of beneficence). Obviously, judgment is needed to decide which perfect duty to act upon and which to violate (or whether the overall principle of beneficence must be sacrificed instead).

This last possibility invokes a conflict between perfect and imperfect duties, one that is commonly thought to be resolved easily in favor of the perfect duty. After all, if one duty is flexible, it seems it should bend to the one that is not; imperfect duties can be satisfied in a number of ways but perfect duties are strict. But this argument focuses too much on the logical structure of the duties and not their substance, the "stronger ground" that Kant said must determine which obligation the agent should follow. Consider a woman who promises to help her friend study for an exam, but then receives a call from her father who needs her help getting to an appointment. Keeping a promise is a strict duty while helping others is a wide one, but we can easily put a thumb on the scales in favor of helping her father. Suppose the promise was simply to accompany her friend to a movie, while her father urgently needs her help to get to the hospital because he is experiencing heart palpitations. As we make the father's situation increasingly dire and the promise to the friend more trivial, the imperfect duty takes on greater importance, even though the perfect duty, technically, can only be satisfied by keeping the promise.[58]

2.2 Judgment via Kant and Dworkin

As we noted above, Kant famously said little about the process of judgment, likening it to intuition or "mother-wit." A number of scholars have expounded on what a Kantian faculty of moral judgment may look like.[59] Briefly, I propose a conception based on the jurisprudential work of Ronald Dworkin, specifically his model of judicial decision-making based on balancing legal principles, which I believe fits well within Kant's description of judgment and the flexibility of his duties, and also shares a focus on character and integrity with virtue ethics (and, as presented above, Kantian ethics itself).

In his jurisprudential work, Dworkin answers a persistent question in legal philosophy: what should judges do in "hard cases" when written law does not provide a clear answer? Placing himself in opposition to positivists, who maintain that only pedigreed legal rules are binding on judges, Dworkin argued that principles that can be found in historical documents, as well as in written constitutions and statutes, are the more basic legal sources for judicial decision-making. A judge facing a hard case must decide first what principles are relevant to the situation and then how to assign different weights to those principles to decide which principle should determine the prevailing side in the case. To discover these principles and their weights, a judge must have constructed a personal theory of the legal–political system that both fits and justifies the principles and rules that comprise it, and use it too make a decision in the case at hand that is consistent with those prior legal materials (what Dworkin called the "seamless web") and thereby maintains the integrity of the legal system.[60]

Dworkin's "integrity theory" of legal decision-making has a number of features in common with Kantian judgment in its most virtue-ous sense. Most obvious, both rely on principles for their basic subject matter and rely on judgment to determine which principle drives the decision-making. For instance, in her work on Kantian judgment, Barbara Herman uses the term *deliberative field* "to represent the space in which an agent's rational deliberation takes place. It is constructed by the principles and commitments that express her conception of value."[61] Also, Dworkin is adamant that there is no formulaic method for identifying principles, balancing them against each other in particular cases or situations, or making the decision that preserves the integrity of the law—all of these are matters for true judgment, not formal, algorithmic methods. Finally, Dworkin posits the existence of a "right answer" to any legal dispute, meaning the one that a thorough analysis of the facts and principles relevant to a case, based on his or her personal legal–political philosophy, leads the judge to support. This correlates with Kant's implication that among conflicting obligations, there is one with the "strongest ground" that we can then identify as the one duty that must be followed.

Besides these features in common with Kantian judgment, already similar to practical judgment as stressed by virtue ethicists, there is another aspect of Dworkin's jurisprudence that draws it into the circle of virtue: the emphasis on character and integrity.[62] Dworkin's language of "the right answer" is very individualized, relying on each judge's unique philosophy of the legal–political system in which they work. This explains how judges on a panel can be equally well informed on the law and facts of the case but still arrive at different decisions (or the same decision for different reasons). This makes the person doing the judging, and his or her character, of critical importance in Dworkin's theory of judicial decision-making.

When translated into a conception of Kantian judgment, Dworkin's integrity-based model of judgment suggests that a person facing a moral dilemma must find her own "right answer," the decision she feels maintains the integrity of her moral character and affirms her core values and how she balances the various principles outlined by autonomy, dignity, and the categorical imperative. In the same way that new judicial decisions contribute to and help transform the seamless web of the law that will then, in turn, influence new decisions, an individual's decisions affect her character in the same self-enforcing, circular process. As Christine Korsgaard describes this process:

> The task of self-constitution involves finding some roles and fulfilling them with integrity and dedication. It also involves integrating those roles into a single identity, into a coherent life. People are more or less successful at constituting their identities as unified agents, and a good action is one that does this well. It is one that both *achieves* and *springs* from the integrity of the person who performs it.[63]

Similarly, referring again to the deliberative field, Herman reinforces the importance of having a moral character, "one in which the moral law belongs to the framework within which desires and interests develop and gain access to the deliberative field."[64] Again, the focus is on the person making a decision, based on her character and her personal view of the moral law through which she balances the various principles resulting from the categorical imperative.

If we consider once more the dilemma of a person faced with either breaking a promise to her friend or helping her father, her process of judgment will take into account the "ground of obligation" to each, the importance of the principles of promise-keeping and beneficence to her, how close she feels to each person, her past history with both of them, and any other factors she considered relevant to the decision. She will weigh and balance the relative importance of these facts and principles to arrive at "the right answer" which affirms who she considers herself to be as a moral agent. Following this procedure will ensure that she makes a choice consistent with her moral character and the principles she regards as most important. It will also be a context-sensitive decision, as any change in circumstances—such as how dire her father's situation is or which friend she made a promise to—affects the balance of the various factors in the choice. Finally, it is an essentially individual decision, not just in the sense of autonomy treasured by Kant, but also in the agent-focused context of virtue ethics. Whatever choice she makes, it is the right choice for her only, not for anybody else (much less for *everybody* else), even in a very similar situation. Even though she makes the choice based on principles as well as facts, at bottom it is *her* choice based on *her* core values, not a universal result based on general rules or formulae. It is this aspect of judgment based on Kant and Dworkin that most directly renders it "virtue-ous" based on its grounding in character as well as principle.

This theory of judgment has numerous economic applications once it is recognized that many economic problems involve multiple concerns that cannot always be put in terms of a common metric, especially when one or more of them takes the form of a qualitative principle. Such conflicts occur in both individual decisions as well as in policy contexts. For an example of the former, consider the consumer who must decide whether to spend more of his scarce budget to purchase fair-trade coffee in support of third-world coffee farmers, a principle that competes for resources with his other needs and wants. Whether he considers this concern a principle or an altruistic preference, it must be balanced somehow with his other preferences, which requires judgment. Another example would be a firm deciding how much of its profit to sacrifice for the sake of better treatment for its employees or safer products for its consumers (assuming both are currently set at the profit-maximizing level and consistent with regulation and industry standards). These are both principles whose pursuit competes with the profit motive but are not commensurate with it, so the leadership of the firm must exercise judgment to determine how far they are willing to go with these initiatives.

The role of judgment is just as important in the area of government policy and regulation, where "purely" economic goals must be balanced against principled concerns such as dignity and equality (as in many hard cases in law). Judgment based on moral principles seems obviously appropriate to government decisions in non-economic areas such as promoting civil rights or exercising military power, but it is important also in areas that are significantly economic or financial in nature. Decisions in the area of fiscal and monetary policy, for example, are not simply technical problems but also moral ones, requiring a sensitivity to matters of justice and fairness, which many policy-makers know but is not captured in most economic models of policy-making. Judgment may be even more important to regulation, which often has a narrower effect than policy but affects people more directly by influencing the nature, cost, and availability of products and services provided by both private firms and the government, which needs to be done with sensitivity to both the well-being and dignity of those whom the regulations are meant to benefit. As with policy, this is rarely captured in economic models of regulation but is practiced by regulators in the real world, as explained by Cass Sunstein in his book *Valuing Life: Humanizing the Regulatory State*, in which he relates his experience heading the Office of Institutional and Regulatory Affairs from 2009 to 2012.[65] Specifically, Sunstein describes the decision-making process behind initiatives such as increasing wheelchair access to public restrooms and decreasing the incidence of prison rape, just two examples in which costs are easily measured in dollar terms but the benefits in terms of human dignity are not—but nonetheless decisions must be made, decisions between conflicting principles that require a faculty of judgment sensitive to such matters.

3. CONCLUSION

In this chapter, I argued that a Kantian-economic model of decision-making, incorporating a conception of judgment based on Ronald Dworkin's jurisprudence, allows economists to explain ethical behavior that does not fit into the simple model of preferences and constraints. In general, duties and principles enable economists to model behavior that is not beholden to preferences alone, and the theory of judgment allows these duties to be arranged among preferences and constraints even when the principles underlying them come into conflict. Most important, this combination of Kant and Dworkin gives economics a new focus on the person as a moral agent, whose decisions are uniquely that person's decisions. In the end, an agent's character, not rules or formulae applied mechanistically and impersonally, determines the choices she will make in moral dilemmas. Of course, the non-algorithmic aspect of this model defies formalization and mathematization, consistent with what Kant and Dworkin wrote. This reflects the fact that moral decision-making itself is not formulaic or algorithmic, nor deterministic in any way. It is essentially qualitative, more accurately captured by narrative than by syllogism, algebra, or symbolic logic. Following this model would entail a radical change in how economics is practiced, and may even prompt economists to reflect on the goals and purpose of economics itself—in other words, on its character. Such considered reflection would surely be virtuous.[66]

NOTES

1. Kant's ethics are summarized in a number of books; a concise but thorough introduction is Roger Sullivan, *An Introduction to Kant's Ethics* (Cambridge: Cambridge University Press, 1994), and he provides an advanced treatment in his *Immanuel Kant's Moral Theory* (Cambridge: Cambridge University Press, 1989). The categorical imperative is analyzed in depth in H.J. Paton, *The Categorical Imperative: A Study in Kant's Moral Philosophy* (Philadelphia: University of Pennsylvania Press, 1947).
2. For more on perfect and imperfect duties, see Mary J. Gregor, *Laws of Freedom: A Study of Kant's Method of Applying the Categorical Imperative in the Metaphysik der Sitten* (Oxford: Basil Blackwell, 1963), chapter 7; and Thomas E. Hill, Jr., "Imperfect Duty and Supererogation," in *Dignity and Practical Reason in Kant's Moral Theory* (Ithaca, NY: Cornell University Press, 1992), 147–75.
3. G.E.M. Anscombe, "Modern Moral Philosophy," *Philosophy* 33(1958): 1–19, at 2.
4. Alisdair MacIntyre, *After Virtue*, 3rd ed. (Notre Dame: University of Notre Dame Press, 2007), 45.
5. Ibid., 236. For a summary of MacIntyre's criticisms of Kant, see Onora O'Neill, "Kant After Virtue," in *Constructions of Reason: Explorations of Kant's Practical Philosophy* (Cambridge: Cambridge University Press, 1989), 145–62, at 148–50.
6. Michael Stocker, "The Schizophrenia of Modern Ethical Theories," *Journal of Philosophy* 73(1976): 453–66, at 459. For more on criticisms of Kant from the viewpoint of virtue ethics, see Robert B. Louden, "Kant's Virtue Ethics," *Philosophy* 61(1986): 473–89, at 473–3; for broader historical context of these debates, see Marcia Baron, "Virtue Ethics in Relation to Kantian Ethics: An Opinionated Overview and Commentary," in Lawrence Jost and Julian Wuerth (eds.), *Perfecting Virtue: New Essays on Kantian Ethics and Virtue Ethics* (Cambridge: Cambridge University Press, 2011), 8–37.
7. Louden, "Kant's Virtue Ethics," 474–6. For a similar description of this contrast, see Thomas E. Hill, Jr., "Kantian Virtue and 'Virtue Ethics,'" in Monika Betzler (ed.), *Kant's Ethics of Virtue* (Berlin: Walter de Gruyter, 2008), 29–59, at 30–3.
8. "There are many persons who are so sympathetically constituted that, without any further motive of vanity or self-interest, they find an inner pleasure in spreading joy around them.... In such a case an action of this kind, however dutiful and amiable it may be, has nevertheless no true moral worth" (Kant, *Grounding for the Metaphysics of Morals*, trans. James W. Ellington, Indianapolis, IN: Hackett publishing Company, 1785/1993, 398; henceforth *Groundwork*).
9. Louden, "Kant's Virtue Ethics," 487 (and in general 484–489); see also Louden, "Moral Strength: Virtue as a Duty to Oneself," in *Kant's Human Being: Essays on His Theory of Human Nature* (Oxford; Oxford University Press, 2011), 16–24, at 19–22.
10. Kant, *The Metaphysics of Morals*, Mary Gregor (trans. and ed.) (Cambridge: Cambridge University Press, 1797/1996), 484.
11. Louden, "Kant's Virtue Ethics," 488.
12. Kant, *Religion within the Boundaries of Mere Reason*, Allen Wood and George di Giovanni (eds.) (Cambridge: Cambridge University Press, 1793/1998), 24n (emphasis removed).

13. Nancy Sherman, *Making a Necessity of Virtue: Aristotle and Kant on Virtue* (Cambridge: Cambridge University Press, 1997), 145. On this point, see also Christine N. Korsgaard, "From Duty and for the Sake of the Noble: Kant and Aristotle on Morally Good Action," in Stephen Engstrom and Jennifer Whiting (eds.), *Aristotle, Kant, and the Stoics: Rethinking Happiness and Duty* (Cambridge: Cambridge University Press, 1996), 203–36.
14. Kant, *Metaphysics of Morals*, 457.
15. On the related issue of the role of desire in motivating dutiful action, see Barbara Herman, "Making Room for Character," in Engstrom and Whiting, *Aristotle, Kant, and the Stoics*, 36–60.
16. As with most of the characterization of virtue ethics in this chapter, this is an overgeneralization; for an account of virtue that does not reject the value of rules, see Rosalind Hursthouse, *On Virtue Ethics* (Oxford: Oxford University Press, 1999), especially 35–9.
17. Kant, *Groundwork*, 393 (emphasis in original).
18. Louden, "Kant's Virtue Ethics," 478.
19. Ibid., 479. However, some are even more skeptical regarding the connection between Kant's "good will" and any notion of character; for instance, see Allen Wood, "The Good Will," *Philosophical Topics* 31(2003): 457–84, at 469–71. (Wood is skeptical in general about the prospect of interpreting Kantian ethics as agent-oriented; see his "Kant and Agent-Oriented Ethics" in Jost and Wuerth, *Perfecting Virtue*, 58–91.)
20. Jeanine Grenberg, *Kant and the Ethics of Humility: A Story of Dependence, Corruption, and Virtue* (Cambridge: Cambridge University Press, 2005), 55.
21. Louden, "Kant's Virtue Ethics," 483, quoting Kant, *Metaphysics of Morals*, 386.
22. Kant, *Groundwork*, 393–4. Nonetheless, on the presence of individual, "thick" virtues in Kant's work, see Philip Stratton-Lake, "Being Virtuous and the Virtues: Two Aspects of Kant's *Doctrine of Virtue*," in Betzler, *Kant's Ethics of Virtue*, 101–21; Grenberg, *Kant and the Ethics of Humility*; Hill, "Kantian Virtue and 'Virtue Ethics,'" 54–8; and Wood, "Kant and Agent-Oriented Ethics," 69–71.
23. Kant, *Metaphysics of Morals*, 380.
24. Hill, "Kantian Virtue and 'Virtue Ethics,'" 40–1.
25. Kant, *Metaphysics of Morals*, 397.
26. Ibid.
27. Ibid., 409. For more on Kant's theory of virtue as strength, see Stephen Engstrom, "Inner Freedom of Virtue," in Mark Timmons (ed.), *Kant's Metaphysics of Morals: Interpretative Essays* (Oxford: Oxford University Press, 2002), 289–315; Hill, "Kantian Virtue and 'Virtue Ethics,'" 40–51; and Betzler, *Kant's Ethics of Virtue*.
28. Louden, "Moral Strength," 19.
29. O'Neill, "Kant After Virtue," 162.
30. See Onora O'Neill, "Kant's Virtues," in Roger Crisp (ed.), *How Should One Live? Essays on the Virtues* (Oxford: The Clarendon Press, 1996), 77–96, at 82–8; and Stratton-Lake, "Being Virtuous and the Virtues," 106–11. See also Sherman, *Making a Necessity of Virtue*, 316 ("The Kantian notion of imperfect duties having latitude and the Aristotelian notion that theory can only present virtues in outline form, roughly parallel each other . . . ").

31. Baron, "Virtue Ethics in Relation to Kantian Ethics," 30.
32. Ibid.
33. Stratton-Lake, "Being Virtuous and the Virtues," 115.
34. O'Neill, "Kant After Virtue," 152.
35. Hill, "Kantian Virtue and 'Virtue Ethics,'" 52 (emphasis in original).
36. Ibid., (emphasis removed).
37. O'Neill, "Kant After Virtue," 161–2.
38. For such criticisms of the role of principle in virtue, see for instance Rosalind Hursthouse, "What Does the Aristotelian *Phronimos* Know?" in Jost and Wuerth, *Perfecting Virtue*, 38–47.
39. Grenberg, *Kant and the Ethics of Humility*, 56.
40. Robert Audi, "Acting from Virtue," *Mind* 104(1995): 449–71, at 469. In general, see also John Waide, "Virtues and Principles," *Philosophy and Phenomenological Research* 48(1988): 455–72.
41. Louden, "Kant's Virtue Ethics," 474.
42. Hill, "Kantian Virtue and 'Virtue Ethics,'" 59, emphasis in original.
43. Kant, *Groundwork*, 389.
44. Immanuel Kant, "An Answer to the Question: What Is Enlightenment?" in *Kant: Political Writings*, 2nd ed., edited by H.S. Reiss and translated by H.B. Nisbet (Cambridge: Cambridge University Press, 1784/1991), 54–60, at 54–5.
45. Onora O'Neill, "Kant: Rationality as Practical Reason," in Alfred R. Mele and Piers Rawling (eds.), *The Oxford Handbook of Rationality* (Oxford: Oxford University Press, 2004), 93–109, at 104.
46. Kant, *Critique of Pure Reason*, trans. Norman Kemp Smith (New York: St. Martin's Press, 1781/1787/1965), A133/B172.
47. O'Neill, "Kant After Virtue," 160.
48. Sullivan, *Introduction to Kant's Ethics*, 40.
49. Hill, "Kantian Virtue and 'Virtue Ethics,'" 52.
50. "Everyone must admit that if a law is to be morally valid, i.e., is to be valid as a ground of obligation, then it must carry with it absolute necessity. . . . And he must concede that the ground of obligation here must therefore be sought not in the nature of man nor in the circumstances of the world in which man is placed, but must be sought *a priori* solely in the concepts of pure reason" (Kant, *Groundwork*, 389).
51. Ibid., 412, and Kant, *Metaphysics of Morals*, 216–17.
52. Sherman, *Making a Necessity of Virtue*, 1; see also chapter 7, especially 325–30, for a comparison of judgment in Aristotle and Kant. On the role of Kant's anthropology in his ethics, see Patrick R. Frierson, *Freedom and Anthropology in Kant's Moral Philosophy* (Cambridge: Cambridge University Press, 2003), and Robert Louden, *Kant's Impure Ethics* (Oxford: Oxford University Press, 2000) and *Kant's Human Being*.
53. Louden, "Moral Strength," 24 (emphasis in original).
54. This model was described in more detail in my *Kantian Ethics and Economics: Autonomy, Dignity, and Character* (Stanford, CA: Stanford University Press, 2011).
55. See, for instance, James Andreoni, "Giving with Impure Altruism: Applications to Charity and Ricardian Equivalence," *Journal of Political Economy* 97(1989):

1447–58, and "Impure Altruism and Donations to Public Goods. A Theory of Warm-Glow Giving," *Economic Journal* 100(1990): 464–77, as well as Amitai Etzioni, The *Moral Dimension: Toward a New Economics* (New York: Free Press, 1988).
56. This simple version of the model assumes perfect rationality and virtue-as-strength, which Kant explicitly disavowed; see White, *Kantian Ethics and Economics*, chapter 2, for an elaboration on this model to incorporate imperfect strength (or weakness of will).
57. On the degree and kind of latitude allowed with respect to imperfect duty, see Marcia W. Baron, *Kantian Ethics Almost Without Apology* (Ithaca, NY: Cornell University Press, 1995), chapter 3; Marcia Baron and Melissa Seymour Fahmy, "Beneficence and Other Duties of Love in *The Metaphysics of Morals*," in Thomas E. Hill, Jr. (ed.), *The Blackwell Guide to Kant's Ethics* (Chichester, UK: Wiley-Blackwell, 2009), 211–28; Barbara Herman, "The Scope of Moral Requirement," in *Moral Literacy* (Cambridge, MA: Harvard University Press, 2007), 203–29; and Sherman, *Making a Necessity of Virtue*, chapter 8.
58. This argument, of course, applies equally to Kant's infamous "murderer-at-the-door" example: even though the duty not to lie to the murderer is strict, the duty to protect your friend from the murderer embodies the stronger ground of obligation. See Kant, "On a Supposed Right to Lie Because of Philanthropic Concerns," originally published 1799, included in the Hackett edition of the *Groundwork* (see Note 8).
59. Barbara Herman, *The Practice of Moral Judgment* (Cambridge, MA: Harvard University Press, 1993) and *Moral Literacy*; Sherman, *Making a Necessity Out of Virtue*, chapter 7; Louden, *Kant's Impure Ethics*; Onora O'Neill, *Acting on Principle: An Essay on Kantian Ethics* (Cambridge: Cambridge University Press, 2013).
60. This paragraph does not, of course, do Dworkin's system justice (no pun intended). For details, see his books *Taking Rights Seriously* (Cambridge, MA: Harvard University Press, 1977) and *Law's Empire* (Cambridge, MA: Harvard University Press, 1986), as well as Stephen Guest, *Ronald Dworkin*, 3rd ed. (Stanford, CA: Stanford University Press, 2013).
61. Herman, "Making Room for Character," 49; see also her *Practice of Moral Judgment*.
62. On the relationship between virtue and jurisprudence—and Dworkin's in particular—see Lawrence Solum, "Virtue Jurisprudence: A Virtue-Centred Theory of Judging," *Metaphilosophy* 34(2003): 178–213; in general, see Colin Farrelly and Lawrence Solum (eds.), *Virtue Jurisprudence* (New York: Palgrave Macmillan, 2008) and Amalia Amaya and Ho Hock Lai, *Law, Virtue, and Justice* (Oxford: Hart Publishing, 2013).
63. Christine Korsgaard, *Self-Constitution: Agency, Identity, and Integrity* (Oxford: Oxford University Press, 2009), 25.
64. Herman, "Making Room for Character," 53.
65. Cass Sunstein, *Valuing Life: Humanizing the Regulatory State* (Chicago: University of Chicago Press, 2004).
66. Early versions of this chapter were presented at an International Network for Economic Method session at the Allied Social Science Associations meetings and the American Philosophical Association Eastern Division meetings. For helpful comments I would like to thank my intrepid co-editor Jennifer Baker as well as Jonathan Wight, Deirdre McCloskey, and various attendants at both conferences.

Part II

Virtue and Economics in Theory

6

On Virtue Economics

Michael Baurmann and Geoffrey Brennan

Why should an economist be interested in virtue? That is a question worth asking because as a matter of fact "virtue" is not a standard term in the mainstream economist's lexicon. In what follows, we attempt to respond to this question by laying out three different possible answers, all of them worthy of some consideration. Explicating these alternative possible answers (that is, possible grounds for a "virtue economics") represents the first part of this chapter. In the second part, we interrogate what the "virtue economics" approach (variously understood) has to say about three issues that seem to us to be of special interest in this connection: invisible hand mechanisms, esteem incentives, and the issue of "virtue allocation." We shall attempt to explain why each of these issues is relevant to virtue when we come to discuss it.

Before we embark on our main task, however, we need to say a little about how we understand the idea of virtue itself. "A little" is, we think, all that's required. Many of the chapters in this volume will be concerned with particular conceptions of virtue and nuances that distinguish the various conceptions that are around in the literature. We do not want to deprecate that kind of enterprise, but it is not the focus of our attention here. For our purposes, it is sufficient to operate with a rather loose—and deliberately capacious—conception of what is entailed in "virtue." This is because we wish to emphasize general considerations that are largely independent of the particular concept of virtue that is deployed, or its detailed content, and that are likely to be entailed in any "virtue economics." In particular, the features that distinguish a *virtue* economics from an economics of a more conventional stripe are largely unaffected by how exactly virtue is defined.

For example, one answer to our initial question might be that the economist *is* interested in virtuous *behavior.* Virtuous behavior is just a sub-class of the entire set of empirically observable forms of behavior. Knowledge of the content of prevailing norms in society (if available) can assist in forming refutable predictions about whether agents will behave virtuously or not.

And anything that can help explain or predict behavior must be grist for the economist's mill.

But we take it that "virtuous behavior" involves not just behavior that is *consistent* with what virtue requires (as for example actions might be by accident) but rather behavior that is (at least in significant measure) *caused* by virtue: in other words, virtuous action presupposes a *virtuous actor*. This understanding of virtuous behavior is consistent with usage in ancient philosophy, later in Adam Smith, and more recently by Philippa Foot. From this perspective, three elements seem to us to be essential:

1. Virtues are not morally acclaimed ways of *acting* but morally acclaimed *dispositions to act*. To talk about dispositions implies that people at least sometimes act according to given personal attitudes and character features—rather than maximizing the outcome for themselves in each and every situation.
2. The disposition to act virtuously includes not only a behavioral tendency to act as virtue demands but to possess a preference order that is shaped by the values which reflect the content of virtues. That means that a virtuous person is, at least over some range, *intrinsically motivated* to act virtuously irrespective of extrinsic incentives or restrictions.
3. Being a virtuous person is to *deliberate* in a particular way. Behaving virtuously involves an inclination to justify one's behavior explicitly by reference to virtues and to denote those virtues as the relevant behavioral motives. Virtuous persons, therefore, are conscious of acting according to virtues and accept and defend such virtues as the driving forces of their behavior.[1]

As we shall show, these properties have upshots that are relevant even for the analyst who remains exclusively concerned with behavior. But we also hope to show that an economistic view of virtue can reveal interesting empirical and explanatory aspects of the role of virtuous behavior for social and economic order—aspects that are philosophically and ethically interesting but lie outside the customary focus of philosophers and ethicists.

1. WHY VIRTUE?

With this as clarificatory background, we turn to our initial question. What might justify the "virtue economics" project?

1.1 Virtue as intrinsically valuable

When we ask what might "justify" a particular project, we are necessarily asking a normative question. The norms in question could be methodological rather than ethical, but economics cannot rid itself of specifically ethical presuppositions if it purports to offer advice on any questions of policy or action (which it has never shown any reluctance to do, despite occasional expressions of doubt about its own competence in ethical matters!).

In this spirit, the first answer to our question is a straightforwardly ethical one: it says that economists ought to be interested in virtue because virtue is of *intrinsic moral worth.* Put another way, the normative framework used in the formulation and design of public policy, as well as the more abstract institutions of society, ought to include some account of how such policies and institutions affect the virtue of the individuals who are subject to them. To take a familiar example, if it is true that market society encourages greed (as many critics have asserted), and greed is a vice, then these considerations are to be taken as a count against markets (whatever else the market's advantages). Equally, if, as Aristotle thought, participation in politics enlarges the spirit and induces in people a greater sense of beneficence and common purpose, and these are virtues, then democracy, by enrolling larger numbers in political activities, is to be applauded for that reason. At the very least, if virtue is of intrinsic worth, then societal circumstances should be such as to enable the exercise of virtue and to open up areas for its practice. That principle might for example favor institutions of self-determination (for example, fields for private charitable behavior) instead of delegating all public (and redistributive) functions to state bureaucracy.[2]

So there are at least two issues relating to institutional design and reform that a virtue perspective raises:

1. Does the institution allow scope for the display of virtue?
2. Does the institution encourage the development of virtue?

So identified, "virtue economics" is the application of virtue ethics to issues of economic policy and institutional design. It supposes that the outcome of a debate, properly pursued in moral philosophy, between virtue ethics and rival claims as to what ultimately matters ethically, has been decided in some sense in favor of virtue ethics.

The subsequent task is to refine the notion of "virtue" in a manner that allows the notion to be deployed in relevant settings, and then to investigate how different policies or different institutions bear on virtue so defined. So, is greed a vice, and is it really true that market society encourages greed? Is it really true that democracy engenders common purpose or enlarged imaginations, and are these necessarily virtues? Is self-governance in public matters actually a promising field for virtue in practice? Or, to take a different case, what is to be said for adversarial as against inquisitorial legal institutions? Do the former institutions encourage individuals to be litigious as, for example, certain caricatures of the US legal system might suggest? And is a propensity to be litigious a vice?

These questions seem to be amenable to both abstract speculation and empirical investigation of the kind that economists have long seen as their staple fare. For example, Adam Smith towards the end of the *Wealth of Nations* (and more extensively in his *Lectures on Jurisprudence*) speculates about the effects of commercial society on its participants.[3] He explicitly laments the likelihood (as he sees it) that the division of labor, characteristic of the market order, will make people narrow and dull, lacking refined sensibilities. He thinks subsidized Sunday schools might be a partial remedy and recommends them on that account. In a similar spirit, he thinks that commercial society encourages people to be more trustworthy and more punctual than otherwise. But he also thinks that commercial society weakens martial spirit: people operating in the market order become mild and non-aggressive in a manner that might make them militarily vulnerable.

Smith's speculations of course demand empirical investigation. His casual observations serve to generate interesting hypotheses, but they do not stand on their own simply on the basis of being consistent with our intuitions or with popular prejudices. To be sure, such investigation has not been a major preoccupation of economists (falling more, perhaps, to sociologists and social psychologists) but this would clearly be one task on the "virtue economist's" agenda. The writings of Herbert Gintis and Paul Seabright would represent two examples of work in this area, and Elinor Ostrom's agenda could also be construed as falling under this rubric.[4]

We noted earlier that virtue economics on this directly normative reading is parasitic on a logically prior debate within moral philosophy. In part that debate is one about the ultimate domain of morality, whether that domain includes the motivations and modes of calculation and dispositions of agents as distinct from the levels of well-being of those agents, some other feature of social outcomes (such as the equality of individuals' well-being), or features of the processes from which those social outcomes emerge. The debate is also in part about whether moral requirements are expressed deontologically in the form of laws, on the one hand, or consequentially in terms of desirable properties, on the other. There seems to be a presumption among many moral philosophers that some one such formulation must be the right one, and that everything else is then derivative from that right formulation. That is, there is some presumption that morality must at base be reducible to a single principle and any failure to discover what that single principle is, means that "there is more work to be done."

In this sense, a position that is natural to the economist is unnatural to the philosopher. The economist may be perfectly content to think that all the aforementioned elements (well-being and its distribution, motives, processes, consequences, and so forth) may all matter ethically—and do so ultimately—to some degree. On the economist's view, elements of utilitarianism, libertarianism, egalitarianism, and justice, for example, may all exist alongside one another, making proper claims on moral attention, and all in principle capable of being of intrinsic moral value. In that case, trade-offs between the competing claims of different moral desiderata will be required in the typical case—but the need to make such trade-offs will just be seen as a necessary part of functioning in a constrained world. In short, for the economist at least, to think specifically that individual virtue matters intrinsically does not in the least commit one to the thought that no other source of value could also matter intrinsically.

Accordingly, a virtue economist may be entirely content that a concern for agent virtue is *part* of the underlying normative framework—and this non-derivatively so—without fully rejecting the quasi-utilitarian (or perhaps contractarian) aspects of a more or less standard welfare economics tradition. And this concession is all that the virtue economist needs in order to justify enquiry about the effects of actions, policies, or institutions on the *virtue* of the individuals who make up the affected community (as well as on their well-being, their liberty, or whatever). So, for example, Smith's argument that specialization is prone to stunt the development of individuals to full humanity can be seen as just one consideration to be weighed against the many advantages that commercial society brings. Ultimately, some trade-off between the two specified ends—human virtue vs. material well-being—will be required.[5]

1.2 Virtue as derivatively valuable

The second possible answer is also normative but of a different kind: it says that virtue is normatively important but not intrinsically so. There are two strands of this line of thought that it is useful to distinguish. The first involves the claim that the virtue of agents is likely to be productive in utilitarian terms. Agents with a disposition to behave cooperatively will, for example, be less likely to free ride in prisoner's dilemmas and in public goods predicaments. Equally, honest agents will be more likely to fulfill contracts and treat their trading partners with fairness. Intrinsically motivated agents obeying a work ethic will be more likely to work hard. Public-spirited citizens will be more likely to pay their taxes and benevolent politicians will be more likely to act in the common interest . . . and so on. If this is so, then there may remain a general concern about the effect of policy action or institutional choice on the virtue of agents even when virtue is derivatively, not intrinsically, valuable.

But even if this were not so—even if agent virtue did not conduce to life going better for everyone in utilitarian terms—it may nevertheless be the case that certain kinds of utilitarianism will require attention to virtue. That would be the case to the extent that the understanding of "utility" is preference-based and agents themselves care either about their own virtue or about the virtue of the agents they deal with. That is, if there is abroad in the community a "taste" for virtue (as we might put it), then that taste needs to be recognized alongside all other tastes as having "preference-satisfaction" status. Virtue becomes a "consumption good" in this community, and having more rather than less of it matters to that extent.

This latter thought is, of course, quite different from the thought that virtue is morally required as an intrinsic good. We say "of course" here because the distinction ought to be obvious. But the habits of economists sometimes run together the moral requirements individuals acknowledge with their tastes and preferences, as if moral requirements just were one kind of preference. We think that view is a mistake as a matter of individual psychology. To acknowledge moral requirements includes a deliberative attitude of justification and a cultivation of behavioral dispositions. But in any event, our concern here involves both the desire that individuals may have to act virtuously themselves and the desire they may have to live in a community of more virtuous people. These desires are clearly not the same, but both desires are relevant for the evaluation of policies and institutions.

As with the first answer, this second answer provides reasons why the economist qua economist should want to be attentive to the effects of actions, policies, and institutions on virtue. In this case the reasons are derivative, dependent on the claim that agent virtue is productive of some things that are intrinsically valued, such as aggregate well-being, or that people prefer to deal with virtuous others for its own sake—that they just find such dealing "more pleasant"—or even that they prefer to be virtuous themselves and want institutions that encourage such virtue!

This second answer opens an additional field of enquiry for the virtue economist. The claim that agent virtue can be productive in utilitarian terms (and therefore of extrinsic worth) is not self-evident. Whether individual dispositions to behave cooperatively are really helpful in solving prisoner's dilemmas and public goods predicaments, or whether honest agents are really important to secure contracts and transactions, are empirical questions open for investigation. Economists are especially well-equipped to contribute to this research agenda as, in the past, they have put a lot of effort and intellectual energy into the project of showing that virtues like benevolence, justice, and public-spiritedness are *not* necessary (or at least of second-order significance) in creating a well-ordered society or flourishing economy. Virtue economists can utilize the results of this tradition even when the focus of their enquiry is itself "untraditional."

1.3 "Virtue" as fact

The third answer is, as far as we can see, not normative at all—it is essentially explanatory—but it has some connection to the second. Let it be the case that individuals do act in certain contexts according to moral dispositions and that they have "preferences over virtue" in themselves or others. In that case, such dispositions and preferences may well help explain particular behavior (or changes in behavior in response to certain stimuli), and explaining or predicting such behavior is presumably a central activity for the mainstream economist. The claim here is that a more nuanced account of the motivational structure of individuals—one that includes the demand for virtue—can provide a more psychologically realistic account of behavior and in some cases more accurate predictions as to behavioral responses to various kinds of stimuli.

For example, suppose that workers come to feel a certain obligation to their employer if the employer demonstrates trust in them and treats them with respect or with some measure of generosity. Suppose that developing such worker loyalty is of value to the employer: workers will, say, work more conscientiously and with less supervision on the employer's behalf if they feel loyal. Then it will pay employers to develop such worker loyalty, perhaps by paying "over-award" wages and providing better working conditions than they otherwise would. Some versions of the "efficiency wage" theory (including Akerlof's original treatment) depend on just some such notion of "the generation of worker loyalty."[6] In contrast with a rival account in which paying more than market-clearing wages operates via providing purely material incentives not to engage in job search, this version depends on the claim that (many) ordinary people have certain dispositions and modes of calculation that are themselves norm-based. Bruno Frey emphasizes the existence of dispositions as motivational forces and examines the conditions under which an increase in reliance on extrinsic incentives can actually destroy (or "crowd out") intrinsic motivation.[7] Interestingly, such dispositional accounts are often referred to (by economists) as "sociological," that is, something other than fully "economic." But we take it that the effects of a disposition to feel loyalty and commitment, together with an account of how that loyalty and commitment may be triggered in the employee, constitutes one example of what we would take to be "virtue economics."

Consider another example. Suppose that nurses are motivated in part by a sense of "vocation": by a desire to care for the sick for the sake of caring itself. To assume this is not to concede that they are not also motivated by other considerations such as higher salary or longer paid holidays. It is just to explain why equilibrium wages in nursing may be lower than exists in professions with comparable training periods: because nurses generally, and more particularly at the margin, enjoy providing nursing services.[8] They "make a difference in people's lives" or they "give back something to the community"—simply put, they care about the quality of the care they give. Now suppose that changes in hospital administration and medical technology mean that nurses spend less time doing the kind of caring work from which they derive their primary intrinsic rewards. Then these changes in administration or technology will involve the equivalent of a loss in total real income to them. Nursing will become less attractive, and in order to maintain a nursing workforce of the same size and quality, the health sector will have to offer a higher monetary component of the total package of salary and benefits. The health sector will become more expensive in terms of dollars.[9] And this is a fact with which those who manage hospital administration and technology policy ought to reckon. They will not, however, reckon with that cost if their working assumption is that the only thing that matters is the financial component of the total compensation package. They will not reckon with that cost, in short, if they do not allow for nurses' professional "virtue"!

A third example may refer to the "dark side" of virtue. Much of the evidence available suggests that the members of fundamentalists groups like al Qaida, Hamas, Gush Emunim, or Islamic State ascribe a supreme value to salvation goods over worldly goods. In the view propounded by such groups, the ultimate fulfillment of human existence requires one to overcome the obsession with mundane happiness and material well-being and to strive instead for eternal redemption (and other ends which are more valuable than profane satisfaction in the life here and now). Salvation goods may not necessarily be religious: to realize the mission of world history, the welfare of mankind, or the recapture of ancient land can also gain supreme value in the sense of gaining lexicographic superiority over worldly aims. To accept an obligation towards the realization of such non-material goods can create a commitment and an intrinsic motivation which trump many other incentives and interests. These are "virtues" only from the point of view of the members of such groups and "vices" seen from outside. But as in other, more desirable cases of behavioral dispositions, we would not be able to understand and deal with the behavior of people who join such groups and sometimes perform horrible deeds if we do not take their special "preferences over virtue" seriously.[10]

The claim that the "virtue economist" makes here is that standard predictions will be off-key to the extent that the working assumption about agent motivations does not track reality. The idea that all agents are motivated exclusively by material self-interest, which they strive to maximize relentlessly in each and every situation, can in some cases be a useful abstraction. But virtue economists are inclined to insist that it *is* an abstraction and that sometimes the sacrifice in terms of empirical accuracy is large. Moreover, even where the assumption of predominant material self-interest does not give false predictions, it may well get the explanation wrong. Some economists of an empirical bent may certainly be able to demonstrate that explanations of social phenomena by appeal to self-interest assumptions "fit the data." The examples are too numerous to justify citing. But this in itself does not show that a better fit on the data would not be secured by operating with a more extended "utility function."

An example of this more limited point might be useful. In much public choice theory, the assumption that voters are motivated by material self-interest in their choices at the ballot box is a very simple empirical generalization. And it seems to have some empirical force. We might observe for example that academics vote for an expansion in higher education funding more than do other voters with similar characteristics. Then we might adduce that academics are voting this way because higher education funding stands to increase academic salaries and hence leave each better off in an expected sense. But another explanation might be that academics have internalized professional norms. They believe in the life of the mind and indeed have dedicated their lives to it. They approve of more extensive and better tertiary education: they have come to believe it to be a good thing and will vote accordingly. As a result, it just seems over-determined whether the relation between electoral support among academics and higher university spending is explained via individual self-interest or broad professional values. But here might be a test: one could examine the voting behavior of academics who are close to or at retirement. The self-interest hypothesis and the professional value hypothesis would here diverge: retiring academics would be expected to retain their professional values, but since they themselves would not benefit from any resultant salary increase, the self-interest hypothesis would predict that they would vote in no way different from the general population. No one as far as we know has done empirical work on this matter, but our point here is that there *are* empirical upshots to the two different motivational hypotheses, so that even a pure empiricist might have cause to want to get the motivational details correct.

Moreover, one of the justifications for methodological individualism in the social sciences, particularly advanced by Mises and the younger Hayek, is that humans have access to an extra level of information relevant to explanation in the social sciences: namely, whether the explanation makes sense introspectively to the participants (or to the analyst adopting imaginatively the "participant's point of view").[11] Max Weber stressed the principle that social scientists, before they try to *explain* the behavior of actors, should *understand* their way of acting—and to understand the behavior of actors for Weber means to identify their motives as the actors themselves interpret them. For Weber it would be a false explanatory approach to present an explanation for a certain kind of behavior that could not be related to the internal point of view of the actors and the way they see the driving forces of their acting themselves.

But among economists there is a propensity to ignore this internal point of view and to claim that anything that might be explained by virtue can "ultimately" be explained by opportunistic choice—that it is "really" self-interest at work. And indeed, sometimes the capacity to offer such self-interest explanations—the more ingenious or offensive to common intuitions, the better—seems to be regarded within much of the discipline as a token of cleverness, a bit like the "Whee! Look, Mummy, no Hands" of the infantile cyclist. But we ourselves mistrust the tendency to replace more psychologically appealing explanations by less appealing ones. And we emphasize that terms like "ultimately" and "really" are entirely gratuitous: they make claims to a deeper level of explanation without any justification as to why that level *is* deeper, or in any other way more satisfactory. (In this connection, appeals to greater explanatory parsimony are unconvincing if the nature of the alternative "self-interest" explanation involves rather rococo models of human interaction.) There is nothing in principle to be said in favor of sticking rigidly to the self-interest assumption; to do so just seems like a failure to distinguish between reality and what might be a useful abstraction in some cases. Of course, none of this is to deny that material self-interest (something like simple income maximization) may not be a predominant motive in many transactions of interest to economists. But it is to deny that when the theorist abstracts from considerations of "virtue"—that is, from the role of norms and values as well as concern with one's own character or the character of those with whom one interacts—she leaves nothing of significance out of account. And when we refer to "significance" here, we mean, among other things, to matters of *explanatory and predictive* significance for ordinary human behavior.

2. APPLICATIONS

With all this as background, we want now to take up three issues that seem to us to be of special interest in the light of the three variants of the "virtue economics" project that we have sketched in the preceding section: the virtue ethics response to "invisible hand mechanisms," the connection between virtue and esteem, and an issue of allocation.

2.1 Invisible hands and agent virtue

So-called invisible hand mechanisms have played an important role in the history of economics, and not least in the evaluation of market-based institutional arrangements. It seems clear that Adam Smith was intrigued by the notion of invisible hand mechanisms and that these played an important role in his general view of the world, even if the explicit references to invisible hands are few and far between in the writing.[12] For Smith, an invisible hand mechanism involves a process whereby individuals are led to act in ways that lead to beneficent outcomes without any (or much) requirement of benevolence—without, that is, the good-making features of the outcomes appearing as a motive (or at least a predominant motive) in the minds of the actors themselves.

There is, however, no evidence that Smith thought that there is any conflict between virtue and securing beneficent outcomes. In this respect, Smith is decidedly at odds with Mandeville, from whom Smith borrows extensively in other ways. It is a characteristic feature of Mandeville's treatment of similar themes that desirable results emerge from individuals' market interactions only if individuals are *not* virtuous: private virtue is for Mandeville a "public vice." Smith was, to be sure, skeptical of businessmen who claimed to be acting from virtue, and he doubtless would have been a critic of any "cooperative spirit" that was hospitable to the creation of monopoly cartels. But there is, for example, little suggestion that Smith thought either that the market made participants "greedy," and still less that their being greedy was necessary for markets to work well. Smith does think that self-interest is a primary motive of human agents and that harnessing that self-interest to beneficent purposes is an especially good thing. He also thinks that there are cases where, when an agent "pursues his own interest," he promotes the interest of "society . . . more effectually than when he really intends to promote it" (society's interest, that is).[13] But the idea that there is a genuine tension between good motivations and good outcomes is not (at least as we see it) a central element in Smith's formulation.

Neither does Smith elaborate much on whether some amount of virtue is actually necessary in participants in the trading nexus. However, he clearly thinks that the market will work better where people observe the basic requirements of justice, understood as an absence of fraud, fulfillment of contracts and respect for (clearly-defined) property rights. (It is worth noting in passing here that if the disposition to abide by the "requirements of justice" is not universal, the market itself may go some way to optimize on the lack of that particular virtue. There will be a demand from potential customers for information about the "trustworthiness" of others, and those who are trustworthy will have a demand for reliable signals that distinguish themselves from their less-trustworthy competitors. If such reliable signals can be found, the trustworthy will do better than the untrustworthy, and this will create incentives for agents to acquire the relevant disposition to be trustworthy—and incentives for parents, who wish to give their offspring the best chances in life, to inculcate the virtue of trustworthiness in their children.)

It should perhaps be emphasized that when we refer to invisible *hand* mechanisms, we are presupposing a normative endorsement of the outcomes. Some commentators prefer to think of "invisible hands" as those mechanisms that give rise to "spontaneous order," where the order in question can be good or bad or indifferent. For these commentators, anything that "promotes an end that was no part of the participant agents' intentions" qualifies as an invisible hand process; they point out that the "hand" can be used to direct a punch as well as to "provide a hand" and that restricting "invisible hands" to cases where the outcomes are normatively defensible is an unnecessary restriction. Our preference, however, is to use a term like invisible foot or invisible backhand for the negative cases.[14] We think this to be more in the Smithian spirit: after all, all of his appeals to the notion of an invisible hand mechanism are examples where the effects are beneficent.

Moreover, there seems to be a useful distinction between what we might term "motive-independent" cases and "motive-divergent" cases of invisible hands. In motive-independent cases, the same equilibrium arises *whatever* the motives of the agents; the processes that determine outcomes are just independent of agent psychology. The obvious example of this case is evolutionary explanations, in which there is some filter that weeds out all outcomes other than the ones that have the relevant property (such as the "genetic fitness" test in the standard biological case). Such mechanisms operate essentially independently of agent motivation: the selection filter works to screen out the genetically less fit whatever the operative motives are. Thomas Schelling likens certain social processes to the party game of "musical chairs," in which it is just a structural feature that there will be one fewer contestant at every round of the game, and nothing the participants think or do can alter that brute fact.[15]

In motive-divergent cases, by contrast, the motives of agents are indeed crucial for the process, but the outcome reveals properties that do not correspond with those motivations. So in Mandeville's case, it is a crucial feature of the collapse of the hive that the bees are motivated by virtue (as Mandeville characterizes it).[16] Smith's understanding of the "invisible hand" of market interactions is rather more like a motive-independent case: whether individuals are motivated by the virtue of benevolence or not, the beneficent outcome tends to emerge (though, as we have noted, certain virtues such as general conformity with the basic requirements of justice are presumed).[17]

The point of this discussion, in the virtue setting, is that invisible hand mechanisms constitute a different kind of issue for the three cases we described in the previous section. For the third (purely explanatory) case, to the extent that outcomes are produced under motive-independent mechanisms, then virtue is simply irrelevant. The primary explanatory role belongs to the institutional factors that explain how the filter operates. To the extent that outcomes are produced under a motive-divergent mechanism, then motives do represent an explanatory input along with the institutional factors: it will be the case that a different set of motives will produce a different set of outcomes. But the same general message, that the relation between motives and justification is not one-to-one, applies.

For the second case, in which virtue is valued instrumentally for its role in achieving good outcomes, then the case for being concerned with virtue seems to be significantly diminished when and insofar as invisible hand mechanisms are operative. "Good dispositions" either produce bad results (in the motive-divergent case) or are unnecessary to producing good results (in the motive-independent case). But the motive-divergent cases pose a challenge for virtue economists. They could lead either to a conclusion in Mandeville's spirit that it would be better if people would refrain from practicing their virtues in such contexts—for example, misguided helpfulness—or to proposals for institutional reform so that "good dispositions" also produce good results—such as the reform of development aid organizations.

All in all, for virtue economists, invisible hand mechanisms seem to be not very significant: there is a limited role for virtue as an explanatory factor and no role at all within such mechanisms for virtue having derivative consequentialist value. Of course, for the first variant of the virtue economist, one who is committed to the value of virtue as an intrinsic moral good, invisible hand mechanisms are either a normative challenge or a normative irrelevance. They are a normative challenge for those who are normative pluralists, because to the extent that virtue produces bad results then there will be a conflict between the intrinsic value of virtue and consequentialist considerations. And they are a normative irrelevance for the pure virtue ethicist because whether good or bad *consequences* flow from virtuous activity is of no normative significance—the sole issue is the extent to which agents are virtuous.

But invisible hand mechanisms could be of interest to the virtue economist from another angle: she could apply the invisible hand approach to the problem of how to supply the desirable virtues in a community. Conventional approaches to this problem focus on socialization, education, or indoctrination—that is, on "visible" mechanisms to produce virtues by conscious and purposeful implantation of desirable behavioral dispositions into people. However, as we already noted, if there is a demand for "trustworthiness" of others in the market or other societal contexts because trustworthy people are more reliable in cooperative relations, and if trustworthiness can be identified with sufficient reliability, then the trustworthy will do better than the untrustworthy. In this way "markets of virtue" could develop and can create incentives for agents to acquire virtuous dispositions without anybody making a "virtuous community" his or her direct aim.[18] And as for markets and invisible hand mechanisms in general, the efficiency of these mechanisms depends on an appropriate institutional framework. Virtue economists could help to examine, design and create such frameworks for flourishing "markets of virtue."

2.2 Virtue and esteem

The demand for virtue in the community might arise because individuals prefer to interact with virtuous others, whether for instrumental or intrinsic reasons, or it might be because individuals themselves have a desire to be virtuous. The natural thought in the latter connection is that some individuals are in part motivated by moral considerations and that one aspect of the moral considerations that weigh with them is their own virtue. There is a further possibility though, lying somewhere between the two "preferences" already noted. This possibility is that individuals as agents typically desire to be well thought of by others, and that individuals as observers think well of people who are more virtuous. As we might put it, individuals both desire the "esteem" of their fellows and they supply such esteem to those who are especially virtuous. Of course, the claim that individuals desire the esteem of others, and the claim that individuals are inclined to give such esteem specifically to those who are virtuous, are both empirical claims that might be rejected. But we think both claims are plausible on their face.[19]

We say that this esteem-based motivation "lies somewhere between the others" because many individuals who do not exhibit virtues in their own actions or deliberations may nevertheless admire the virtue of others. A soldier who is not especially courageous can admire heroism in others; an academic who is not especially gifted admires those among her fellows who do brilliant work. Even a person with rather weak moral motivations, not sufficient to induce moral conduct except when temptation to do otherwise is negligible, may nevertheless esteem the saints in his midst. In this way, individuals can be suppliers of esteem just by virtue of their spontaneous attitudes towards those who exhibit estimable qualities. It might be observed that most of us have fairly decent moral values even though our own behavior is morally lackluster. And this is because our attitudes arise in us willy-nilly, just as an effect of our being observers, whereas to *behave* morally often costs us a great deal in terms of energy, time, or material resources, which have uses that are more pleasurable for us. There is, it seems, nothing in the least inconsistent about saintliness being rare while at the same time admiration for the saints is extensive.

But if the esteem of others connects to virtuous behavior, and if social esteem is an object of desire among most of us, then individuals can be led to act virtuously in order to obtain the esteem that so acting brings them. Each will have reason to "up her game" in the virtue stakes so as to earn greater esteem (or less disesteem). When we refer to "acting virtuously" here, we do not mean acting in a manner that is merely consequentially desirable. We do not even mean acting as the virtuous agent would. In most relevant cases, it is not so much the action that is admired as the agent herself, and the attributes of the agent that garner esteem are the dispositions and motivations that her action exhibits.[20] In other words, it is not enough to act *as if* out of considerations of virtue: the agent must be thought to be genuinely virtuous.

So, for example, in market situations, individuals are not esteemed *because* they act in the interests of others: their so acting can be fully explained in terms of their fulfilling their own narrow self-interest. Adam Smith's famous butcher and baker are not esteemed for their providing others with dinner: they are presumed to act out of (plentiful) "self-love" rather than "humanity." Equally, the individual whose actions can be explained in terms of his desire for the esteem of others cannot normally hope to garner that esteem—or at least he can only garner that esteem because he can induce in observers the belief, which is by hypothesis false, that he acts out of the virtue itself. So if we observed that a certain individual only gave money to street beggars when there were others present to observe the generosity, we would not be inclined to esteem the giver even though the beggar is made better off to the same extent whatever the giver's motives. In other words, the desire for esteem is potentially self-defeating: esteem is a motive that dare not speak its name.

Where there are no material advantages to acting in a particular way, there may well be esteem benefits on offer, but accruing those benefits will in many instances depend on observers believing that the desire for esteem is not the motivation that leads to the action. In many instances, the objects of esteem are the agent's virtuous dispositions themselves, not his possession of "a morbid love of admiration."[21] To the extent that agents' motives in action are transparent,[22] then there will be no incentive for the esteem-hungry to alter their behavior *qua* behavior. To the extent that motives are not transparent, then esteem can provide a motive for acting as the virtuous agent would, but the amount of esteem on offer will be predictably lowered because observers cannot be sure whether the actor is genuinely estimable or not. This does not mean that incentives disappear in the transparent case. Rather, the esteem-hungry individual will have reason, not just to behave virtuously, but to become genuinely virtuous, to acquire and cultivate the dispositions and modes of calculation of which true virtue is constituted. The incentives will operate at the dispositional level!

And at that level, we take it, the fact that a desire for esteem explains the acquisition of virtue does not in any way undermine the esteem itself: if the agent is esteemed for being virtuous, and if the virtue is indeed possessed, then the reason for the virtue's being possessed is neither here nor there. In other words, the desire for esteem is only self-defeating at the action level not at the dispositional level. We esteem individuals for their virtuous dispositions because we marvel at the fact that they act virtuously even when extrinsic incentives are absent. If individuals genuinely possess virtue, that is all that matters; how they came to possess the virtue they do possess is irrelevant for the esteem they enjoy.

Of course, one might query the extent to which virtue is available for acquisition in the manner suggested. One might think that the acquisition of virtue is path-dependent in a manner that rules out its being acquired for certain kinds of non-virtue-based reasons. But virtue theorists have not typically been inclined to deny that virtue can be cultivated, that ways of thinking and modes of deliberation can be acquired by habit, or training under an appropriate guide. And even if one thought that virtue can only be augmented, so that one requires *some* virtue to begin with in order for the project of becoming "more fully virtuous" to be feasible, we do not think that requirement would be very restrictive. Almost everyone has some moral sense, some positive judgment about virtue, as well as some desire for esteem and material well-being. Indeed, since "prudence" is itself one of the virtues, some sense of one's own material well-being is a necessary component of virtue, aggregatively viewed.

The bottom line is that one might have a variety of motives for wanting to become more virtuous, of which the desire for (greater) esteem might be one.[23] So, under appropriate circumstances, might be material self-interest. That latter possibility is, as we see it, the central upshot of the literature on trustworthiness, in what some have called "the basic game of trust."[24] The "appropriate circumstances" here involve enough transparency of motive that the gains from actually being trustworthy exceed the gains from merely appearing trustworthy, just as in the esteem case itself. Virtue does not have to be "its own reward" exclusively. Indeed, in a well-ordered society there may be a variety of incentives encouraging virtue and hence there will be reason to augment the institutions that make those incentives effective. In the esteem case specifically, those institutions include arrangements for augmented publicity in appropriate cases because greater publicity increases the force of esteem incentives and thereby the incentives (given sufficient transparency) for agents to acquire the virtues of which observers generally approve.[25]

So far, we have emphasized virtue (or behavior in accord with what virtue requires) as a natural object of esteem. But there is a further connection between virtue and esteem that is no less significant. Recall that, at the outset, we defined virtue in terms of possessing certain dispositions to act and having certain attitudes. And we have noted that, as in the heroism case, many (perhaps most) individuals may have those values without necessarily *acting* in accord with them. If the values are not strong enough in the individual's "utility function" to induce action, the standard economic approach would involve treating the attitudes as behaviorally irrelevant. The esteem story shows that that dismissal is way too quick because even if the values of individuals are not strong enough to induce virtuous action in themselves, their evaluative attitudes can be strong enough, via esteem effects, to induce behavioral changes *in others*. To supply esteem is a low-cost activity that can produce high-cost behavior in its addressee. In fact, it is entirely possible that, in a community of weakly virtuous individuals, individuals who would not act virtuously on the basis of the virtue alone, may be induced to act virtuously by the aggregated force of esteem.

The point here is that the working of the esteem mechanism depends on the fact that not only the actors but also the observers have the relevant evaluative attitudes. Possessing such attitudes is constitutive of virtue: on the side of the virtuous actor, the virtue operates as a disposition to perform the virtuous act, and on the side of the observer it operates as a disposition to esteem those who act in this way. To concede that esteem may have behavioral effects—and there is overwhelming evidence for that claim—is, therefore, just to concede that individual attitudes matter. Virtue economics brings those attitudes to the explanatory table; the behavioral impact of esteem is something that virtue economics delivers, and that the standard paradigm totally overlooks.[26]

2.3 The allocation of virtue

Consider a virtue economist of the "mixed kind," one who values virtue both for its own sake and for the good consequences available if there are larger numbers of more virtuous people around, and one who believes that the desire to act as virtue requires does actually motivate behavior in at least some agents.

Then there arises an additional matter about the optimal use of the virtue that is available, namely the "optimal allocation" of virtuous persons among the various activities that make up the division of labor in society. The basic thought is simple: virtue can be thought of as a form of human capital that is differentially productive in different social locations. Specifically, locations where desirable action is produced reliably from largely "invisible" processes do not require virtue from participants. But locations in which we depend upon a certain "virtue and honor among mankind," as Alexander Hamilton put it in *Federalist* #76, will be ones in which virtuous participants will outperform non-virtuous ones in consequentialist terms.

Consider for example an occupation where it is relatively easy to monitor the performance of workers—where, say, the returns to each are determined on a piece-rate system, so that each has an appropriate incentive to be productive. In such a case, there is no need to "select" among workers according to their internal dispositions. The contrasting case is where it is relatively hard to monitor the quality of performance, and where the quality of output is opaque, so that the consumer is at the mercy of the producer to some extent. Paradigmatic examples include the plurality of experts like the medical or legal professions, where patients or clients have considerable difficulty in assessing the quality of the services they are receiving and where they are vulnerable to poor service. In such cases, the professional *conscientiousness* of the doctor or lawyer in question is a relevant attribute, no less relevant perhaps than her pure practical competence.

To take an example likely to be familiar to readers of this chapter, consider the processes that academic departments typically go through in the employment and tenuring of colleagues. Of course, departments assess applicants in terms of the quality and quantity of their written work and their record of classroom performance. But the primary concern is not with an applicant's past but with her future. Is the research running out of steam? Has classroom activity in the past largely been driven by a desire to get tenure? Recognizing that there are limited mechanisms for subsequent reward and punishment, and difficulties in assessment of performance anyway, departments select on the basis not only of record but also of promise. They want to assess the applicant's dispositions: whether she has internalized the values of the "life of the mind" and is professionally committed to living by them. Departments seek, in short, to assess her "academic virtue"—and partly by necessity and partly by choice, they know that they will be relying mainly on "selection" devices to make the right choice, and rather less on incentive devices to secure greater performance quality once that selection is made.

Alternatively, consider the political case. Rational choice political theory has concentrated most of its energies on assessing the incentive properties of democratic processes. The central question has been whether, and under what circumstances, electoral competition provides significant incentives for candidates to offer policies that are broadly consistent with voter interests (or sometimes electoral preferences if these are different) and to deliver on those policy platforms if elected. The standard assumption about candidate motivation has been the routine assumption in principal–agent settings: namely that candidate-agents will exploit any discretion they possess to further their private interests at the expense of citizen-principals. Therefore, the challenge for citizen-principals is to create an institutional framework with sufficient control and incentive structures to counterbalance these risks.

We do not deprecate that kind of approach, but we want to insist that it represents only part of the story. Democratic institutions are not just incentive devices: they are also importantly *selection* mechanisms. And this is true not only as a normative matter but also as a matter of description. That is, voters—as a matter of fact—are involved in a personal assessment of alternative candidates. They seek to discern the qualities of those candidates in terms not just of their competence but also of their honesty, trustworthiness, integrity, courage—in short, their virtue! And arguably, they are better equipped to make those assessments than they are assessments of the qualities of policies the candidates offer.[27] After all, evolution has provided us with skills for the assessment of the virtuous qualities of other persons, whereas the assessment of alternative policies in most cases requires extensive specialist study in policy analysis. Moreover, for the political observer to conceive of policy platforms as if they are designed to appeal to voters directly may be to get things seriously wrong. It may be that candidates use policy choices, rather, to demonstrate something of their own personal qualities and political commitments; in short, policy is primarily a mechanism for signaling candidate virtue as distinct from giving the voters what they want. When Churchill famously promised the electorate nothing but blood, sweat and tears, or when Kennedy urged voters to ask what they could do for their country rather than what their country could do for them, these famous figures were to be understood as showing something of their own commitments rather than promising to deliver what the voters really wanted.

Two general provisos are in order here. We have indicated that there is a normative issue involved in allocating virtuous agents to their highest value uses and that in that sense the social theorist needs to attend to selection mechanisms as well as incentive ones. But we do not mean to imply that there is a necessary conflict between the selection and incentive functions of alternative institutions. Indeed, even where there is an indispensable role for agent virtue, it is important to recognize that virtue has its limits. It would be a mistake to expose even the best of human agents to temptations that are likely to prove irresistible. And indeed it would be a waste of such virtue as there is in society to allocate its bearers to settings where even saints would lapse. (So the rule of allocating virtuous individuals to those employments that place the greatest demands on virtue is not a good general rule.)

The second proviso is really an implication of the foregoing argument that directs attention, not so much to the allocation of virtuous persons across employments, but rather to the distribution of virtue across persons. Assessing virtue in terms of a consequentialist normative system—of the kind that economists routinely deploy—raises a further question about comparing a society with a small but significant number of saints with one where virtue is much more widespread but no one person is exceptionally virtuous. We have assumed in the foregoing discussion that agents are heterogeneous in terms of the virtue they possess (some more virtuous than others). But here we raise a question about the normative implications of the degree of heterogeneity itself.

Our thought in this connection is that it may well be better to have less virtue in aggregate if the virtue available is concentrated in a smaller number of people. After all, the ancient challenge "*quis custodet ipsos custodies*" ("who will guard the guardians?") admits a reasonable response if there exists with society a sufficient group of reliably virtuous persons and if we can with tolerable accuracy discern them as such. A society that is much more virtuous in aggregate but where none are especially virtuous is not likely to function as well, not least because of the fact, as learned from Smith and Mandeville, that even when virtues can promote the general welfare of a society, there are large areas, especially in market societies, in which demands for virtue and virtuous behavior are of less concern. To be "too" virtuous in these areas can be a waste (unless the virtue is valued for its own sake).

Of course, monists about agent virtue, who think that questions of virtue entirely exhaust the moral domain, will be underwhelmed by any such observations. For them, whether a society "functions well" is *defined by* how much virtue there is around. But for the rest of us, as less extreme virtue theorists, questions about the instrumental uses of virtue and how virtue may be used more productively remain of critical interest. A concern with such questions is something the virtue *economist* can usefully bring to virtue ethics.

3. CONCLUSION

The basic conclusion reached in this chapter is that, although "virtue economics" is not an entirely mainstream activity within the economics profession, there is a perfectly respectable niche within economics for scholars with a concern for virtue as an analytic category. Furthermore, there are clearly many aspects of the "virtue economics" agenda that cry out for serious analytic and empirical treatment.

Our modest contribution to that exercise has been to emphasize several distinctions that will shape the way analysis and empirical enquiry will properly go: namely, whether virtue is understood as a means or as an end (or both), and whether virtue is construed primarily as a consumption or a production good. We have also suggested that how virtue operates in society is dependent not just on details about its precise content (about which we have said next to nothing) but also on certain other factors operating within society, such as: whether there is ready access to invisible hand mechanisms; how virtue interacts with the "economy of esteem"; and how virtue is allocated across the range of social locations.

We have taken our audience for this chapter to be two largely independent groups. To those scholars who characterize themselves as virtue theorists, we want to say that economics (or, more accurately, a broad rational-choice mode of social analysis) has something important and distinctive to offer their enquiry. And to the economists, we want to say that a sensitivity to virtue can enrich the capacity to explain and predict human behavior and contribute insights relevant for policy analysis and institutional design that are important and largely overlooked within the discipline as it stands.

NOTES

1. We do not mean to imply that virtuous people are necessarily preoccupied with their own virtue, as might be implied by inserting "virtue" in the agent's utility function. We mean that the considerations that are entailed in virtue are ones that weigh with the actor. We also mean to suggest that, if the actor were persuaded that she was mistaken as to whether those considerations were indeed entailed in virtue, she would change her disposition to act as those considerations suggest.
2. This observation demands a more detailed enquiry as to the extent to which collective activity, such as voting (or deliberately delegating), exhibits virtue vis-à-vis direct individual action. That enquiry strikes us as interesting and important but we cannot pursue it here.
3. Adam Smith, *The Wealth of Nations*, R.H. Campbell and A.S. Skinner (eds.) (Indianapolis: Liberty Fund, 1776/1982), and *Lectures on Jurisprudence*, R.L. Meek, D.D. Raphael, and P.G. Stein (eds.) (Indianapolis: Liberty Fund, 1982).

4. Herbert Gintis, *Moral Sentiments and Material Interests* (Cambridge, MA: The MIT Press, 2005); Paul Seabright, *The Company of Strangers* (Princeton: Princeton University Press, 2010); Elinor Ostrom, *Governing the Commons* (Cambridge: Cambridge University Press, 1990) and *Understanding Institutional Diversity* (Princeton: Princeton University Press, 2005).
5. Those scholars who wish to reclaim Smith as a "virtue theorist" need to bear this in mind. To recognize a place in the Smithian normative scheme for virtue is not to deny the general utilitarian spirit of much of his overall argument.
6. George Akerlof, "Labor Contracts as Partial Gift Exchange," *Quarterly Journal of Economics* 97(1982): 543–69.
7. Bruno Frey, *Not Just for the Money* (Cheltenham, UK: Edward Elgar, 1997).
8. Individuals will predictably self-select into professions they "enjoy," that is, from which they get "intrinsic rewards." But this fact will not generate equilibrium wage differences unless the nurse who derives least such intrinsic reward gets *some* intrinsic reward vis-à-vis comparable employments.
9. It is worth noting that this shift away from intrinsic towards financial rewards will also change the composition of the nursing workforce away from those who derive a larger share of their total return in the non-financial component. But that effect probably means that more monitoring of nursing activity is required: there will be fewer nurses who do their tasks for their own sake and a larger number who do those tasks only because they are paid to do so. The effect on nurse "morale", on the culture of the profession, may be considerable. But, of course, such effects can only be allowed for if the analyst admits the possibility of such "culture" effects in the first place.
10. Michael Baurmann, "Rational Fundamentalism? An Explanatory Model of Fundamentalist Beliefs," *Episteme: Journal of Social Epistemology* 4(2007): 150–66.
11. Methodological individualism is, of course, a principle that economists are inclined to consider a core piece of their "way of thinking."
12. For an attempt to downplay the role of invisible hand thinking in Smith, see Tony Grampp, "What Did Adam Smith Mean by the Invisible Hand," *Journal of Political Economy* 108(2000): 441–69.
13. Smith, *Wealth of Nations*, IV.2.9.
14. In German, one might contrast "unsichtbare *Hand*" with "unsichtbare *Wand*" (invisible wall).
15. Thomas Schelling, *Micromotives and Macrobehavior* (New York: W.W. Norton, 1978).
16. Bernard Mandeville, *The Fable of the Bees* (Oxford: Oxford University Press, 1705/1924).
17. Schelling's famous case of neighborhood segregation is an instance of (partial) motive-independence ("Models of Segregation," *American Economic Review* 59 (1969): 488–93). The point of his model is that radical racial separation can emerge even when that is not desired by any of the parties, provided that they have a much weaker desire—namely that their race or group constitute a majority within the community. The complete segregation outcome is in that sense quite consistent with everybody's "optimal" outcome being a minimal 51–49 split.

18. Michael Baurmann, *The Market of Virtue: Morality and Commitment in a Liberal Society* (Dordrecht: Kluwer Law, 1996/2002).
19. We owe this point to Jennifer Baker.
20. This is another example of the blindness of standard economics in regard to the facts of life. In the artificial world of *homo economicus,* where all actors make decisions from case to case, the granting of esteem could not be explained because in this world dispositions *qua* dispositions are irrelevant.
21. As Gilbert and Sullivan's Bunthorne has it in their comic opera *Patience* (1881).
22. As the game theorist might put it, to the extent that there is a separating equilibrium in the signaling game.
23. The bracketed addition of "greater" is to register that we are including reduced disesteem as well as enhanced positive esteem as part of the esteem package.
24. For treatments by the present authors see Geoffrey Brennan, "Democratic Trust: A Rational-Choice Theory View," in Valerie Braithwaite and Margaret Levi (eds.), *Trust and Governance* (New York: Russell Sage Foundation, 1998), 197–217; Geoffrey Brennan and Hartmut Kliemt, "Finite Lives and Social Institution," *Kyklos* 47(1994): 551–72, and Baurmann, *The Market of Virtue.*
25. For more extended discussion, see Geoffrey Brennan and Philip Pettit, *The Economy of Esteem* (Oxford: Oxford University Press, 2004).
26. In his paper on the evolution of social norms, Robert Ellickson argues in line with our thoughts that the implementation of social norms depends crucially on the applause from the "audience" for the active norm enforcer ("The Evolution of Social Norms: A Perspective From the Legal Academy," in Michael Hechter and Karl-Dieter Opp (eds.), *Social Norms,* New York: Russell Sage Foundation, 2001, 35–75).
27. Michael Baurmann and Geoffrey Brennan, "What Should the Voter Know?" *Grazer Philosophische Studien* 79(2009): 159–86.

7

The Separation of Economics from Virtue

A Historical–Conceptual Introduction

Eric Schliesser

> The official attitude (of which Robbins is perhaps the best known contemporary exponent) now became more austere: the study of ends was held to be a problem in ethics and the economist *qua* scientist had no special competence in this field, even as applied to economic policy. Quite recently there has been a return to the view that the treatment of welfare problems is an integral part of economic analysis. The new welfare economists claim that many policies can be shown (to other economists?) to be good or bad without entering a dangerous quagmire of value judgments.
>
> George J. Stigler (1943)[1]

The aim of this chapter is to explain what philosophical commitments drove mainstream professional economists to understand their own discipline as leaving no space for ethics (including virtue) between, say, 1883 and 1977. In particular, I argue that economics embraced a *technocratic conception of politics and science.* An important theme of my chapter is that philosophers, too, embraced and continue to embrace a number of commitments about philosophy and science that entrench a sharp division of labor between philosophers and economics and that keep not just ethics, but virtue, outside of economics. Many of these philosophers' commitments were adopted by economists, such that they could assume, in practice, that there is a self-sufficient apolitical domain of pure economics.[2] So, in effect, this chapter explores the origin and nature of a conceptual split between economics and ethics.

There are two subsidiary themes in my chapter that are not fully worked out in it, but play a non-trivial role in the development that I sketch. First, I pay some attention to the role of so-called epistemic virtues that good economic inquirers need to possess by virtue of the split between economics and ethics. By "epistemic virtue" I mean to refer to the moral character or moral properties of the scientific economist. I will not discuss the epistemic virtues commonly associated with scientists, such as patience, objectivity, disinterestedness, and humility, although these do operate in the background, but I will call attention to those epistemic virtues that take on special urgency in light of the larger development. Second, I also consider the ways in which the expert economist can (and cannot) assume to be agreeing with the values of the society she studies and hopes to advise as a policy scientist.

By "technocratic conception of politics and science," I mean here to capture the following three features of a resilient and influential image within economics.[3] First, it is characterized by the ideal that, with social knowledge and its progress, substantial political disagreement can be eliminated. For example, as Milton Friedman claims in his 1976 Nobel lecture:

> Many countries around the world are today experiencing socially destructive inflation, abnormally high unemployment, misuse of economic resources, and, in some cases, the suppression of human freedom not because evil men deliberately sought to achieve these results, nor because of differences in values among their citizens, but because of erroneous judgments about the consequences of government measures: errors that at least in principle are capable of being corrected by the progress of positive economic science.[4]

Second, and in particular, this ideal of conflict-free politics presupposes (as is clear from the quoted passage above) considerable value-unanimity in society. So, for example, in a famous 1977 article, the Chicago-school economists George Stigler and Gary Becker write that "one may usefully treat tastes as stable over time and similar among people," and that establishing this point "is the central task of this essay."[5] When value unanimity is granted, one is allowed to assume representative agents and ordinary welfare economics is possible as a kind of (social) engineering science.[6]

Third, the conception requires an image of science in which one of the central aims of policy scientists is to achieve consensus (or lack of disagreement). In economics this idea goes back, as I show, at least to Henry Sidgwick's (1883) *Principles of Political Economy*.[7] In this chapter, I note that the adoption of certain mathematical tools was, in part, designed to facilitate such consensus generation. It is worth emphasizing, however, that (a) I am not claiming that all consensus generation tools were introduced with a technocratic conception in mind, and (b) that the expectation of consensus was by no means universal even among those firmly committed to a mathematical approach. Milton Friedman's sometime co-author, L.J. Savage, for example, insists in *The Foundations of Statistics*, that "we must be prepared to find reasoning inadequate to bring about complete agreement."[8] But Savage's view became a minority position.[9]

Before I turn to my argument, I wish to explain the choice of dates that I have adopted. The concluding date (1977) was chosen because several of the most important papers I mention were published in that year. I could have chosen more recent statements to illuminate the claims I make,[10] but, as the chapters in this volume suggest, professional economics may be changing so that the question of virtue's role in economics can be asked anew. In particular, my chapter does not touch on the increasing use of data-mining and so-called natural experiments within economics, and this is why I do not wish to convey completeness.

The starting date is a bit more arbitrary (although not entirely): it is the year in which Sidgwick published the first edition of *The Principles of Political Economy*, a textbook designed for a self-standing discipline of (political) economics, distinct from moral philosophy, at Cambridge University, a department that was eventually (within a decade) co-founded with Alfred Marshall.[11] This textbook, and works by Alfred Marshall and J.N. Keynes (a Cambridge logician-methodologist of economics and the father of the more famous Keynes) which I discuss below, also helped facilitate the shift of economics away from the so-called Historical and Moral Sciences Tripos to a self-standing Economics Tripos in 1903.[12] Sidgwick was the leading ethicist of his time (and arguably one of the most enduringly influential philosophers of the English language) and extremely sophisticated philosophically.

For, the character of political economy changed between, say, Adam Smith's "moral science" (his *Wealth of Nations* was published in 1776) and the period in which economics became thought of as a "social science."[13] To be clear, and to avoid a common confusion, the 18th century term "moral science" (or "moral philosophy"—"philosophy" and "science" are often treated as synonyms at the time) does not quite mean what we might think it means.[14] Condorcet, for example, understood "by this term all those sciences that have as their object either the human mind itself, or the relations of men to another."[15] Moral sciences were opposed to physical sciences and distinguished by the kinds of causes to be discussed. Moral sciences dealt with moral causes, wherein "moral" meant something like "social." For example, institutions, norms, education, language, emotions, and property-relations were all thought of as *moral* causes; by contrast, geography, climate, mechanics, and matter-theory were physical causes.

Therefore, eighteenth century "moral" science and twentieth century "social" science are closer in outlook than is commonly thought. Even so, the two practices have different presuppositions: social science often presupposes a version of the fact–value distinction, whereas in moral science, "the natural course" or "nature" is often itself normative. If acting according to nature, or properly cultivated nature, is a key criterion or means towards the practice of virtue—as it is in many traditions—then moral science might be a guide to the practice of virtue.

Now, Smith has a traditional and demanding understanding of virtue. His most explicit and simultaneously very demanding definition is as follows: "virtue is excellence, something uncommonly great and beautiful, which rises far above what is vulgar and ordinary."[16] By "vulgar" Smith does not mean somebody rude in our sense, but rather something akin to our "run-of-the-mill" (which can encompass rudeness). Few people writing today would accept such a demanding standard of virtue, which is apt for a classical sage. (Most chapters in this volume work with a less demanding standard.) Smith's political economy did not presuppose, expect, or describe virtuous people in this demanding sense, although he did hope that by reducing human misery and power differences, commercial society would make it more likely that such virtue, and also less demanding virtues, could be practiced within the rule of law.[17]

As many other commentators have noted, Smith did think of prudence as a virtue:

> In the steadiness of his industry and frugality, in his steadily sacrificing the ease and enjoyment of the present moment for the probable expectation of the still greater ease and enjoyment of a more distant but more lasting period of time, the prudent man is always both supported and rewarded by the entire approbation of the impartial spectator, and of the representative of the impartial spectator, the man within the breast.[18]

So, moral science, as practiced by Smith in his political economy, presupposed and made explicit further, less demanding moral values, such as humanity, equity, flourishing, and prudence, that are often thought extrinsic to the practice of late nineteenth century social science.[19] This is, in part, due to a new conception of "science" in the wake of Whewell coining the term "scientist" (while reviewing a book by Mary Somerville) and Comte's positivist interpretation of "science." The normative conception of "nature," while not wholly eliminated, was not part of the official self-understanding, or image, of science. Sidgwick, whose *Methods of Ethics* and *History of Ethics* still frames philosophy's self-understanding, was not a passive bystander to this historical transformation, and so we have to understand his recasting of political economy as a principled decision.[20]

In what follows, I give a historical sketch of the adoption of the technocratic conception of politics and science within mainstream economics. Along the way, I call attention to the key distinctions that left no place within economics for virtue in the demanding sense quoted from Smith, as well as in the less demanding sense, such as equity, humanity, prudence, and so forth, that he wished to promote in his political economy. I proceed roughly chronologically: in the first section I focus primarily on the late nineteenth century, and in the second section I focus on the period after World War II in which economics became the dominant policy science. I will emphasize the links between the two periods by way of the now-forgotten John Neville Keynes.

1. SIDGWICK, KEYNES, AND THE DISTINCTION BETWEEN POSITIVE ECONOMICS AND ETHICS

> Utilitarianism was, and still is perhaps, the most influential longest continuing tradition in English speaking moral philosophy. While it perhaps can claim no writer of the stature of Aristotle and Kant (their ethical works being in a class of themselves), taking the tradition as a whole, and viewing its extent and continuity and ever increasing refinement in certain parts of the view, utilitarianism is perhaps unique in its collective brilliance. One must remember that utilitarianism is historically part of a doctrine of society, and is not simply a detached philosophical doctrine. The utilitarians were also political theorists and had a psychological theory. Also, utilitarianism has had considerable influence in certain parts of Economics. Part of the explanation for this is that if we look at the more important economists in the English tradition before 1900 and the well-known utilitarian philosophers, we'll find that they're the same people; only Ricardo is missing. Hume and Smith were both utilitarian philosophers and economists . . . Sidgwick and the great economist Marshall were both in the same department at Cambridge, when they decided to found a separate department of economics around 1896.
>
> Since that time there has been a split, although utilitarianism still influences economics, and welfare economics has a close connection to the utilitarian tradition. Still, since 1900 the tradition has divided into two more or less mutually-ignoring groups, the economists and the philosophers, to the reciprocal disadvantage of both . . . The division is not easy to rectify given the pressures of specialization, and much else. It is also very difficult nowadays to get a sufficient grasp of topics in both subjects for one person to intelligently discuss them.
>
> —John Rawls[21]

In this section I first turn to Sidgwick and explain how he and his successors promoted a conceptual split between economics and ethics. Conceptually and methodologically the split required the embrace of a certain image of science. By an "image of science" I mean to call attention to a list of characteristics that function as a kind of shorthand for representing science; these characteristics are used in polemical or educational contexts often to justify or rely on the epistemic authority of a practice described as "science." This image is often accompanied by a privileged list of scientific or epistemic virtues. I call it an "image" to highlight that when such an image is deployed, there tends to be lots of tacit commitments about the nature of knowledge, the nature of reality, the nature of society, and also the nature of science.

In the epigraph to this section, John Rawls, himself a great student of the history of economics and philosophy,[22] notes that in the wake of Sidgwick there has been a "split" between "philosophers and economists" even *within* the "utilitarian tradition" as well as the two disciplines generally. Here I leave aside the (opportunistic and somewhat misleading) characterization of Hume and Smith as belonging to the utilitarian tradition.[23] Rawls does not attribute the "split" to Sidgwick, but I follow Rawls in assuming that in the final decade of the nineteenth century, Sidgwick and Marshall were part of an attempt at a decisive change.[24] I use "attempt" because part of the point of what follows is that the "attempt" did not, despite disciplinary and educational splits, wholly succeed and I exhibit this by showing ongoing mutual explicit and implicit influence by philosophers and economists.

In the introduction to his *Principles*, Sidgwick is explicit that his aim is to salvage "the really sound and valuable results of previous [economic] thought" from "the waves of disputation"—in other words, to "eliminate unnecessary controversy." For "[*Principles*] is written in the belief that the reaction above described against the treatment of Political Economy as an established science was inevitable and even salutary; but that it has been carried too far."[25] Sidgwick's project within economics is to create a technical apparatus that produces consensus among experts; without this, the political economist has no special standing as the expert worth listening to by policy-makers. Beyond the area of agreement, all existing further disagreement has either to be caused by conflicting facts (as Sidgwick acknowledges in context) or by fundamental differences in values (as Sidgwick describes in great detail in his later discussion of the legacy of Adam Smith). Thus, his project is to create a (mathematical) body of doctrine (about economic causes) that economists could rally around, so it could become the most important policy science. As Sidgwick writes:

> In those parts of this work in which I have used chiefly deductive reasoning, I have made it my special aim to state explicitly and keep clearly in view the limited and conditional applicability of the conclusions attained by it.
>
> With this view I have been generally careful to avoid any dogmatic statements on practical points. It is very rarely, if ever, that the practical economic questions which are presented to the statesman can be unhesitatingly decided by abstract reasoning from elementary principles. For the right solution of them full and exact knowledge of the fact of the particular case is commonly required; and the difficulty of ascertaining these facts is often such as to prevent the attainment of positive conclusions by any strictly scientific procedure.[26]

According to Sidgwick, economics is (in part) an abstract policy science whose advice guides the "statesman," but the mathematical and theoretical framework that is capable of generating consensus has "limited and conditional applicability." For, economic policy advice does not merely require deduction from foundational economic theory to particular consequences, but also knowledge of (relevant) particular facts. While there is consensus among experts over economic theory, there would be (more) consensus over policy advice if (a) all relevant facts were known and (b) policy experts relied on the same core principles from which they deduce their (conditional) advice. It is no coincidence that the collection of massive amounts of data and the development of mathematical theory have become an increasing priority.[27]

In the passage quoted above, Sidgwick relies on a distinction regarding economics between the theoretical consensus it can generate and the univocal policy guidance it could offer if there were better data and consensus over values (which is one reason why the theoretical framework is "conditional"). He develops the idea and makes it more explicit as follows in describing the status of *laissez faire* in scientific economics:

> It must be obvious, however, as soon as it is pointed out, that the investigation of the laws that determine actual prices, wages and profits, so far as these depend on the free competition of individuals, is essentially distinct from the inquiry how far it is desirable that the action of free competition should be restrained or modified . . . So far as the purely scientific economist studies primarily the results that tend to be produced by perfectly free competition, it is not because he has any predilection for this order of things—for science knows nothing of such preferences—but merely because its greater simplicity renders it easier to grasp. He holds that a knowledge of these simpler relations precedes, in the order of study, the investigation of more complex economic problems that result from competition modified by disturbing causes. But the adoption of a perfectly free competition as a *scientific* ideal—a means of simplifying the economic facts which actual society presents, for the convenience of general reasoning—does not imply its adoption as a *practical* ideal, which the statesman or philanthropist ought to aim at realising as completely as possible.[28]

Here Sidgwick articulates a sharp division between the study of a (simplified) model or abstract reality and the articulation or discovery of what is desirable. The former is capable of generating consensus, whereas the latter, the development of a "practical ideal" that is implemented by a "statesman or philanthropist," is not a matter of *economic* science, but instead belongs properly to ethics. As it happens, Sidgwick also thinks ethics can be made into something like a science: "ethics seeks to attain systematic and precise general knowledge of what ought to be, and in this sense his aims and methods may properly be termed 'scientific.'"[29] But he makes a sharp distinction between the agreement over beliefs with "other members in our society" and the agreement over "new beliefs" that is subsequent ethical argument.[30]

So, *within* economics it is not permitted to take such ethical science for granted. That is to say, the key epistemic virtue presupposed by a Sidgwickian scientific economist is self-command (or self-limitation); if she wishes to avoid needless conflict, she limits the scope of her claims to a model (or hypothetical) reality.[31] In fact, Sidgwick thinks the virtue of "self-control," which is a "habit of resistance to desires and fears," *just is* "practical wisdom" (so far as practical wisdom "is a virtue").[32] That is to say, a true Sidgwickian economist would possess practical wisdom.

To be sure, Sidgwick's image of science in which science generates consensus is not the only possible image of science, despite the fact that it would seem quite natural to those of us trained up on Kuhnian notions of "normal" science as consensus. This is not the place to explore alternative images of science more permissive of permanent disagreement; but these were developed by influential contemporaries of Sidgwick.[33]

To sum up my treatment of Sidgwick, in effect he proposes a threefold distinction between theoretical political economy, practical political economy, and ethics. The first and third are theoretical enterprises in which consensus is possible; the second guides policy and is implemented by a statesman or philanthropist, and in it there is no consensus because of uncertainty over particular facts.[34] Therefore, we have in Sidgwick already the broad outlines of the technocratic conception of science and politics.[35]

The scheme sketched in Sidgwick is elaborated and made precise in much greater detail by his Cambridge colleague, John Neville Keynes, whose now all-but-forgotten work *The Scope and Method of Political Economy* was probably the first self-standing contribution to what we might call "philosophy of economics" in the English language.[36] Keynes, too, makes a distinction between economic science and ethics: "it is not . . . the function of the [economic] science to pass ethical judgments."[37] But Keynes is not a slavish follower of his more famous colleague. He writes:

> There is a further reason why a positive science of political economy should receive distinct and independent recognition. With the advance of knowledge, it may be possible to come to a general agreement in regard to what is or what may be in the economic world, sooner than any similar agreement is attainable in regard to the rules by which economics of individuals and communities should be guided. The former requires only that there shall be unanimity as to the facts; the latter may be prevented by conflicting ideals, as well as by divergent views as to the actual or the possible.[38]

Unlike Sidgwick, Keynes does not expect (foreseeable) agreement over social values. The reason for this is not that he expects moral pluralism (along, say, the lines of Max Weber, who thinks that the increased complex division of labor of modern society would generate plurality of values),[39] but rather that he thinks that people's modal expectations will be non-uniform (or "divergent").

We might say that he expects that, when it comes to what ought to be the case, Keynes thinks that people's sense of reality is going to be different.[40] In fact, he introduces enduring terminology to describe the practice that relates to social ideals, calling it "normative economics" (or "applied ethics"), which is a "body of systematized knowledge relating to criteria of what ought to be;" furthermore, it's "about the ideal as distinguished from the actual," and normative economics consists of "judgments."[41] Crucially, normative projects, even the ones that pertain to economic phenomena, should be kept outside economics (which is why "applied ethics" is a better term for the enterprise). Again, we see that one of the key assumed theoretical virtues that a practicing positive economist should have is a kind of self-command in order not to overstep the boundaries of positive science.

Not unlike Sidgwick, Keynes expects economics to generate agreement over the model reality ("economic world") and its possibilities ("what may be"). The domain that can be subject to consensus he calls "positive economics," which is just a "body of systematized knowledge of what is."[42] These facts, once established, are not supposed to be controversial. Again, similar to Sidgwick, Keynes thinks that there ought to be a bridge between positive economics and actual policy-making. This he calls the "art of economics," which is a "system of rules for the attainment of a given [policy] end."[43] He does not seem to have thought that the art of economics is capable of generating a consensus (again in agreement with Sidgwick); rather, it's the domain of (defeasible) maxims and practical precepts. As I explain in Section 2, this threefold distinction among the art of economics, positive economics, and normative economics is turned into a cornerstone of Milton Friedman's methodological writing about economics.

But Keynes is not merely a terminological innovator over Sidgwick. He also adds a temporal dimension to the image of science that is relevant to positive economics. Keynes thinks that sciences can be more or less mature: for example, economics is a less mature (or less "definitive") science than, say, "physics and astronomy." For Keynes relies on the idea that a science develops through different stages, including a "descriptive or classificatory" stage before reaching an ultimate (or "definitive") "deductive" stage.[44] In fact, sciences, including economics can undergo "revolutions." One important example of this is the so-called "marginal revolution" of Walras, Menger, and Jevons (of the 1870s); Keynes singles out Menger, in particular, as one such revolutionary, who is also self-reflective about the method and history of economics.[45] So, in Keynes's image of science there is, over time, development from primitive science (without consensus) to mature science (with consensus) as well as the possibility of revolutions between mature theories.[46]

I mention Keynes' image of science not just because of its intrinsic interest (and the ways in which it prefigures Kuhnian philosophy of science), but also because this image gets deployed in order to keep ethics outside of positive economics. As Keynes writes:

> If political economy regarded from the theoretical standpoint is to make good progress, it is essential that all extrinsic or premature sources of controversy should be eliminated; and we may be sure that the more its principles are discussed independently of ethical and practical considerations, the sooner will the science emerge from its controversial stage. The intrusion of ethics into economics cannot but multiply and perpetuate sources of disagreement.[47]

We can see that the independence of positive economics from both applied ethics and the art of economics is, in fact, treated as a (nearly) necessary precondition for progress in positive economics. It follows from this that Keynes thinks of applied ethics as a source of permanent disagreement. Keynes' key move, thus, is not the distinction between (a) a realm of facts and their generalizations that may lead to unanimity and (b) a realm of values that are sources of disagreement. Rather, the key is that he deploys some such distinction in the context of a "theory" of scientific "progress" in which a field develops from the immature, conflict-ridden stages to mature stages characterized by considerable agreement. He sketches a route to progress in knowledge only if economics can be cleansed from ethics.

Sadly, Keynes does not reflect on all the difficulties with the idea of making theoretical or positive economics independent of ethical judgments. But, in disciplinary practices, Keynes' position is attractive to those economists who wish to "get on" with their research and possibly sell its fruits to others (politicians and philanthropists), as well as to those philosophers who are enamored by the idea that they are the experts of pure ethical matters. Keynes's position becomes second nature to those educated or disciplined as *professional* economists or philosophers; it is how they (we) learn to see the world.

A generation later, Lionel Robbins captures the upshot of Sidgwick's and Keynes' position nicely when he writes that "economics deals with ascertainable facts; ethics with valuations and obligations," while recasting the nature of economics subtly:

> And, quite apart from all questions of methodology, there is a very practical justification for such a procedure in the rough-and-tumble of political struggle, differences of opinion may arise either as a result of differences about ends or as a result of differences about the means of attaining ends. Now, as regards the first type of difference, neither Economics nor any other science can provide any solvent. If we disagree about ends it is a case of thy blood or mine—or live and let live, according to the importance of the difference, or the relative strength of our opponents. But, if we disagree about means, then scientific analysis can often help us to resolve our differences. If we disagree about the morality of the taking of interest (and we understand what we are talking about), then there is no room for argument. But if we disagree about the objective implications of fluctuations in the rate of interest, then economic analysis should enable us to settle our dispute . . . Surely, for the sake of securing what agreement we can in a world in which avoidable differences of opinion are all too common, it is worthwhile carefully delimiting those fields of enquiry where this kind of settlement is possible from those where it is not to be hoped for—it is worthwhile delimiting the neutral area of science from the more disputable area of moral and political philosophy.[48]

Here the "neutral area" of positive economics has explicitly become what one might call "instrumental reason." What Robbins describes is, by Sidgwick's lights, a species of "technical skill" which selects "the best means to given ends in a certain limited and special department of human action," a form of "worldly-wisdom."[49] In limiting economics' scope as a conditional science, it becomes possible to generate the hoped-for agreement. Economics here has the character of an engineering science that works within given constraints. Robbins himself thought this meant that so-called "welfare economics" was illegitimate (and so he could block social engineering). But in his landmark 1947 work *Foundations of Economic Analysis*, which inaugurated the so-called mathematical revolution in economics, Paul Samuelson (correctly) noted that all this entails is that if there are values, then the economist's job can be to analyze what follows from them: "it is a legitimate exercise of economic analysis to examine the consequences of various judgments."[50]

By contrast, according to Robbins there is little hope to generate agreement over ends: recall, from the passage quoted above, that "it is a case of thy blood or mine—or live and let live, according to the importance of the difference, or the relative strength of our opponents." Moral and political philosophy now have become a field of permanent disunity—no surprise he would have thought so during the 1930s with communism, fascism, and liberalism being deadly rivals—disconnected from economics.[51] While Robbins himself was no friend of technocratic social engineering, it is—with the benefit of hindsight—no surprise too that his understanding of economics carried the day within economics after World War II. It provided the economists (as was his intention) with a way of understanding and selling themselves as neutral experts and inaugurated a great age of a technocratic conception of economics. The aim of Section 2 is to argue that this technocratic conception was shared by post-world-war Keynesians and Chicago-school pro-free-market-types.

This is not to deny that the engineering conception bequeathed by Robbins was not contested. John Maynard Keynes hated it[52] and so did his ideological rival, the Chicago economist Frank Knight;[53] but while they made many telling and undeniably sound criticisms, ultimately their resistance was swept away by the cold-war growth of mathematical economics (despite opposition from economists like Kenneth Boulding).[54] From the vantage point of the technocratic conception of politics and science, what was required was (a) a commitment to consensus in society and (b) ways to remove conceptual barriers to embracing consensus in science.

In Section 2 my focus is exclusively on (a), but on (b) let me just note two significant developments during the early period of the formal revolution in economics (from 1945 to 1955). First, in polemical exchanges (known in part as the Koopmans-Vining debate),[55] Tjalling Koopmans defended the use of econometric techniques because they could generate policy-relevant predictions.[56] Second, while leading, ideologically diverse economists of the 1920s and 1930s, such as John Maynard Keynes and Frank Knight, embraced epistemic and metaphysical versions of uncertainty, their views were tacitly rejected and displaced by commitments to probable risk and uncertainty re-interpreted as randomness, both of which were friendly to mathematical treatment.[57] For example, the Nobel-winning Chicago economist (and student of Milton Friedman), Gary Becker, argues that agents "will be represented by a probabilistic model in which decisions are determined so to speak, by the throw of a multisided die."[58]

2. POSITIVE AND NORMATIVE ECONOMICS AND THE TECHNOCRATIC CONCEPTION OF POLITICS

During the 1930 and 1940s, an age of "revolution" in economics, the "new welfare economics" (NWE) became an autonomous, highly technical discipline within mathematical economics.[59] This revolution is associated with Paul Samuelson's *Foundations of Economic Analysis*.[60] While its formulae were developed within a utilitarian, moral philosophical framework, by focusing on so-called "revealed preferences," NWE dispensed with the psychological commitments of utilitarianism so it could explore the *formal* characteristics of social choice without, as it claimed, highly contested psychological and moral judgments.[61] This development fit well with the technocratic self-conception of a burgeoning field that was about to become the privileged policy science, displacing law, history, and civil engineering, and winning out over sociology and political science.

Samuelson's vision was contested in a fierce, brief exchange with George Stigler at the height of World War II in the pages of the *American Economic Review*. Their polemic reveals the significance of the issues central to this chapter. Stigler, winner of the 1982 Nobel Prize in economics, argued in 1943 that NWE assumes a question-begging consensus over values in a given society.[62] Stigler criticizes what soon became the dominant approach within professional economics that combined sophisticated mathematical technique, a focus on revealed preference, and an understanding of economics (inspired by Robbins) as resource maximization under constraint. Near the end of his discussion, Stigler writes:

> Talcott Parsons probably had economists in mind when he wrote: "For it is a fact that social existence depends to a large extent on a moral consensus of its members and that the penalty of its too radical breakdown is social extinction. This fact is one which the type of liberal whose theoretical background is essentially utilitarian is all too apt to ignore—with unfortunate practical as well as theoretical consequences." *At the level of economic policy, then, it is totally misleading to talk of ends as individual and random; they are fundamentally collective and organized. If this conclusion be accepted, and accept it we must, the economist may properly exceed the narrow confines of economic analysis.* He may cultivate a second discipline, the determination of the ends of his society

> particularly relevant to economic policy. This discipline might be called, following J.N. Keynes, applied ethics.[63]

While the *American Economic Review* was already the most important journal within economics, Stigler's article opens with a long epigraph from Aristotle's *Nicomachean Ethics*.[64] Stigler then targets the formal revolution with an argument that was philosophical, not mathematical. In particular, Stigler argues that economists presuppose a moral and political consensus when they are doing *policy* science. Stigler—who is here echoing his teacher Knight—takes for granted that the economic sphere is framed or constrained by political or social ends.[65] (It is on this point that Stigler cites Parsons approvingly.[66]) Thus, Stigler's argument distinguishes between pure economic analysis, in which ends are thought of as individual and random, and policy science (or applied ethics), where ends are unified; and it is this distinction that drives him to accept Keynes' own distinction between positive economics and applied ethics.

Stigler's point is not that economists should avoid policy science. Echoing Sidgwick and Keynes, he thinks that economists ought to cultivate such applied ethics, and that this can be pursued scientifically:

> It is quite another thing to conclude that therefore ends of good policy are beyond the realm of scientific discussion.
>
> For surely the primary requisite of a working social system is a consensus on ends. The individual members of society must agree upon the major ends which that society is to seek. If any large share of the population actively disagrees with the society's ends, and in particular if it believes that the system is unfair by the group's criteria, the social system will surely disintegrate, probably with violence. This is almost axiomatic in modern social theory.[67]

It might seem that, for Stigler, economists should try to discover empirically *what* the "consensus" over society's "major ends" involves. But this is not what happened. Rather, economists ran with the other implication: *that* there is such a consensus can be discerned by the lack of civil strife (or even war).[68]

So, Stigler's criticism of the main thrust of the formal revolution (as characterized by the NWE), while perhaps motivated by displeasure with the political direction that welfare economics might take, is not ultimately political but philosophical; he insists that the normative presuppositions of NWE ought to be different than the assumptions in pure (positive) economics. Stigler argues for greater self-understanding on the part of economists about the *essentially* political nature of welfare economics when applied to societies. In context, Stigler's point is meant to warn against two tendencies: first, the tendency to import the representative agent into the pure part of economic analysis, and second, the tendency to forget the contentious nature of assuming that that society's ends are unified.[69] Stigler's argument presupposes, of course, that there is a self-sufficient apolitical domain of pure economics.

In response, Samuelson never denies this; instead, he focuses on some technical mistakes in Stigler's examples, ridicules Stigler's tacit elitism ("frankness necessitates the regrettable admission that neither the old nor new welfare economics qualifies as sprightly conversation in the Dale Carnegie, the Oscar Wilde, or even the Oxford Movement sense") and insists that NWE applies only to "a *limited* set of pairs of situations, [between which] it does tell us which *would* be better *if* we had the choice between them" (emphases in original).[70] Samuelson insists that NWE rests on "the relatively mild assumptions that (1) 'more' goods are 'better' than 'less' goods; (2) individual tastes are to 'count' in the sense that it is 'better' if all individuals are 'better' off."[71] While there are serious metaphysical and axiological issues that haunt these two assumptions, this seems to have ended debate over NWE within economics for several decades.[72]

Officially, the stance of the profession echoed Samuelson's deflationary position about the aspirations of NWE,[73] but in practice it provided a "professional consensus" for so-called "applied" welfare economics, "to increase, to society's general benefit, the influence on public policy of good economic analysis." I am quoting from a piece by Arnold Harberger, the intellectual mentor of the so-called Chicago-Boys and a colleague of Stigler and Friedman at Chicago in the 1960s and 1970s.[74]

A few years later, in reviewing Samuelson's *Foundations*, Stigler alludes to his exchange with Samuelson:

> I persist in my belief that this [NWE] is one of the less fertile areas that modern economists till; it is symptomatic that we have elaborate instructions on how to form welfare judgments that do not depend on value judgments, but we have no illustration of the application of this technique to a real problem of contemporary policy. Samuelson indeed offers much support for this skeptical view, by this enumeration of the assumptions of the new welfare economics... most of which are held to be partly invalid. But he fails to examine other facets of the problem, one of which, I think, is especially significant. When economists are writing freely on desirable policy, that is, when they are not writing on methodology, the disputes are almost always over how the economic system works, and not over the goals that should be sought.[75]

Despite criticizing Samuelson, Stigler here anticipates the central commitment of the technocratic conception—consensus over fundamental values—made by Friedman in his 1953 methodology essay: "I venture the judgment, however, that currently in the Western world, and especially in the United States, differences about economic policy among disinterested citizens derive predominant from different predictions about the economic consequences of taking action—differences that in principle can be eliminated by the progress of positive economics."[76] So, given the embrace of the technocratic conception of economics and science, political conflict can be eliminated once economics has become mature.

Note, however, that in his review of Samuelson, Stigler assumes consensus over values among the experts ("economists . . . writing freely on desirable policy"), *not* necessarily the public.[77] In fact, in the concluding paragraph of the review, Stigler advocates that Samuelson make his work intelligible to fellow experts, other economists, not the public at large. This is a matter of "responsibility" to "scholarly canons," not society. By Stigler's lights, then, economists have *duties* to the guild of experts or, perhaps, he thinks there is an ethics of inquiry; but these duties are not necessarily to society. (If economists are also treated as ordinary agents, then one can say about them what Stigler notes about "particular entrepreneurs," that they are "in the industry because it is the most profitable place to be.") Of course, once economists are trained in or recruited from the ranks that understand "advanced calculus, higher algebra, and differential equations," and it is assumed that they agree on fundamental values (which they are taught is not part of their subject matter), then the door is opened to economists-as-social-engineers who, once the technocratic conception of politics and ethics is accepted, neither question given ends *qua* scientists and may overlook tacit normative commitments of their theories and concepts. (Stigler does not offer an analysis of the distinction between fundamental and lesser values.)

Thus, in the context of criticizing the main theoretical workhorse of economics as a technocratic policy science, Stigler explicitly accepts J.N. Keynes' contrast between positive economics and normative economics. But rather than rooting normative economics in a distinct science of ethics, Stigler, after reflecting on his exchange with Samuelson, claims (with a nod to Talcott Parsons) that its normative principles are either major ends that must be presupposed by any existing political community or, at least, are presupposed by the community of experts. So, Stigler does not deny that a community of experts requires shared values or even an ethics. (He had, in fact, an enduring interest in the sociology of knowledge.[78]) But he insists that it is not a *proper* part of economics to reflect on values.

When Stigler's life-long friend, Milton Friedman, articulated his methodological commitments in 1953—after intensive correspondence and discussion with Stigler[79]—he begins by explicitly embracing Keynes's distinctions:

> In his admirable book on *The Scope and Method of Political Economy* John Neville Keynes distinguishes among "a positive science . . . a body of systematized knowledge concerning what is; a normative or regulative science . . . a body of systematized knowledge discussing criteria of what ought to be . . . an art . . . a system of rules for the attainment of a given end"; he comments that "confusion between them is common and has been the source of many mischievous errors"; and urges the importance of "recognizing a distinct positive science of political economy.[80]

As we have seen, in 1953, Friedman is not entirely assured that economics is fully mature.[81] But on the whole, during subsequent decades, the discipline embraces the idea and Kuhnian tropes and rhetoric became ubiquitous in economics.[82]

One further reason to highlight Friedman's 1953 essay is that it also articulates a conception of scientific objectivity in terms of rule-following and a publicity requirement.

> In seeking to make a science as "objective" as possible, our aim should be to formulate rules explicitly in so far as possible and continually to widen the range of phenomena for which it is possible to do so. But, no matter how successful we may be in this attempt, there inevitably will remain room for judgment in applying the rules.[83]

In relying on a public ("explicitly") rule-following conception of objectivity, Friedman thereby minimizes the requirement of theoretical virtue(s) among scientific practitioners. As he recognizes, of course, he cannot eliminate the requirement of good judgment among scientific practitioners entirely.

To forestall twofold misunderstanding, I am not claiming that the technocratic conception of politics is an autonomous invention by economists or only adopted by them. In particular, the technocratic conception of politics is also fully embraced in the seminal text of twentieth century political philosophy, John Rawls' *A Theory of Justice*. Rawls' approach can be understood as offering a decision procedure that generates unanimity.[84] In fact, in doing so, Rawls appeals to Knight's claim that "legislative discussion" is an expert "objective inquiry" and not a contest between interests![85] So, Rawls accepts the third condition of the technocratic conception of economics even outside science, for "moral philosophy."[86]

Moreover, Rawls writes:

> By way of summing up, the essential point is that despite the individualistic features of justice as fairness, the two principles of justice are not contingent upon existing desires or present social conditions . . . By assuming certain general desires, such as the desire for primary social goods, and by taking as a basis the agreements that would be made in a suitably defined initial situation, we can achieve requisite independence from existing circumstances. The original position is so characterized that unanimity is possible; the deliberations of any one person are typical of all. Moreover, the same will hold for the considered judgments of the citizens of a well-ordered society effectively regulated by the principles of justice. Everyone has a similar sense of justice and in this respect a well-ordered society is homogeneous. Political argument appeals to this moral consensus.[87]

Here Rawls clearly subscribes to the first two features of the technocratic conception. Even so, we should be alerted at once that Rawls' position is idiosyncratic because he resists securing liberties by "uncertain and speculative actuarial calculations."[88] But I leave this non-trivial complication (and the role of uncertainty more generally in Rawls) aside.

3. CONCLUSION

Thus, within the technocratic conception of politics and science there is little room for theorizing about the exercise of virtue of economic agents and, more reflexively, by economic theoreticians. The theorized agents (and markets) are increasingly thought of as responding to incentives[89] and constraints as well as to be otherwise random in their behavior. Even the intellectual virtues of the theoreticians tend to be assumed or they get displaced by conceptions of objectivity as primarily, disinterested rule-following. In this latter way, the economist qua scientist gets conceived of as a kind of Weberian bureaucrat.

However, this (often tacit) conception of the scientist as rule-follower is now being displaced by a conception of science promoted by grant agencies that seeks to make the scientist respond to scientometrically-informed incentives. For, in this chapter I have not discussed the "demand" side: that governments, foundations, grant agencies, and university administrators have also shaped disciplinary discussions.[90]

In this chapter, I have focused on how philosophical ideas, developed within economics and philosophy, shaped the way economists conceived of their expertise and how they conceive of the nature of science. I have also argued that these ideas also created an intellectual division of labor among experts who deal with economic facts and experts who deal with moral facts. While that division may have originated, in part, in an embrace of the fact–value distinction, once the divided expertise becomes associated with different professional disciplines it does not require the acceptance of that distinction to sustain itself.[91]

NOTES

1. George J. Stigler, "The New Welfare Economics," *American Economic Review* 33(1943): 355–9, at 355.
2. In what follows, I ignore the role of governments, foundations, and others that created incentives in facilitating the rise of this conception.
3. Obviously, the term and the topic are the territory of critical theory (Horkheimer, Adorno, Marcuse, and Arendt) and sociology of knowledge (Mannheim). My focus is narrower than theirs.
4. Milton Friedman, "Nobel Lecture: Inflation and Unemployment," *Journal of Political Economy* 85(1977): 451–72. Friedman's Nobel lecture was given in a highly charged, political context resulting from his visit to General Pinochet in Chile a few years before, and shortly after Friedman's most important critic—the Chilean economist Orlando Letelier—had been assassinated by the Chilean secret police. Even so, it is notable that in the sentence quoted above, Friedman entirely denies the significance of value disagreement in explaining political conflict. See Eric

Schliesser, "Friedman, Positive Economics, and the Chicago Boys," in Ross Emmett (ed.), *The Elgar Companion to the Chicago School of Economics* (Cheltenham, UK: Edward Elgar, 2010), 175–95.

5. George J. Stigler and Gary S. Becker, "De Gustibus Non Est Disputandum," *American Economic Review* 67(1977): 76–90, at 77.
6. See, for example, the arc that runs from Paul A. Samuelson, "Further Commentary on Welfare Economics," *American Economic Review* 33(1943): 604–7, to Arnold C. Harberger, "Three Basic Postulates for Applied Welfare Economics: An Interpretive Essay," *Journal of Economic Literature* 9(3): 785–97. For incisive criticism, see M. Ali Khan, "On Measuring the Social Opportunity Cost of Labour in the Presence of Tariffs and an Informal Sector," *Pakistan Development Review* 31(1992): 535–64.
7. In what follows I quote from Henry Sidgwick, *The Principles of Political Economy*, 2nd ed. (London: Macmillan, 1887).
8. Leonard J. Savage, *The Foundations of Statistics*, 2nd rev. ed. (New York: Dover, 1972), 7; see also 3, 67ff.
9. The locus classicus is Robert J. Aumann, "Agreeing to Disagree," *Annals of Statistics* 4(1976): 1236–9. For a critique of Aumann, see Merel Lefevere and Eric Schliesser, "Private Epistemic Virtue, Public Vices: Moral Responsibility in the Policy Sciences," in Carlo Martini and Marcel Boumans (eds.), *Experts and Consensus in Social Science* (Dordrecht: Springer, 2015), 275–95.
10. So, for example, I would not have to change much about my argument to accommodate a recent, influential methodological statement (Faruk Gul and Wolfgang Pesendorfer, "The Case for Mindless Economics," in Andrew Caplin and Andrew Schotter (eds.), *The Foundations of Positive and Normative Economics*, Oxford: Oxford University Press, 2010, 3–42).
11. I used "arbitrary" because undoubtedly there are earlier anticipations of Sidgwick's position throughout the nineteenth century. The views I am about to describe can be traced back to Mill: "Mill's methodological views dominated the mainstream of economic theory for well over a century... Mill's vision survived the so-called neoclassical revolution in economics beginning in the 1870s and is clearly discernible in the most important methodological treatises concerning neoclassical economics, such as John Neville Keynes' *The Scope and Method of Political Economy* (1891) or Lionel Robbins' *An Essay on the Nature and Significance of Economic Science* (1932)" (Daniel M. Hausman, "Philosophy of Economics," *Stanford Encyclopedia of Philosophy*, 2012, <http://plato.stanford.edu/entries/economics/>). I focus on Sidgwick because of his importance in (both) the institutionalization of economics and his significance in Rawls' analysis.
12. John Maloney, *The Professionalization of Economics: Alfred Marshall and the Dominance of Orthodoxy* (New Brunswick, NJ: Transaction Publishers, 1985/1991).
13. The two classic, big picture works are Joseph A. Schumpeter, *History of Economic Analysis* (London: Routledge, 1954) and Mark Blaug, *Economic Theory in Retrospect* (Cambridge: Cambridge University Press, 1997). For recent work, inspired by Foucault, see Mary Poovey, *A History of the Modern Fact: Problems of Knowledge in the Sciences of Wealth and Society* (Chicago: University of Chicago Press,

1998); Margaret Schabas, The Natural Origins of Economics (Chicago: University Of Chicago Press, 2007); and Germano Maifreda, *From* Oikonomia *to Political Economy: Constructing Economic Knowledge from the Renaissance to the Scientific Revolution* (Surrey: Ashgate, 2012).

14. The following few paragraphs were first published with some variations as <http://digressionsnimpressions.typepad.com/digressionsimpressions/2015/05/on-the-moral-sciences.html>.
15. Quoted from Ian Hacking's translation in *The Taming of Change* (Cambridge: Cambridge University Press, 1990), 38; as his source, Hacking (ibid., 220n3) gives "Eloge de M. Burquet," in A Condorcet-O'Connor and F. Arago (eds.), *Oeuvres de Condorcet* (Paris: Firmin Didiot Frères, 1847), 2: 410. Condorcet is also among the first thinkers to use "social science" in something like the modern sense. See K.M. Baker, "The Early History of the Term 'Social Science,'" *Annals of Science* 20 (1964): 211–26; and Robert Wokler, "Saint-Simon and the Passage from Political to Social Science," in Anthony Pagden (ed.), *The Languages of Political Theory in Early-Modern Europe* (Cambridge: Cambridge University Press, 1987), 325–38. (I thank Michael Kremer and Jeroen Van Bouwel for help on this note.)
16. Adam Smith, *The Theory of Moral Sentiments* (1759), D.D. Raphael and A.L. Mackie (eds.) (Indianapolis: Liberty Fund, 1759/1982), I.1.5.6. For an excellent treatment see Ryan Patrick Hanley, *Adam Smith and the Character of Virtue* (Cambridge: Cambridge University Press, 2009).
17. Lisa Herzog, "Higher and Lower Virtues in Commercial Society: Adam Smith and Motivation Crowding Out," *Politics, Philosophy & Economics* 10(2011): 370–95.
18. Smith, *Theory of Moral Sentiments*, 6.1.11.
19. Eric Schliesser, "The Measure of Real Price: Adam Smith's Science of Equity," in Sandra J. Peart and David M. Levy (eds.), *The Street Porter and the Philosopher: Conversations on Analytical Egalitarianism* (Ann Arbor: University of Michigan Press, 2008), 228–38.
20. Henry Sidgwick, *The Methods of Ethics*, 7th ed. (Indianapolis: Hackett Publishing, 1907/1981) and *Outlines of the History of Ethics for English Readers* (London: Macmillan, 1892).
21. John Rawls, *Lectures on History of Political Philosophy* (Cambridge, MA: Belknap, 2008), 162–3.
22. David M. Levy and Sandra J. Peart, "Efficiency or a 'Fair' Game: John Rawls Contra Lionel Robbins," working paper, 2007, available at: <https://researchgate.net/publication/237278013_Efficiency_or_a_Fair_Game_John_Rawls_Contra_Lionel_Robbins>. See also, Daniel Little, "Rawls and Economics," in Jon Mandle and David A. Reidy (eds.), *A Companion to Rawls* (Hoboken, NJ: Wiley, 2013), 504–25; David Coker "Rawls and Knight: Connections and Influence in A Theory of Justice" <http://jepson.richmond.edu/conferences/adam-smith/papers2015/DCokerSIPaper.pdf>. In what follows I sometimes use passages from Rawls as signposts in my argument.
23. Sidgwick and Rawls agree on the characterization, and they can propose good reasons for it, especially in treating Hume this way. (For an alternative, see David Gauthier, "David Hume, Contractarian," *Philosophical Review* 88(1979): 3–38; I thank Donald Ainslie for calling my attention to this.) But Smith is only a

genuine consequentialist when it comes to evaluating social institutions not when it comes to evaluating individual character or the propriety of behavior. For some discussion see David M. Levy, "The Partial Spectator in the *Wealth of Nations*: A Robust Utilitarianism," *European Journal of the History of Economic Thought* 2 (1995), 299–326, and D.D. Raphael, *The Impartial Spectator: Adam Smith's Moral Philosophy* (Oxford: Oxford University Press, 2009), 43–8. (I thank Sam Fleischacker for referring me to this reference.)

24. It suits Rawls' purposes to accept Sidgwick's invention of a continuous tradition, so that Rawls has a stable (and worthy, "long line of brilliant writers who learned from each other") target for criticism; Rawls, in turn, invents retrospectively and simultaneously extended an opposing, alternative (social contract) tradition. (I thank Chris Brooke for discussion.)
25. Sidgwick, *Principles of Political Economy*, 7; see 5–6 for Sidgwick's analysis of the varied sources of polemics.
26. Ibid., 7–8.
27. The Statistical Society of London was founded earlier in the nineteenth century (1834) and among its founding members were important political economists. The founding of mathematical statistics is commonly associated with names like Edgeworth, Galton, and Pearson. Of the three, Edgeworth was also a major economist at Oxford. All three were also major eugenicists; the concern over population was shared by eugenics and political economy in this period (although some economists were anti-eugenics). Darwin-inspired proponents of eugenics rejected any role for sympathy in political economy. See David M. Levy and Sandra J. Peart, "Sympathy Caught Between Darwin and Eugenics," in Eric Schliesser (ed.), *Sympathy: A History* (Oxford: Oxford University Press, 2015).
28. Sidgwick, *Principles of Political Economy*, 23–4 (emphasis in original).
29. Sidgwick, *Methods of Ethics*, 1 (although, in context he explains why he does not refer to ethics as a "science" in order to avoid terminological confusion with some of the human sciences).
30. Ibid., 16. I ignore here the further question if Sidgwick thought such consensus, even among ethical experts, would be enduring or even possible given what he calls "dualism of the practical reason" in the preface to *Methods of Ethics*.
31. I ignore here to what degree Sidgwick thought the actual economy approximated the model.
32. Ibid., 234–5. I thank David Gordon for directing me to the proper section in Sidgwick.
33. For historical (and polemical) details, see Joseph Agassi, *Science and Its History: A Reassessment of the Historiography of Science* (Dordrecht: Springer, 2008).
34. I leave it ambiguous to what degree Sidgwick advocated taking the conclusions of ethics as some of the axioms in economics.
35. I am ignoring complex issues pertaining to the question to what degree Sidgwick was a "Government House" utilitarian that also embraced esotericism (and, thus, would not expect the second criterion of the technocratic conception to be really true).
36. John Neville Keynes, *The Scope and Method of Political Economy*, 3rd ed. (London: Macmillan, 1904). Obviously, serious reflection on the philosophy of economics

precedes Keynes. It is probable, as Jens van 't Klooster suggested to me, that he was inspired by Carl Menger, *Untersuchungen über die methode der socialwissenschaften: und der politischen oekonomie insbesondere* (Berlin: Duncker & Humblot, 1883).

37. Keynes, *Scope and Method*, 60.
38. Ibid., 52.
39. See Fred Beiser, *The German Historicist Tradition* (Oxford: Oxford University Press, 2011), chapter 13.
40. I am indebted to Anna de Bruyckere for this terminology. See also Matthew Ratcliffe, *Feelings of Being: Phenomenology, Psychiatry and the Sense of Reality* (Oxford: Oxford University Press, 2008).
41. Keynes, *Scope and Method*, 34. (A Google search reveals that Keynes did not invent the phrase "normative economics," but it was a term that had only recently become more widely used.)
42. Ibid. Keynes tends to slide between treating positive economics as a simplified abstraction and a purely factual science.
43. Ibid., 34–5.
44. Ibid., 5.
45. Ibid. Adam Smith's "History of Astronomy" (published posthumously in 1795 and included in *Essays on Philosophical Subjects*, W.P.D. Wightman, J. C. Bryce, and I.S. Ross (eds.), Indianapolis: Liberty Fund, 1982), offers a historical narrative about successive revolutions among (psychologically) incommensurable systems of thought in the sciences, which have regular patterns of development between each revolution. Carl Menger knew about this work; see his *Untersuchingen uber die Methode der Socialwissenschaften und der Politischen Oekonomie insebsodere* (Leipzig: Duncker & Humblot, 1883), 24. (I am unsure if Keynes was aware of Smith's "Astronomy" and that Menger knew of it.)
46. This image of science does not generate relativistic concerns in Keynes.
47. Keynes, *Scope and Method*, 51.
48. Lionel Robbins, *An Essay on the Nature and Significance of Economic Science*, 2nd ed. (London: Macmillan, 1935), 132, 150–1.
49. Sidgwick, *Methods of Ethics*, 231–2.
50. Paul A. Samuelson, *Foundations of Economic Analysis* (Cambridge, MA: Harvard University Press, 1947), 220.
51. For critical discussion of Robbins' separation, see Amos Witztum, "Ethics and the Science of Economics: Robbins's Enduring Fallacy," *Journal of the History of Economic Thought* 33(2011): 467–86. See also A.B. Atkinson, "Economics as a Moral Science," *Economica* 76(2009): 791–804, who calls useful attention to the ways in which value judgments inform tacit principles of application even in purportedly neutral areas.
52. As Lord Keynes wrote to Sir Roy Harrod on July 4, 1938, "As against Robbins, Economics is essentially a moral science. That is to say, it employs introspection and judgement of value" <http://economia.unipv.it/harrod/edition/editionstuff/rfh.346.htm>. For discussion, see John B. Davis, "Keynes's View of Economics as a Moral Science," in Bradley W. Bateman and John B. Davis (eds.), *Keynes and Philosophy: Essays on the Origins of Keynes's Thought* (Aldershot, UK: Edward Elgar, 1991), 89–103.

53. For Knight's main statements on the relationship between ethics and economics, see Frank H. Knight, "Ethics and the Economic Interpretation," *Quarterly Journal of Economics* 36(1922): 454–81, and "The Ethics of Competition," *Quarterly Journal of Economics* 37(1923): 579–624. For excellent discussion, see Ross Emmett, "Frank H. Knight on the Conflict of Values in Economic Life," *Research in the History of Economic Thought and Methodology* 9(1992): 87–103.
54. Kenneth E. Boulding, "Economics as a Moral Science," *American Economic Review* 59(1969): 1–12. For good discussion, see M. Ali Khan, "On the Irony in/of Economic theory," *Modern Language Notes* 108(1993): 759–803.
55. For the full exchange, see the May 1949 issue of *Review of Economics and Statistics*, 31(2), available here <http://cowles.econ.yale.edu/P/cp/p00a/p0029.pdf>. For discussion see, especially, Edmond Malinvaud, "The Scientific Papers of Tjalling C. Koopmans: A Review Article," *Journal of Economic Literature* 10(1972): 798–802; see also the commentary in David F. Hendry and Mary S. Morgan (eds.), *The Foundations of Econometric Analysis* (Cambridge: Cambridge University Press, 1995).
56. Tjalling C. Koopmans, "Measurement without Theory," *Review of Economics and Statistics* 29(1947): 161–72, at 167.
57. For useful accounts see, J. Barkley Rosser, Jr., "Alternative Keynesian and Post Keynesian Perspectives on Uncertainty and Expectations" *Journal of Post Keynesian Economics* 23(2001): 545–66; Charles R. McCann, Jr., *Probability Foundations of Economic Theory* (London: Routledge, 1994); and Geoffrey M. Hodgson, "The Eclipse of the Uncertainty Concept in Mainstream Economics," *Journal of Economic Issues* 45(2011): 159–76. On the significance of randomness, see the concluding page of the important review article by Kenneth J. Arrow, "Alternative Approaches to the Theory of Choice in Risk-Taking Situations," *Econometrica* 19(1951): 401–37, and the reference to the final paragraph of Armen A. Alchian, "Uncertainty, Evolution, and Economic Theory," *Journal of Political Economy* 58(1950): 211–21.
58. Gary S. Becker, "Irrational Behavior and Economic Theory," *Journal of Political Economy* 70(1962): 1–13, at 5 (the entire page is relevant, and Becker cites Alchian's "Uncertainty, Evolution, and Economic Theory"). For an interesting, alternative discussion, see Michel Foucault, *The Birth of Biopolitics: Lectures at the Collège de France, 1978–1979* (New York: Palgrave MacMillan, 2008), 269.
59. Roger E. Backhouse, "The Transformation of US Economics, 1920–1960, Viewed Through a Survey of Journal Articles," *History of Political Economy*, Number Supplement 30(1998): 85–107. Some of the material in this section draws from Eric Schliesser, "On Joseph Cropsey's 'What is Welfare Economics?'", *Ethics* 125(2015): 847–50.
60. In 1970 Samuelson won the second Nobel Prize in economics for "raising the level of analysis in economic science" ("The Sveriges Riksbank Prize in Economic Sciences in Memory of Alfred Nobel 1970," <http://nobelprize.org/nobel_prizes/economic-sciences/laureates/1970/>). Joseph Cropsey puts it thus: "Professor Samuelson's position among mathematical economists is such that one who seeks an example is not unjustified in turning to his works. I therefore recur to his *Foundations of Economic Analysis*" ("What Is Welfare Economics?" *Ethics* 65(1955): 116–25, at 122).

61. An early survey is E. J. Mishan, "A Survey of Welfare Economics, 1939–59," *Economic Journal* 70(1960): 197–265.
62. Stigler, "New Welfare Economics."
63. Ibid., 358 (emphasis added); he quotes from Talcott Parsons, *The Structure of Social Action* (New York: McGraw-Hill, 1937), 395.
64. *Nicomachean Ethics*, 6.7. The sub-text of Stigler's positions seems to be that Samuelson (like Thales and Anaxagoras) trades in highly technical, esoteric, and useless knowledge, not knowledge of human affairs; he lacks knowledge about the nature of expertise in political society.
65. David M. Levy and Sandra J. Peart, "Stigler, George Joseph (1911–1991)," in Steven N. Durlauf and Lawrence E. Blume (eds.), *The New Palgrave Dictionary of Economics Online*, 2nd ed., 2008, <http://dictionaryofeconomics.com/article?id=pde2008_S000262>.
66. Stephen Stigler informs me that his father owned a copy of the first 1937 edition of Parsons' *The Structure of Social Action*: "He read it but with few notes. Inside the back cover he marked 3 page numbers: 392, 395, 248 (in that order). In addition there are marginal dashes on pages 232, 256, and 566" (personal communication, March 31, 2010). All six pages concern the common moral values and ends of a political community; they provide the background to the claim with which Stigler ends "New Welfare Economics." For more on the connection between Stigler and Parsons, see Eric Schliesser, "The Surprising Weberian Roots to Milton Friedman's Methodology" in *Explanation, Prediction, and Confirmation* (Netherlands: Springer, 2011), 533–43.
67. Stigler, "New Welfare Economics," 357.
68. It does not follow, of course, that all civil strife is over major ends.
69. In 1953 Friedman assumes that in advanced societies values have converged. For the significant afterlife of the issue, see Schliesser, "Friedman, Positive Economics, and the Chicago Boys," and Ross Emmett, "Realism and Relevance in the Economics of a Free Society," *Journal of Economic Methodology* 16(2009): 341–50.
70. Samuelson, "Further Commentary on Welfare Economics," 606.
71. Ibid., 605. Cropsey quotes a version of this argument from Samuelson's *Foundations of Economic Analysis* (223), at the start of "What Is Welfare Economics?" (116).
72. Cropsey, who was still an economist, published a metaphysical critique ("What Is Welfare Economics?") in *Ethics*, but this was largely ignored; John Rawls' *A Theory of Justice* (Cambridge, MA: Harvard University Press, 1971) was a more successful response.
73. The official, limited interpretation was reinforced by Arrow's famous impossibility results. See S.M. Amadae, *Rationalizing Capitalist Democracy: The Cold War Origins of Rational Choice Liberalism* (Chicago: The University of Chicago Press, 2003).
74. Harberger, "Three Basic Postulates for Applied Welfare Economics," 786; for criticism, see again Khan, "On Measuring the Social Opportunity Cost of Labour."
75. George J. Stigler, "Review of *Foundations of Economic Analysis* by Paul Anthony Samuelson," *Journal of the American Statistical Association* 43(1948): 603–5.
76. Milton Friedman, "The Methodology of Positive Economics," in *Essays in Positive Economics* (Chicago: University of Chicago Press, 1953), 3–43, at 5.

77. This is a bit of a shift from the 1943 essay, where Stigler allows that some economists can be social reformers that deviate from the socially shared consensus, but that in doing so they stop being "scientists" (see "New Welfare Economics," 359, especially note 9).
78. Stigler was much impressed by his Columbia colleague Merton; see also his G.J. Stigler, "Does Economics Have a Useful Past?" *History of Political Economy* 1(1969): 217–30.
79. See Daniel J. Hammond and Claire H. Hammond (eds.), *Making Chicago Price Theory: Friedman-Stigler Correspondence 1945–1957* (London: Routledge, 2006). See also Eric Schliesser, "The Surprising Weberian Roots to Milton Friedman's Methodology" in Dennis Dieks et al. (eds.), *Explanation, Prediction, and Confirmation* (Dordrecht: Springer, 2011), 533–43.
80. Friedman, "Methodology of Positive Economics," 3.
81. For more details on the history of the idea of immaturity of economics in the period, see Eric Schliesser, "Inventing Paradigms, Monopoly, Methodology, and Mythology at 'Chicago': Nutter, Stigler, and Milton Friedman," *Studies in History and Philosophy of Science Part A* 43(2012): 160–71.
82. For evidence see ibid. and Michel de Vroey, "The Transition from Classical to Neoclassical Economics: A Scientific Revolution," *Journal of Economic Issues* 9(1975): 415–39.
83. Friedman, "Methodology of Positive Economics," 25.
84. Rawls, *Theory of Justice*, 106, 232–3; Rawls directly confronts Arrow's charge that this demand is peculiar to "the political philosophy of idealism" on 232–3.
85. Ibid., 314n16. In the note Rawls cites *both* Arrow and Knight, focusing on their (limited) agreement and ignoring the deeper disagreement. As Rawls adds (in his own footnote): "in both cases see the footnotes!"
86. Ibid., 233.
87. Ibid., 232.
88. Ibid., 139. In "Some Reasons for the Maximin Criterion" (*American Economic Review* 64(1974): 141–6), Rawls sharply distinguishes his use of maximin (as an "equity criterion") and the then standard use of it in conditions of (probabilistically interpreted) uncertainty in economics.
89. Gordon Tullock, *The Organization of Inquiry* (Durham, NC: Duke University Press, 1966).
90. This also changes how we should think about the moral character of scientific communities, see Lefevere and Schliesser, "Private Epistemic Virtue, Public Vices."
91. This chapter has benefited from careful and generous comments by Jennifer Baker, Marieke de Goede, Lisa Herzog, Jens van 't Klooster, Anna de Bruyckere, Rutger Claassen and the editors of this volume. I would also like to thank audiences in Athens, Ghent, Lieden, and Johns Hopkins University.

8

The Space Between Choice and Our Models of It

Practical Wisdom and Normative Economics

Andrew M. Yuengert

Two men in a hot-air balloon have lost their bearings in a cloudbank. The mist clears long enough for the men to see another man on the ground. They ask him where they are, and he tells them, "you're up in the air," whereupon one of the balloonists says to the other, "that man must be an economist. What he told us is undeniably true but utterly useless."

The economic account of rational choice confirms the punch line to this joke: it rings true, but is not particularly helpful as advice for making a decision. The rational choice model in its simplest form is an optimization problem:

$$max_X \ U(X), s.t. p'X \leq Y$$

where $U(\cdot)$ is a single-valued objective (or utility) function, X is a vector of goods, p is a vector of prices, and Y is income. We may complicate this model by adding uncertainty, resource endowments, multiple time periods, and strategic considerations, of course, but it will remain an optimization exercise.

The outline of rational choice is straightforward and plausible: specify your objectives, know your constraints, estimate probability distributions for things you do not know for certain, and choose the best feasible bundle. Nevertheless, it is not sufficient to make an *actual* decision; it is not *practical*. Rational choice does not help us to discover what our objectives should be, or what is feasible in a given circumstance, or the risks we face. Even the behavioral economist's account, with its seemingly more realistic emphasis on rules of thumb that may describe some observed behaviors more accurately, does not help one to make an actual decision—to choose which rule of thumb to use, or when to abandon a well-worn rule and experiment with another.

There is a "space between" the economic account of decision-making and what it is like to make an actual decision. This chapter is about the existence of this "space between," about what fills it, and about the implications of this "space" for normative economics. Section 1 argues for the relevance of the question, "are there aspects of actual decision-making which *cannot* be incorporated into the economist's optimizing framework?" Section 2 introduces *practical wisdom* as an account of what fills the "space between." In practical wisdom, the Aristotelian tradition offers a self-consciously comprehensive account of decision-making that highlights aspects of actual choice that are beyond the reach of the economic model. The unformulability of practical wisdom poses a challenge for normative economics: if practical wisdom is crucial to actual decisions but invisible to economic models, how should economists think about their models when giving policy advice? To get insight into this challenge, Section 3 looks to three different social science research programs that explore the shortcomings of formal accounts of choice and the implications of those shortcomings for the practical usefulness of formal method. Section 4 summarizes what these examples mean for economists seeking to take practical wisdom seriously even though they cannot explicitly model it in an optimizing framework.

1. HOW THE "SPACE BETWEEN" MATTERS: THE NORMATIVE USES OF POSITIVE MODELS

The first question about the space between the economic model of choice and actual choice is whether what fills it can be incorporated into the economic account without radically altering the economic account. To jump from a generally specified optimization model (shown in the equation above) to an actual decision, does the decision-maker simply insert his objective function, prices, and income (say, $U(X) = x_1^4 x_2^5$, $p_1 = 4$, $p_2 = 6$, $Y = 100$)? Is the actual decision simply a specific instance of the general optimization problem? Or is the actual decision something more, even something radically different—the exercise of a non-technical kind of reason whose logic is not captured by the optimization of single-valued objective functions?

I will argue that there is something more to decision-making than optimization, something that cannot be captured by more complex models. The non-optimization aspects of decision-making may matter for positive analysis—that is, might result in better predictive models—but that is not my concern here. I am content to entrust any potential positive improvements to the many ambitious economists who devote themselves to positive economics. Whatever the positive implications of the "space between," its nature has important normative implications.

To see the normative importance of the "space between," imagine that actual decisions are nothing more than specific instances of the general model specified in the equation above. In this case, the transition from positive to normative analysis will be a transition from one sort of optimization problem (a simple equation like that above) to another sort of optimization problem (the satisfaction of multiple objective functions subject to aggregate constraints). In this case both positive and normative analyses will be technical. Moreover, in both accounts the individual's objective function will have primary normative weight. However one frames the policy-maker's problem—as the assignment of individual utility weights in a social welfare function, or as a search for Pareto optimal allocations—the existence of utility functions is foundational.

This transition from technically conceived positive problem to technically conceived normative problem is smooth if the only thing needed to make the economic account practical is knowledge of individual utility functions and resource constraints. However, if the "space between" is filled with something more than the specific details of our simple equation, then normative analysis will require more than information about individual utilities, as well as the social welfare functions and Pareto criteria that utility makes possible. Normative analysis will require a deeper understanding of the "space between." The non-calculative skills, judgments, and habits which fill that space—their generation and maintenance, their function in the operations of markets and society, and their contribution to well-being—will be normatively important.

Although economists suspect that non-optimizing accounts of choice lack rigor and consistency, there are in fact established traditions of careful philosophical and social science reflection on the meaning and implication of practical decision-making and action. These disciplines highlight what is systematically absent from economic accounts and the normative implications of these gaps. Section 2 introduces the Aristotelian practical wisdom tradition, which offers a careful account of what is left out of the economic model, and the relationship between formal accounts of action and actual decisions, while the following section examines three examples of social scientific research on the practical implications of the "space between" for theory and practice.

Practical wisdom is the virtue by which people act well in the world. It is precisely those aspects of choice that are simultaneously difficult to formalize and crucial to actual decision-making that constitute practical wisdom. Economists should be interested in the practical wisdom tradition for two interrelated reasons. First, practical wisdom describes crucial aspects of choice which can never be modeled, and thus defines definite limits to the modeling enterprise. The invisibility of practical wisdom to economic accounts of choice suggests a second reason why economists should be interested in practical wisdom: because practical wisdom is crucial to decision-making, its generation and preservation is an important policy concern. Its existence thus provides a challenge to economists who wish to offer good policy advice: how do you take into account something as important as practical wisdom in your policy advice when you cannot hope to model it fully?

2. PRACTICAL WISDOM FILLS THE "SPACE BETWEEN"

Economists are quick to acknowledge that their models are approximations of actual decision-making, but nowhere do they offer a full account of decision-making against which the approximation could be gauged.[1] Comprehensive accounts of choice are, however, available. The Aristotelian tradition in moral philosophy, beginning with Aristotle's *Nicomachean Ethics* and later interpreted through Aquinas and his modern interpreters, offers just such a comprehensive account of choice.[2] Aristotle's account of practical wisdom, "a reasoned and true state of capacity to act with regard to human good," is an account of decision-making which attempts to be comprehensive, leaving no aspect of choice out of its account by method, and which builds into its account a recognition that there are aspects of practical wisdom which cannot be fully formulated.[3] Given the ambition of its vision—to give a full account of what it is like for a person to decide on a course of action—the Aristotelian tradition offers an account of what economists leave out when they simplify the process of decision-making.

The unbridgeable differences between practical wisdom and rational choice originate in the radically different environments in which practical wisdom must operate. The first and most important characteristic of that environment is its "contingency."[4] In the complex, uncertain world of Aristotelian contingency, no two sets of circumstances are identical, and a small change in circumstance may result in disastrous consequences from the same action. In such a world, there is little data from which to construct probability distributions; to group circumstances together into something like a statistical sample, one must overlook differences in material, social, and personal circumstances which may be crucially important.[5]

The contingency of circumstance cannot be circumvented by the collection of data and the construction of probability distributions; most decisions must grapple with contingency directly. Irreducible contingency touches on every aspect of decision-making, including the second aspect of the decision-making environment of practical wisdom, the nature of the objectives of action. When economists assume a single-valued utility function $U(X)$, they ignore the process by which agents reason about and discover what is good in a contingent environment. Although "ultimate goods," such as life, health, friendship, truth, justice, beauty, and freedom, are obviously and certainly good, they are not chosen directly.[6] Instead, people choose goods (*Xs*) which are desired only as instrumental means to the ultimate goods.[7] The relationship between instrumental goods and the ultimate goods they promote is not obvious in a contingent environment, but must be discerned in each situation.[8] As a result, the acting person cannot consult a pre-existing utility function. His objectives develop as he acts and he moves towards (or away from) his own fulfillment and happiness. The sorts of skills and habits which aid this process of discovery are not calculative.

A third aspect of the environment within which decisions must be made is the existence of internal conflicts that require the development of virtue (or habit). Contingency is found in internal as well as external matters; differences in character must be taken into account when making a decision.[9] A person may reason that a particular course of action is good but be unable to pursue it due to an inability to postpone gratification or resist fear. Most people are not helpless in the face of these internal conflicts, but may develop habits or other strategies for self-management. This internal dimension complicates already complex decisions, and makes observed choices an imperfect guide to individual welfare.[10]

A fourth aspect of the environment in which practical wisdom must operate is its intensely personal nature.[11] The economic model is abstract and impersonal; if decisions were simply a matter of specifying a particular version of our equation above, then any person who understands calculus could make a decision for any other person. To the person making the decision, however, there is more at stake than abstract utils. No one makes a decision *in general*—she makes a decision about her own life and flourishing. Likewise, individuals care little about abstracted probability distributions over the outcomes of choice, but care instead about the realization they will experience. There is every incentive to change the odds, to discern the risks, and avoid the worst outcomes.

These four aspects of the decision-making environment—its contingency, the nature of objectives, the need for virtues, and the personal nature of action—make it impossible to treat the objectives of action and the choice set as if they were unproblematically given, as if the only decision skill needed were calculus. The skills needed to decide in this environment are perceptual, not calculative; they embody the need to perceive the barest hints of possibility for action in complex environments and to manage both the external challenges of contingency and the internal challenges of developing and maintaining character. Aquinas, in a detailed outline of the virtues needed to make good decisions, lists non-calculative virtues like memory (which allows us to draw on past experience), docility (receptiveness to advice from those who have more experience), understanding (the knack for discerning the possibilities for action when they are not obvious), foresight, circumspection, and constancy (the ability to stick to a decision once it is made).[12]

These aspects of the decision environment and the virtues that decision-making requires in this environment together explain the unformulability of practical wisdom. If the exercise of decision-making were identical to optimization subject to constraints, then all knowledge of decision-making could be contained in manuals and formulae, and skill in decision-making would be nothing more than knowledge of how to formulate and solve constrained optimization problems. But practical wisdom is not formulable; it is passed from person to person, not as one passes a book of instructions from hand to hand, but as one learns a craft, a way of life, through imitation and apprenticeship.[13]

There is a partial overlap between practical wisdom and rational choice: their shared means–ends structure. When a person reflects *ex ante* on the stakes of a decision to be made, or looks back *ex post* on the advisability of an action already taken, she will call to mind the purposes and goals of the action and the suitability of the means employed. This sort of reflection, and the means-end structure to which practical reflection gives rise, is itself a part of mature practical wisdom, which develops with experience.[14] We orient ourselves through means–ends reasoning.

Nevertheless, a practically wise person is much more than a means–ends optimizer. Filling in the means–ends outline requires a kind of reasoned judgment which brings into play experience and a wide range of non-calculative habits of perception and self-management. Neither is a practically wise person a mere deliberative plodder, specifying a set of ends and grinding away along well-worn decision paths. Practical wisdom most often operates as an ability to perceive options and act quickly (even subconsciously), in ways that do not always follow the plans we ascribe to, before or after we observe its operations.

Neither the contingent environment nor the aspects of practical wisdom that are fitted to that environment can be captured in an economic optimization model. These are not simply phenomena which *do not happen* to be captured by the economic model of choice—they *cannot* be captured by the logic of optimization subject to constraints. If we accept that the "space between" economic models of choice and human behavior must always exist, and is filled with a crucial human virtue, how then should we view the economic model? As I said at the beginning of this chapter, researchers attempting to overcome the limitations of the optimization framework may generate improved positive models. I am content to leave potential improvements to the many positive economists, and instead wish to raise neglected questions about the normative uses of economic models in light of their inescapable shortcomings.

What kind of normative framework do necessarily incomplete economic models of choice offer us? Should the existence of practical wisdom, incapable of being captured by formal economic methods but nonetheless crucial to decision-making, affect the advice economists offer about the economy? To answer these questions, Section 3 discusses three separate areas of inquiry (only one of which is purely "economic") in which the inability of formal accounts to describe actual decision-making affects the uses of formal methods.

3. NORMATIVE INSIGHTS FROM THREE SOURCES

The Aristotelian tradition is not alone in its recognition that there are activities and kinds of knowledge which resist formalization, but which are nonetheless crucial to healthy social interaction and social order. This section discusses three different analyses of the relationship between formal accounts of action and the reality thereof, and offers reflections on the usefulness of formal accounts in light of this relationship. The three examples are:

a) Lucy Suchman's analysis of machine–human interaction.[15]
b) James Scott's analysis of the failures of "high modernist" social planning to account for informal skills and modes of intelligence on which successful social order depend.[16]
c) Vernon Smith's analysis of the relationship between constructivist and ecological rationality, building on the analysis of Friedrich Hayek.[17]

Each example offers answers to four questions relevant to our inquiry into practical wisdom:

1) What is the formal approach to decisions?
2) What is the informal reality?
3) How are the formal approach and informal reality related?
4) How should we think about the practical application of the formal approach in light of its relationship to the informal reality?

3.1 Plans and situated actions

In *Human-Machine Reconfigurations*, Lucy Suchman reports on research into the difficulty of designing interactive interfaces for copy machines.[18] Her research, begun in the 1980s, locates the difficulty in the gap between the theory of action and communication which informs machine programming and the behavior of human beings trying to make copies. Suchman organizes her analysis around "two alternative views of action" (p. 51). The view which informed early attempts to program computer-user interfaces for copier machines "locates the organization and significance of human action in underlying plans" (p. 51). Suchman defines a "plan" as "a sequence of actions designed to accomplish some preconceived end (p. 52). To specify a plan is to identify a current state, a desired end state, and the path from one to the other. Although the goals of plans are more general than the preference maximization favored by economists (a plan will get you to a specified goal, without asking whether or not it is optimal), the formal structures of plans and optimization are similar: specify ends and the means to achieve them. In both cases, all action is described as a form of problem solving; on this account, action is inconceivable without a plan.

Within this framework, a "smart copier" utilizes a carefully designed plan for communicating with human users, who are also assumed to act according to carefully pre-specified plans when they make copies. The problem with this approach is that human action is not captured cleanly by plans, but is instead "situated":

> The coherence of situated action is tied in essential ways . . . to local interactions contingent on the actor's particular circumstances . . . A consequence of actions' situated nature is that communication must incorporate both a sensitivity to local circumstances and resources for the remedy of troubles in understanding that inevitably arise. (pp. 51–2)

Plans are abstract representations of situated action: they simplify both of the goals to be achieved and the contingency of circumstances within which action occurs. As such, plans are always "vague." Situated action must take into account the contingencies of place, of social context, and of the actor's understanding and misunderstanding of her situation. On this account, all action is situated. Human beings adjust to their particular environments and collaborate with others in those environments to construct an intelligible course of action. The intelligibility of action is not just dependent on the material environment; it is a mutual, co-produced intelligibility between the situated actors. Crucial to this construction is the ability to detect and repair mistakes in understanding and communication.

Suchman traces the observed failures of copy machine user interfaces to the inability of machine plans to fully describe the situated actions of users. The background knowledge needed to fully interpret the intentions of users can never be fully coded into a plan. Moreover, the full range of human communicative resources (gestures, pauses, expressions) is not available to machines. As a result, "there is a profound and persisting asymmetry between people and machines, due to a disparity in their relative access to the moment-by-moment contingencies that constitute the conditions of shared interaction" (pp. 182–3).

The "situated action" described by Suchman requires more than a plan can deliver: an ability to wade into highly contingent circumstances, circumstances that include the actions and intentions of other actors. The situated actor *feels* her way into a situation, discovering what ends are possible, what means are available, and even what counts as means and ends. Resources for correcting misunderstandings and learning from those misunderstandings are crucial. Situated action bears a strong resemblance to practical wisdom in its need to make sense of material and social contingency.

In the same way that practical wisdom has a means–ends logic, and thus resembles the optimizing models of economists, Suchman notes that, when human beings reflect on their situated actions, they often invoke the means–ends structure of plans. However, in contrast to an account in which plans are prior to situated actions—in which action merely fills in the gaps left in a purposefully vague general plan—Suchman asserts that plans are a product of situated action. Plans are one of the ways that we make sense of our circumstances, but plans do not determine action, because they are abstractions from background knowledge of material and social context (p. 52). For example, a person organizing her thoughts about a decision will often invoke a plan, and someone who reflects back on a decision will often structure his reflection within the framework of a plan, because plans are, as Suchman writes,

> efficient formulations of situated actions. By abstracting uniformities across situations, plans allow us to bring past experience and projected outcomes to bear on our present actions. As efficient formulations, however, the significance of plans turns on their relation back to the unique circumstances and unarticulated practices of situated activities. (p. 184)

Because Suchman's distinction between plans and situated action is similar to the distinction between economic accounts of decision-making and practical wisdom, the practical advice for machine programming which results from her analysis is highly relevant to the central question of this chapter: how should economists think about the normative implications of their models in light of the gulf between optimizing models of behavior and actual behavior governed by practical wisdom?

Although the plans of programmers cannot replicate the contingency-respecting processes of situated action, programmers can respect and take advantage of situated action. Instead of discarding plans altogether, they must "understand what kind of resource [plans] are" (p. 183). Accordingly, programmers in the fields of Computer Assisted Cooperative Work and Participatory Design have begun to structure their approach around the orienting function of plans in human decision-making—as a way to organize situated action and give it room to evolve (pp. 277–8). The programmer provides a framework within which the means, ends, and practices of the community of users can develop, not substituting his own fully formed purposes but allowing them to emerge from situated actions which he cannot fully describe but whose purpose and fruitfulness he wants to promote. This changes the role of the designer from the one who anticipates and plans the interaction with the machine (the all-seeing expert) to the one who puts into place a programming structure which takes full advantage of situated action: "the object of design must shift. Rather than fixed objects that prescribe their use, artifacts... comprise a medium or starting place elaborated in use" (p. 278).

Suchman's description of the relationship of formal descriptions of action (plans) to action itself (situated action) parallels the relationship between the economic account of choice and the choices people actually make. The economic account is intelligible in the means-ends framework of optimization, but that framework is insufficient for decision-making, and may be a reflection of decision-making, not a necessary precursor. Just as Suchman's programmers must respect the reality of situated action when designing computer systems, in their normative advice economists ought to respect the operation of practical wisdom, even though they cannot explicitly incorporate it into an optimization model.

3.2 Seeing like a state

In *Seeing Like a State*, James Scott investigates the failures of certain plans of social reform, locating their failures in the planners' blindness to the existence of local and personal information, judgments, and actions that are necessary to social order.[19] State plans of reform must rely on schematic representations of society, and whatever does not fit the simplified description is often invisible to the planner. Because Scott's analysis is practical in that it is intended to inform policy, it offers an informative look at the normative shortcomings of abstract models, and how one might use models in spite of their shortcomings.

Scott contrasts two kinds of knowledge, "authoritarian high modernism" and "*mētis*." Authoritarian high modernism is the attempt to rationalize society through the systematic application of scientific and technocratic methods: "High modernism is... a particularly sweeping version of how the benefits of technical and scientific progress might be applied—usually through the state—in every field of human activity" (pp. 89–90). The improvement of society, undertaken by the state, requires a high degree of simplification. "Society" must be defined as something capable of improvement. The planner must abstract away from certain aspects of human behavior and well-being in order to focus on those aspects which are the focus of government regulation and control (p. 87). Among the details left out when planners simplify are variations in material and social characteristics which are important challenges and resources at the local level, but which cannot be viewed in detail through the synoptic lens of the planner's model. Scott argues that the past successes of technology and science breed an overconfident reliance on abstract plans, increasing the planner's disregard for local contingencies, because they apparently have been unimportant in the past (p. 95).

Scott documents the failures of several large-scale plans that ignored the local knowledge and practices which were necessary to the success of the plan. This local knowledge he calls *mētis*, which "represents a wide array of practical skills and acquired intelligence in responding to a constantly changing natural and human environment" (p. 313). *Mētis* is similar to practical wisdom, although it is typically expressed in activities of smaller scope than is practical wisdom (which is life-as-a-whole). Like practical wisdom, *mētis* arises to manage irreducible contingency in environments where the personal stakes of action are high (pp. 313–19). It emerges through experience reflected on and expressed within a community of practice, and is unarticulated and embedded in character. *Mētis* develops through the experience of repeated actions conducted in similar but not identical settings. It adjusts to differences in environment which are difficult to articulate but crucial to performance. *Mētis* is made necessary by just those contingencies which are invisible to state planners. Scott also notes that *mētis* arises in those situations which are least abstract: when the personal stakes are high, such as the starvation of one's family, fatal injury, or financial ruin, and where abstract analysis has less relevance and involves more risk (p. 318).

Like Suchman, Scott emphasizes the dependence of formal plans on informal practice, although plans and *mētis* are not as closely connected as Suchman's plans and situated action. Because planners are not involved in the local practices of *mētis*, their plans are abstract representations of the problem as planners (not locals) perceive it. This creates a greater disconnect between Scott's planners and *mētis* than exists between Suchman's plans and situated action. Nevertheless, Scott emphasizes that plans are dependent on the exercise of *mētis* for their practical success, even though planners often ignore *mētis* or even consider it a sort of unruly resistance to the plan: "Formal order . . . is always and to some considerable degree parasitic on informal processes, which the formal scheme does not recognize, without which it could not exist" (p. 310).

Scott does not denigrate all planning; neither does he praise all *mētis*. Plans can bring about great social improvement, and *mētis* can be embedded in and perpetuate local oppression. He is most critical of plans which operate as if *mētis* does not exist or is not relevant. Scott locates the failure of large-scale plans of social reform in their failure to recognize the operation of *mētis*, and its necessity to the plan's success (p. 340). Plans that do not recognize the operation of *mētis* often inadvertently disrupt its operation through the dislocation of populations, and the imposition of rationalized methods, which displace sometimes superior local knowledge.

In light of Scott's analysis, how should planners view the project of social reform and the place of technical plans in that project? Scott asserts that the abstraction of planners is "not a problem once it is seen to be incomplete" (p. 346). What are the consequences of this incompleteness for wise planning?

Scott offers several pieces of advice for how plans should incorporate respect for *mētis*. First, plans should favor small reversible steps; since planners can observe neither the operation of *mētis* nor the contingencies which make *mētis* necessary, they should be ready for the unexpected and not put too much weight on the goals of the plan. Second, planners should plan for surprises and allow space for human inventiveness (*mētis*) to meet and overcome challenges in unpredictable ways (p. 344). Although plans abstract away from contingency, communities still must grapple with it, and the resources for dealing with it exist among the communities subject to the plan. Third, to better meet the challenges of contingency, planners should consider institutions which are "multifunctional, plastic, diverse, and adaptable," even if it is not clear what purposes these characteristics serve in the plan (p. 353). Just as computer programmers design software that is flexible enough to develop in unexpected ways when it meets the unpredictable complexities of the user, planners ought to design plans which can take advantage of *mētis*.

Scott offers an additional caveat to planners: authoritarian high modernism can undermine *mētis*. As he writes, "high modernist designs for life and production tend to diminish the skills, agility, initiative, and morale of their intended beneficiaries" (349). Because *mētis* cannot be incorporated explicitly in a plan, it appears to serve no purpose, but its loss may undermine the plan and impoverish the community whose purposes and goals are not simply the goals and purposes of the plan. Planners ought to value *mētis* for its own sake, and regard its diminishment as a loss.

3.3 Constructivist and ecological rationality

In *Rationality in Economics*, Vernon Smith reflects on the field of experimental economics and its connections to Friedrich von Hayek's work on planned versus spontaneous social order.[20] In his case against planned economies, Hayek contrasted two kinds of rationality: constructivist and evolutionary (or ecological).[21] Constructivist rationality is calculative and optimizing; Smith defines it as "the deliberate use of reason to analyze and prescribe actions judged to be better than alternative feasible actions that might be chosen" (p. 2). According to Hayek, by assuming that agents have full information about their preferences and options, economists give the impression that this information can be known prior to the evolutionary market interactions without which the information will not be revealed.[22] This gives rise to the impression that society can be planned and that planners "should redesign society and its institutions so that all our actions will be wholly guided by known purposes."[23] In his ambition, the planner criticized by Hayek is similar to Scott's "authoritarian high modernist."

In contrast to constructivist rationality, ecological rationality begins with the observation that individuals do not consciously behave as if they were constructivist maximizers, but that the rules of thumb and the behaviors they adopt are nevertheless fitted to the order which emerges from social interaction (p. 2). The behaviors, norms, and institutions which evolve in markets are undesigned by any one mind possessing a comprehensive view. They are however, reflexively reasonable, the product of mutual adaptation: "The behavior of an individual, a market, an institution, or other social system involving collectives of individuals is ecologically rational to the degree that it is adapted to the structure of its environment" (p. 36). The logic of ecologically rational institutions and behaviors is often invisible to those attempting to rationalize the system from a planner's perspective.

Hayek's and Smith's ecological rationality is difficult to connect cleanly to practical wisdom, although it bears a strong resemblance to the mental processes of decision-making they describe. Hayek's early work in neuroscience grounded his work on the limits of constructivist reason: because he was convinced that it was a logical impossibility for the human brain to formulate a comprehensive account of its own functioning, he was understandably skeptical that human practical reason could be described in purely constructivist terms.[24] Human practical reason is driven by the pursuit of goals and purposes, but its process is intuitive, not calculative, reliant on a combination of rules of thumb and norms of behavior and its ability to adapt those rules when they no longer work.

Smith takes a similarly naturalistic approach to human cognition and choice, adopting the two-tiered cognitive system of modern cognitive science: constructivist reasoning requires cognitive effort, and the brain economizes on this effort by relying on non-constructivist reason for most of its decisions.[25] These non-deliberative modes of thought are able to relate present circumstances to previous experience, and draw on context-specific rules and norms of behavior without explicitly evaluating them (p. 32).

I do not want to overstate the congruence between Hayek's and Smith's naturalistic accounts of decision-making and the practical wisdom tradition: in Hayek's account, even the mind and its categories of reason are subject to evolutionary development,[26] and Smith argues that the existence of a deliberating mind is itself only a useful evolutionary illusion masking automatic brain processes (p. 33). Nevertheless, the dichotomy between conscious deliberation (which often takes constructivist form) and the less describable, more habitual mechanisms by which most decisions are made, mirrors the same divisions in the practical wisdom tradition; for this reason their discussion of the relationship between the two modes of reason is relevant.

In the relationship between constructivist and ecological modes of reasoning, both Hayek and Smith give primacy to ecologically sensitive reason. Constructivist frameworks are useful for understanding the logic and efficiency of evolved norms and institutions, but existing norms and institutions are not generated by constructivist method, and their evolution cannot be predicted by constructivist analysis—they survive a process of selection which is invisible to constructivist reason.

In light of the inability of constructivist reason to comprehend the emergent order in markets, how useful is constructivist reason as a tool for policy? Both Smith and Hayek argue strenuously against exclusive reliance on constructivist reason in policy design. According to Smith, policy design is inherently constructivist, but the success or failure of any program is a product of ecological forces that determine which institutions and norms are efficient (p. 322). Hayek adds that not only is constructivist planning unable to predict the evolution of institutions, but it is also unable to evaluate the institutions which will emerge, because human values also evolve: "Men's goals are open, that new ends of effort can spring up . . . even what we consider good or beautiful is changeable."[27]

According to Hayek and Smith, policy should both promote the free initiative of its citizens (which drives evolutionary innovation) and safeguard those institutions which give the largest space within which efficient institutions can emerge (the right of possession, the right of alienation by consent, and the enforcement of contracts).[28] In other words, what should be "constructed" are the conditions which allow emergent orders to work freely, "for in fact we are able to bring about an ordering of the unknown only by causing it to order itself."[29]

3.4 Implications for economic models and practical wisdom

Each of these three examples explores the space between formal accounts of decision-making and action and their reality. All three draw similar connections between formal accounts and informal behavior: formal accounts are sketches of a more complicated reality, but are not sufficient as a means of making decisions. Each example offers lessons for the practical usefulness of formal accounts in light of those crucial aspects of decision and action which it cannot capture.

Suchman's analysis of machine–human interactions suggests that plans can provide a useful orientation towards action, but should be designed to provide space for situated action to unfold. Consequently, programmers should place less emphasis on the specified ends of their programs, which may be superseded by unforeseeable contingencies as humans make use of the program. Plans should allow space for the creative but unpredictable directions that situated action may take. Similarly, Scott's analysis of large-scale social planning suggests that planners and reformers must allow a place for the surprises that will certainly occur as a result of irreducible contingency, leaving room for the creative innovations and adaptations of *mētis* by reducing community disruptions and emphasizing flexible, multi-use institutions. The realization that their models are incomplete should induce a certain amount of humility in planners, who should plan incremental, reversible steps, and not seek wholesale redesign of social systems that they cannot fully comprehend. Hayek and Smith, like Suchman and Scott, urge planners to safeguard the social spaces in which informal adjustments and emergent norms and institutions operate, even though the nature of those adjustments is impossible to predict or evaluate with constructivist approaches. A framework in which property is secure and alienable, and in which promises are enforced, gives rise to emergent orders which are superior to planned order.

In each of these three areas, researchers urge a certain humility about the usefulness of formal plans and models of action: formal models should not be employed in a way that is heedless of informal human actions and institutions that are both invisible to informal method and crucial to social order. To leave room for these informal processes, planners should hold lightly to the goals of their plans, allowing those goals to change if the creative adjustments of human beings in society reveal new goals and more efficient institutions.

How are the practices of situated action, *mētis*, and ecological rationality related to practical wisdom? They are similar to practical wisdom in their operation, but their scope is narrower. The domain of practical wisdom is the entirety of a person's life, while specific situated actions, the exercise of *mētis* in local affairs, and the search for adaptive behaviors can contribute to the entire life project over which practical wisdom acts. A person of practical wisdom must make all of these decisions; any decision which must address contingent circumstances and affects well-being and character comes under the government of practical wisdom.[30]

As a result, the advice drawn from these three examples can help us to think about the uses and limits of economic models in normative analysis. Although economic optimization models are unable to capture radical uncertainty and the ambiguities of objective functions and constraints, the practical wisdom which navigates these uncertainties is crucial to the functioning of markets. The conditions that foster and sustain practical wisdom, and give it room to adjust creatively, are economically important even though they cannot be explicitly modeled. Practical wisdom can be given its due in policy advice by economists who are aware of its importance, in spite of its absence from their models.

When practical wisdom is viewed in its broadest perspective—not the perspective of someone trying to make copies, or to organize purchases or business practices, but the perspective of an entire life to which all purposeful action is directed—its exercise takes on a greater significance. When the operation of practical wisdom is seen in mundane actions, such as using a copier, buying a car, or starting a job, its value is more likely to be instrumental, bringing about more efficient outcomes than externally directed plans or guidance. When instead, practical wisdom is the self-direction of a person in her entirety towards her end, practical wisdom becomes itself a basic human good: the freedom of self-government. Its exercise becomes valuable not simply because it leads to better narrowly-defined outcomes; in the exercise and development of practical wisdom, the person's autonomy and self-direction are at stake.

It thus becomes incumbent upon economists to give normative weight to human freedom, not just because it is instrumentally useful in getting people what they want, but also because it is an ultimate good, like life, friendship, and truth.[31] Amartya Sen, in *Development as Freedom*, notes that people value freedom not simply because they are able to choose better for themselves than someone else can, but because they value the ability to decide for themselves, to direct themselves towards their own fulfillment, however imperfectly.[32] Thus, even imperfectly exercised practical wisdom is valuable as part of human development.

4. CONCLUDING THOUGHTS

When the account of decision-making in the practical wisdom tradition is contrasted with the economic account of rational choice, it becomes clear that the gap between the economic theory of action and the practical reality of choice cannot be bridged through the development of more complex models. This poses a challenge for the use of economic models for policy analysis: they cannot help but leave out of their formal analysis aspects of actual decision-making, namely practical wisdom, which are crucial to the operation of the economy. There is consequently an inescapable incompleteness in any normative analysis which makes use of the economic model of decision-making.

Insights from three different treatments of the gap between the formal analysis of choice and the reality of human behavior offer guidance for how economists might modify the insights of their models of choice when offering policy advice. Common to all three examples is advice to consciously structure institutions to leave space for the operation of practical wisdom, including informal skills in decision-making and creative adjustment to contingency. In addition, policy-makers should hold lightly to the goals of their plans, because the goals of institutions may change unpredictably under the adjustments to unmodeled contingency. Finally, the virtues and informal skills which elude formal modeling ought to be valued even when they cannot be given a formal rationale in economic models.

This advice may seem strange to model-inclined economists, but it is already being followed implicitly in several economic disciplines. The concepts of tacit knowledge in industrial organization,[33] and social capital in development economics,[34] are examples of phenomena which do not enter directly into models but find a place in cost functions and human capital earnings functions without a clear account of how they work. Despite ongoing efforts to model these concepts, and dissatisfaction with them because they resist formalization, they merit a place in economic analysis.[35] They should provide encouragement to economists, that concepts which lie outside of our modeling efforts can still find a place in our analysis and our policy advice.[36]

NOTES

1. See Andrew Yuengert, *Approximating Prudence: Aristotelian Practical Wisdom and Economic Models of Choice* (New York: Palgrave MacMillan, 2012), 11–14.
2. Aristotle, *Nicomachean Ethics*, in *The Basic Works of Aristotle*, Richard McKeon (ed.) and David Ross (trans.) (New York: Random House, 1941); Thomas Aquinas, *Summa Theologica*, trans. Fathers of the English Dominican Province (New York: Benziger Brothers, 1948); John Finnis, *Natural Law and Natural Rights* (Oxford: Clarendon Press, 1980); Kevin Flannery, *Acts amid Precepts: The Aristotelian Logical Structure of Thomas Aquinas's Moral Theory* (Washington, DC: Catholic University of America Press, 2001); John Bowlin, *Contingency and Fortune in Aquinas's Ethics* (Cambridge: Cambridge University Press, 1999); and Eleonore Stump, *Aquinas: Arguments of the Philosophers* (London: Routledge, 2003). Although this chapter makes use of the Aristotelian account of practical reason, it is conceivable that economists could draw also on Kantian or Humean alternatives for this exercise. For more on these alternatives, see Mark D. White's chapter in this volume as well as his *Kantian Ethics and Economics: Autonomy, Dignity, and Character* (Stanford, CA: Stanford University Press, 2011), and Robert Audi, *Practical Reasoning and Ethical Decision* (London: Routledge, 2006).
3. Aristotle, *Nicomachean Ethics*, 6.5, 1.3.
4. Contingency is similar to Knightian "uncertainty"; see Frank Knight, *Risk, Uncertainty, and Profit* (Mineola, NY: Dover Publishing, 1921/2006).
5. Yuengert, *Approximating Prudence*, 70–7.
6. See Finnis, *Natural Law*, 85–90, for discussion of the challenge of drawing up a complete list of ultimate goods.
7. Aristotle, *Nicomachean Ethics*, 1.1.
8. Yuengert, *Approximating Prudence*, 56–7.
9. Bowlin, *Contingency and Fortune*, 37.
10. Yuengert, *Approximating Prudence*, 116–19.
11. Ibid., 126–7.
12. Aquinas, *Summa Theologica*, II-II, 49–54. See also Stump, *Aquinas*, chapter 9.
13. Yuengert, *Approximating Prudence*, 144–6.
14. Flannery, *Acts Amid Precepts*, 49; see also Alasdair MacIntyre, *After Virtue: A Study in Moral Theory*, 3rd ed. (Notre Dame: University of Notre Dame Press, 2007), chapter 15.
15. Lucy A. Suchman, *Human-Machine Reconfigurations: Plans and Situated Actions*, 2nd ed. (Cambridge University Press, 2007).

16. James C. Scott, *Seeing Like a State: How Certain Schemes to Improve the Human Condition Have Failed* (New Haven: Yale University Press, 1998).
17. Vernon L. Smith, *Rationality in Economics: Constructivist and Ecological Forms* (Cambridge: Cambridge University Press, 2007); Friedrich A Hayek, *The Constitution of Liberty* (Chicago: University of Chicago Press, 1960), *Law, Legislation, and Liberty, vol. 1: Rules and Order* (Chicago: University of Chicago Press, 1973), and *The Fatal Conceit* (Chicago: University of Chicago Press, 1988).
18. Suchman, *Human-Machine Reconfigurations*, 8–12; all in-text citations in this subsection are to this work.
19. Scott, *Seeing Like a State*, 6–7; all in-text citations in this subsection are to this work.
20. Smith, *Rationality*, 1–10; all in-text citations in this subsection are to this work.
21. Hayek used the term "evolutionary rationalism" (*Law, Legislation, and Liberty*, 29–30), while Smith used the term "ecological rationality" (*Rationality*, 36).
22. Friedrich A. Hayek, "The Use of Knowledge in Society," *American Economic Review* 35(1945): 519–30.
23. Hayek, *Law, Legislation, and Liberty*, 8–9.
24. Bruce Caldwell, *Hayek's Challenge: An Intellectual Biography of F.A. Hayek* (Chicago: University of Chicago Press, 2004), 249.
25. See Daniel Kahneman, "Maps of Bounded Rationality: Psychology for Behavioral Economics," *American Economic Review* 93(2003): 1449–75.
26. Hayek, *Constitution of Liberty*, 23–4.
27. Hayek, *Constitution of Liberty*, 35.
28. Ibid., 4; Smith, *Rationality*, 324.
29. Hayek, *Fatal Conceit*, 83.
30. Aristotle, *Nicomachean Ethics*, 6.5.
31. Finnis, *Natural Law and Natural Rights*.
32. Amartya Sen, *Development as Freedom* (New York: Anchor Books, 1999).
33. See Richard Nelson and Sidney Winter, *An Evolutionary Theory of Economic Change* (Cambridge, MA: Harvard University Press, 1982). For a more recent survey, see Peter Thompson, "Learning by Doing," in Bronwyn Hall and Nathan Rosenberg (eds.), *The Handbook of the Economics of Innovation* (Amsterdam: Elsevier/North Holland, 2009), 429–76.
34. Steven N. Durlauf and Marcel Fafchamps, "Social Capital," in Philippe Aghion and Steven Durlauf (eds.), *The Handbook of Economic Growth* (Amsterdam: Elsevier, 2005), 1639–99.
35. See Yuengert, *Approximating Prudence*, 150–3, for a discussion of the limits of a formal treatment of tacit knowledge.
36. Many thanks to those colleagues who have suggested the works from very different fields which are the material for this chapter: Dan Morrison, who lent me Lucy Suchman's book after a conversation at the division copier, and Chris Udry and Joel Fetzer, who strongly recommended James Scott's work. None of these knew the connections I would try to draw between these works and economics, so they cannot be blamed for any unwarranted connections or misreadings I may have perpetrated here.

Part III

Virtue and Economics in Practice

9

Virtues of Productivity versus Technicist Rationality

Christine Swanton

Much thinking about the relation between virtue, economics, and business ethics has taken off from Alasdair MacIntyre's skepticism about business ethics expressed in his book *After Virtue*.[1] The events of 2008 appear to show that this skepticism is justified. The apparent conflict between the imperatives of productivity and economic growth on the one hand, and virtue on the other, has led to demands for considerable regulation to ensure better outcomes. It may be thought that this is unnecessary since economic management in banks and elsewhere is a technical matter, one of following certain economic/mathematical rules. However, according to Daniel H. Freedman, a lesson of 2008 is that mathematics in the form of risk models was a potent cause of economic calamity, for they "omitted a major variable affecting the health of a portfolio: liquidity, or the ability of a market to match buyers and sellers."[2] Although he claims that in the future the only real option is not to trust such models, Freedman is skeptical that this will happen; he writes, quoting Robert Jarrow, that "there has never been any incentive to distrust the models because the people in control keep making lots of money using them."[3] The solution to this appears to be regulation, requiring banks to hold more cash or at least a higher ratio of liquid assets to total liabilities, but the downside of this requirement is limiting growth and efficiency.

This conundrum is avoided if the goal of "people in control" is not seen as "making lots of money" but rather virtuous productivity, and people at the helm of business think and behave accordingly. The task of this chapter is to explore the notion of virtuous productivity, thereby avoiding MacIntyrean skepticism about virtue in business. But first what is the basis of this skepticism?

1. PROFIT AS THE INTERNAL GOAL OF BUSINESS

For MacIntyre business is inherently an activity that undermines virtue. How does he reach this conclusion? Let us present his argument as a series of premises:

1. Institutions of a given type (such as business) are justifiable if and only if they facilitate or are (partially) constitutive of the good life.
2. In order for institutions to bear this relation to the good life they must sustain practices, in which a practice is "any coherent and complex form of socially cooperative human activity through which goods internal to that form of activity are realized in the course of trying to achieve those standards of excellence which are appropriate to, and partially definitive of, that form of activity."[4]
3. Virtues are acquired dispositions which facilitate the achievement of goods internal to practices.[5] As such, they are excellences of character as opposed to traits which are "effective" in the achievement or obtaining of "external" goods such as money.
4. Business, the goal of which is to secure external goods in the form of profits, cannot respect or sustain virtue because it does not constitute or sustain practices. Instead, business secures the "goods of effectiveness" rather than the goods of excellence.

The key issue here in relation to business is MacIntyre's assumption that profit is like money in being an external good. However, this view relies on a certain conception of profit. To see profit as the internal goal of business is not necessarily to see profit as "unconstrained maximized profit"; still less does "profit" mean "shareholder profit only."[6] Profit as such is a thin notion which can be thickened in a variety of normative theory-laden ways, including the theory-laden way of virtue ethics as well as the theory-laden way of conceiving profit in terms of shareholder profit only. The internal goal of business on the view developed here is not profit as such, but profit constrained by virtue in ways commensurate with the distinctive business purpose. The way this theory-laden thickening of "profit" is conceived is the topic of this chapter; here we engage in the preliminaries.

What has gone wrong? Unsurprisingly, what has gone wrong is at the level of conceptualization. First, there has been confusion between the external good of money and profit. Profit is something essential to business; without making profit businesses would eventually go under. Though money as such is an external good, profit is money under another description, one internally related to business practice. This by itself, however, does not make profit an internal *good of excellence*. The issue is: what needs to happen for profit-making to count as a good of excellence internal to business practice? The thesis of this chapter, elaborated in subsequent sections, is that, to be such a good, profit has to be infused with productive virtue.

Let us be clear about the nature of this thesis. It is not being claimed that virtue is simply a means or even a necessary means to success in achieving the internal goal of business—profits. It is claimed rather that the internal goal of business (profit) should be conceived as an internal *good* where the good is internally related to business practice and consists in profit appropriately constrained by relevant virtue. John Dobson claims that writers such as Richard T. DeGeorge "confuse strategic cooperation with moral cooperation," allegedly illustrated by DeGeorge's claim that "competing successfully with integrity is in fact the *aim* and norm of individuals who compete with integrity."[7] However, what makes for success in the profit-making enterprise need not be understood in a thin way where the role of virtue is merely strategic. What counts as *success*, as DeGeorge suggests, is competing-successfully-with-integrity. Making *more* profit but with lack of integrity would not count as success.

MacIntyre is correct to claim that money *as such* is an external good: it is only contingently related to practices. One can obtain money in a number of ways other than through business practice, such as through fraud, winning prizes, burglary, gambling, or inheritance. Making a profit, by contrast, is a way of making money that is internally related to business, and for making profits to be a good of *excellence* internally related to business as opposed to a good of (mere) effectiveness, we need to have a conception of the virtues internal to the practice of business. These are the virtues of productivity. We move then from a picture of profit as a thin concept, to a conception of excellence in a profit-making practice, a conception according to which excellences in a profit-making practice exemplify virtues of productivity.

Aristotle has the same general picture: external goods such as power, money, friends, honors, and pleasure are not "good without qualification" unless they are infused with relevant virtue, or at least uncontaminated by certain vices. Money acquired unjustly, honors that are undeserved, and pleasure that is sadistic are not to be regarded as good, even *pro tanto*, even though they are still the *external goods* of money, honors, and pleasure, respectively. In this respect, virtue-ethical conceptions of goodness or value are intrinsically related to excellence, and thereby differ from traditional axiology of the kind espoused by Thomas Hurka.[8] The picture is made more complex insofar as the goods in question are related to practices within which virtue is expressed. In the case of money, for example, we need to know within what practice money is obtained, whether or not the practice is part of a good life, the nature of the excellences characterizing that practice, and the virtues expressed by individuals operating in roles within that practice. It is here claimed that business can be a practice that is part of a good life (a practice in MacIntyre's sense) provided that business exhibits virtues of productivity internally related to business.[9]

Second, the way MacIntyre draws the distinction between internal and external goods, goods of excellence and goods of effectiveness, is faulty. Instead of saying that business *cannot* be a practice because it pursues an external good, he should claim that money and profit can be turned into internal goods (goods without qualification) provided the pursuit of such goods is conducted within a practice in his highly normative sense. Certainly business may be corrupted, even all too readily so, but that is not to say that business cannot be a practice.

Why would MacIntyre think that business cannot be a practice? Part of the explanation is his apparent view that the rationality defining business is a rationality of mere effectiveness. He claims that

> The manager treats ends as given, as outside his scope; his concern is with technique, with effectiveness in transforming raw materials into final products, unskilled labor into skilled labor, investment into profits. The therapist also treats ends as given, as outside his scope; his concern also is with technique . . . Neither manager nor therapist, in their roles as manager and therapist, do or are able to engage in moral debate.[10]

The crucial distinction between what may be called "technicist rationality" and the rationality of virtue or *phronēsis* (where ends are not treated as given), and their connection with virtues of productivity, are the topics of later sections. But here let us consider this: why should it be thought that the "manager" cannot engage in moral debate?

The answer, I think is that in our society the manager is not for MacIntyre a role occupier in a genuine practice, but rather what MacIntyre calls a "character":

> the requirements of a *character* are imposed from the outside, from the way in which others regard and use *characters* to understand and to evaluate themselves. With other types of social role the role may be adequately specified in terms of the institutions of whose structures it is a part and the relation to those institutions of the individuals who fill the roles. In the case of a *character* this is not enough. A *character* is an object of regard by the members of the culture generally or by some significant segment of them. He furnishes them with a cultural and moral ideal. Hence the demand is that in this type of case role and personality be fused. Social type and psychological type are required to coincide. The *character* morally legitimates a mode of social existence.[11]

Maybe MacIntyre is right about the power of the ossified notion of "manager-as-character" and to think of such a type as deeply corrupting. But as he himself claims, we are not victims of social determinism; traditions, cultural paradigms and the status of characters can be and are questioned. In particular we can and do question the "character" roles of manager and therapist in relation to what business and therapy can be at their best.

Third, conceptual confusion may arise from just how we conceive of business at its best. Robert Solomon, unlike MacIntyre, is prepared to think of business at its best as a practice which has an internal good and whose practitioners manifest associated virtues.[12] Business can possess the goods of excellence as opposed to the goods of mere effectiveness. But if our conception of profit, contaminated as it is with the opprobrium of it being deemed a mere external good, is a conception in which it cannot be construed as the internal good of business, confusion arises.

This problem is manifest in forms of stakeholder theory and the even broader social responsibility theory. Solomon, for example, deploys what I have called the Expansionist Strategy in determining the purpose of a business organization, a strategy that expands that purpose to embrace "the good life" in general.[13] For example, he questions the orthodox view of the point and function of business, claiming "the good life is the goal of business—not profits, not competition, not management or the work ethic."[14] In his book *Ethics and Excellence: Cooperation and Integrity in Business*, Solomon has another account of the purpose of business, which is also very broad: "The purpose of business is to promote prosperity, to provide essential and desirable goods, to make life easier."[15] At the root of this expansionist conception is a distinction that Solomon makes between goal and purpose, illustrated by reference to the game of (American) football. The goal of a competitive game of football is to win (within the rules). The purpose in such an end is to let out aggression and enjoy the game.[16] Similarly in business "making a profit is the aim but the purpose is producing a product or service that will make people's lives better."[17]

This distinction between goal and purpose on my view is a distinction without a difference. To think of the purpose of competitive sport as providing enjoyment is to confuse mere entertainment with competitive sport. Any genuine fan will tell you that it is better to "win ugly" than to "lose pretty." Indeed, playing a boring game may be just the thing to beat a team with superior talent or speed, and fans may be justifiably angry when this necessary tactic is not part of the game plan. Nor are players there to enjoy themselves: they are there to put their bodies on the line for the sake of winning. Of course, if players do not characteristically get enjoyment from playing, they may decide on another career, but then again they may not—they may be earning too much money. To think that the purpose of business is to make people happier or their lives easier is to confuse business with, perhaps, politics. Again, both the purpose and aim of educational institutions is to educate, not to, for example, provide fun and enjoyment for students (even if, alas, we teachers are now expected to entertain). Where that is a means towards the educational purpose, as opposed to a distraction, it might be fine, but it is not the purpose.

What may have gone wrong is a failure to recognize a distinction between the assessment of a type of institution as contributing to the good life of human beings (or otherwise) for various types of reason, and the characterization of the distinctive aim or purpose of institutions of that type. Business as a whole and competitive sport as a whole are deemed to be worthy institutions since they enhance or contribute to the good life (for different reasons), but the purpose of individual businesses and sports teams is good performance as a practice with distinctive internal goals. And the goal or aim of an individual *qua* role occupier within that practice is also good performance: exemplifying the virtues that facilitate the achievement of goods internal to that practice.

2. *TECHNÊ* AND *PHRONĒSIS*

In the previous section I outlined some of the conceptual issues that may prevent one from thinking of business as a practice having an internal good of excellence, one essentially related to virtue and distinctive of the business purpose. But there is a much more deep-seated source of the problem: the distinction between what MacIntyre calls *bureaucratic rationality* and a form of rationality associated with the internal goods of a practice. Bureaucratic or *technicist rationality* is characterized by the idea that rationality is not something directed at ends but only at the means to those ends (the goods of "effectiveness"). As we have seen, MacIntyre seems to think that business is essentially beholden to technicist rationality, and it is this conception of rationality that is the enemy of virtue.

But why should productive enterprises be answerable only to technicist rationality? At the heart of the problem is the notion of *technê* itself and the Aristotelian distinction between *technê* and *phronēsis* (practical wisdom). This section aims to expose this problem, leaving scope for the notion of a rationality of production involving *phronēsis*, namely productive virtue. Such virtue supplies standards defining a specific kind of "good of excellence." In relation to business the good in question is the internal good of business as a specific kind of productive enterprise: one that is profit-making.

The distinction between technical and practical reason, inherited from Aristotle's distinction between knowledge and rationality (*phronēsis*) fitted to action (*praxis*), and knowledge and rationality (*technê*) fitted to production (*poesis*), has created distortions in our thought about ethics in relation to not just economics and production in general, but to our institutions in general. Why is this? As MacIntyre rightly claims, although institutions are necessary to sustain practices, they are inherently liable to corruption for the following basic reason:

> Institutions are characteristically and necessarily concerned with what I have called external goods. They are involved in acquiring money and other material

> goods; they are structured in terms of power and status, and they distribute money, power and status as rewards.[18]

There is on this view a separation in institutions between the "bureaucratic" (technicist) rationality of effectiveness and virtue-driven evaluation of both ends and means, proper to the institution as a sustainer of practice. This separation presupposes in turn a separation between two conceptions of rationality. That of *phronēsis* presupposes the virtues essential to the correct discernment of complex particulars, and for virtue there needs to be a correct appreciation of ends appropriate to a good life. By contrast, *poesis* (production or making) apparently requires merely technical excellence, an excellence not inherent in action for its own sake but directed at production or making. For this one requires mastery in the form of knowledge of general principles and causes, and how these relate to "materials" whether in the form of wood or stone for the production of sculpture,[19] or mathematical formulae in the case of economics.

Difficulty occurs when this narrow technicist model of rationality is applied to what ought to be thought of as practices in the full MacIntyrean sense. Examples abound; here is one from education supplied by Joseph Dunne. In the late 1970s, Dunne and his fellow teacher trainees were subjected to what was called the "behavioral objectives model" as the "blueprint in planning and conducting lessons." It is described thus:

> The pre-specification of intended learning outcomes would be the primary requirement for effective teaching. It would be the basis on which teachers could determine how their instruction should be organized with respect to methods, classroom activities, and learning materials, and at the same time it would provide a clear-cut criterion for evaluating the success of their endeavors: to succeed now would simply mean to achieve one's objectives. The objectives model thus seemed to be the royal road to *efficiency* in teaching.[20]

The real difficulty with the model on Dunne's view was the notion of "objective" itself: a scientistic measurable verifiable output which could be recognized "by a detached observer who could not be assumed to have any familiarity with the teacher's situation or background" or a "shared contextual understanding" involving interpretation. Admittedly, just as profit is the internal goal of business (as opposed to going bankrupt), so learning is the internal goal of educational practice (as opposed to rendering or causing to remain ignorant). However the notion of learning can be thickened in various theory-laden ways, in a virtue-theoretic way, for example, or in a "technicist" way in terms of the behavioral objectives model. In the latter form of thickening, the goal of learning becomes divorced from MacIntyrean practice. It is uninformed by a rich understanding of pedagogical virtue (apart from efficiency)—in other words, uninformed by teaching as a practice. In a climate such as this, the relevant institutions become preoccupied with external goods, as MacIntyre believed.

When the technicist model of rationality is applied to what ought to be thought of as practices, they are inherently liable to corruption and, as we have seen, for MacIntyre necessarily so. This is a bleak picture. Why should narrow technicist models be necessarily applied to institutions? Why are institutions thought to be *necessarily* concerned with external goods in a competitive way, as opposed to realizing the internal goals of practices which institutions are supposed to sustain? Where we have an impoverished notion of the objectives of an institution such as profit as such, or learning outcomes which are easily measurable, as well as a virtue-impoverished notion of a reward structure tied to success in relation to those objectives, a competitive attitude to external goods in the form of prestige, such as placement on league tables (in relation to schools) and so forth, becomes almost inevitable. In this corrupting situation, technicist rationality rather than *phronēsis* holds sway, and institutions become divorced from practices as properly understood.

The claim of necessity is tied to an entire critique of modernity in which *phronēsis* has been replaced by *technê*. As a result of this trend in modernity, the distinction between *phronēsis* and *technê* has caused upheavals in Western thought. First, notably in Heidegger, there is an attack on *technê* in the form of modern technology understood as resource-based thinking.[21] Second, and from a somewhat opposed direction, rather than criticize technology, the privileging of *praxis* over *technê* is undercut by rethinking what true *poesis* really involves. Such a move is evident in Heidegger's "The Origin of the Work of Art."[22] In modern times the most widely read thinker who valorizes productivity, whether in business or practices, and where genuine productivity is properly understood through a virtue theoretic treatment, is Ayn Rand. Her much misunderstood virtue ethics of productivity—misunderstood because of her unfortunate usage of the notion of selfishness—is further discussed in the Section 3.[23]

In a virtue-centered approach along these lines, *poesis* should not be downgraded as an inferior kind of knowledge or rationality—instead, rationality should be upgraded to the status of *phronēsis*. This process is assisted by the fact that, in the *Nicomachean Ethics*, the distinction has already become blurred. "The reasoned state of capacity to make" (*hexis meta logou poietike*)[24] when applied to the *technai* of navigation and medicine is not fully governed by general principle and requires knowledge of the particular.[25]

Does this understanding of rationality also require virtue? What seems clear is that, in the move from the general to the particular in at least many forms of *technê*, correctness or excellence involves more than mastery of general principles. But does this excellence require virtue as opposed to what Aristotle calls *mētis*, a kind of resourceful cunning intelligence? Note that this form of rationality is not to be confused with *deinotes*, translated as "cleverness," "a faculty . . . such as to be able to do the things that tend toward the mark we have set for ourselves, and to hit it. Now if the mark be noble the cleverness is laudable, but if the mark be bad, the cleverness is mere villainy."[26] Cleverness in medicine can be directed at producing ill health and death, as in Agatha Christie novels, but it seems that strategic, bureaucratic technicist rationality in business and education does not (intentionally) foster ends opposed to those of education or business (that is, learning outcomes or profit thinly described). After all, the *telos* of *technê* is production, not destruction or despoliation, and the *telos* of education is learning, not fostering ignorance. *Mētis*, not *phronēsis*, then may be the notion of rationality best suited to business. Resourceful but not necessarily virtuous managers may be all that is needed. That is what I believe to be the orthodox view in much professional ethics opposed to virtue ethical treatments: *deintotes* is insufficient for excellence in *technai*, but *mētis* is sufficient and *phronēsis* unnecessary.

I now wish to question this claim. Are learning outcomes, profit, and mere curing the correct full descriptions of the ends of education, business, and medicine? Although the ends of education or business should be seen as distinctive and not defined in terms of the expansionist strategy, their distinctive ends should as far as possible harmonize, and be integrated, with the good life. Learning outcomes must be seen as part of a richly described end of education where pedagogical virtue such as caring for, respect for, and sensitivity to children is paramount; communication with their parents occurs in the right way; children are inducted into a long-lasting curiosity and drive to learn what is significant; learning is not a superficial commitment to memory; and so forth. In medicine a doctor must be committed to health involving care and respect for patients and colleagues, and not mere efficiency: "the technical competence of such a doctor will be infused with a solicitude for his patients that will incline him to respond to late night calls" where his medical practice has not become "a vehicle for his acquisitiveness."[27] In the case of business, profit as an end is part of a richly described end of business which involves a wide variety of productive virtues—to which we now turn.

3. PRODUCTIVE VIRTUE

To understand productive virtue we need to explore three theses.

(1) The centrality of productiveness to human nature.

(2) The broadening of the field of the "moral" so that it is more friendly to the inclusion of productiveness and related virtues of creativity, as well as virtues (such as industriousness) on which those traits depend for their status as virtues.

(3) The nature of productive virtue, and the virtues on which productive virtue depends.

We begin with the first of these issues. Both the connection between production and *technê*, and the contrast between *technê* and *phronēsis*, have been a potent cause of the association of business with technicist rationality, for two related reasons. First, in a tradition inherited from Aristotle, human nature is intrinsically associated with the fineness and nobility of rationality understood in terms of *phronēsis* rather than *technê*. As a result, "morality" as the highest and most stringent form of normativity has not been associated with *poesis* but rather with *praxis*. Second, the separation of *technê* and *phronēsis* as distinct forms of rationality has had baneful effects on the conception of institutions and business in particular. Rather than embodying or potentially embodying virtue by being or sustaining practices, they are seen as, in their very nature, corrupting of virtue. Even if we can remove or enrich technicism—for example, with the "behavioral objectives model"—it may be thought that business is inherently a productive enterprise, and as such is designed for *production* and not action for the sake of virtue. As noted above, the problem is worsened with an Aristotelian conception of the essence of human beings as rational, where to be rational in its fullest sense is to act for the sake of the fine and the noble, in accord with virtue and for its sake, as *opposed* to action for the sake of production.

The relation between rationality understood in terms of rationality in *praxis* and rationality in *poesis* was turned on its head with the ethical writings of Ayn Rand. For her, the standard of evaluation for the assessment of a life of a human being is what is proper to the *survival* of man *qua* man, and on Rand's view the application of that species standard reveals that productive work is the central purpose of any human life. In "The Objectivist Ethics" (in *The Virtue of Selfishness*), Rand claims that "the two essentials of the method of survival proper to a rational being are thinking and productive work."[28] Furthermore, her view of the essence of man as productive is a virtue-centered conception, as her novels display vividly. For that purpose to be pursued in a way proper to human life, it must be pursued rationally, with integrity, from an orientation of self-love (what Rand calls self-esteem), with determination, honestly, and courageously. Once *poesis* is front and center of the conceptions of human essence, Aristotelianism can be applied to production, as indeed Rand's ethical writings exemplify.

We turn briefly now to the second thesis: the need to broaden the range of the "moral" so that it is friendlier to the inclusion within its purview of productiveness and related virtues of creativity, such as industriousness. The moral as a taxonomic notion has had baneful effects on substantive normative theorizing. The common view that the "moral" is overriding, when joined with the narrow taxonomic sense of "moral," has basically confined the properly "moral" to benevolence and justice, with attendant neglect of productivity and its normative importance. Not only that, but a range of virtues on which virtuous productivity depends, such as amiability, industriousness, and toughness (see below), has been basically confined to the non-moral or even the anti-moral, even within virtue ethics itself. For example, Julia Annas explicitly excludes tidiness, wittiness, affability, punctuality, and being hard-working as virtues.[29] They are seen merely as neutral "traits." But most of these are intimately connected with productive virtue, particularly industriousness, one of the most salient traits of Rand's industrial and professional heroes, and also highly salient in much of Hume's work. A disposition to be punctual—an aspect of reliability—is also obviously related to efficiency, which too is a productive virtue. Even a disposition to tidiness, such as office tidiness (as I discover all too often), promotes productivity as a result of not having to waste time finding important documents. All of this is surely obvious but rendered invisible as a result of tendentious conceptions of the moral. My solution, which I discuss elsewhere, is to follow Aristotle in not speaking of "moral" virtue at all, but simply of virtue as an excellence of character individuated by fields or spheres of concern that are all, in their different ways, part of a good life.[30] And if Rand is right, a centrally important field of virtue is production.

We finally turn to a discussion of productive virtue itself. In what Martha Nussbaum describes as its "thin" description, productive virtue is not behavior directed at a mere output or result, nor is it even a mere efficient generation of outputs, but a disposition to be well disposed in production.[31] That in turn requires *phronēsis*, which not only concerns deliberation about means but also involves a correct conception of productive ends relative to the kind of institution involved in production, whether art, business, or hobbyist enterprise. What Nussbaum describes as the thick account of a virtue is an account that provides a substantive understanding of what it is to be well disposed in relation to production.

An interesting feature of productive virtue is that it is dependent on many other virtues. Some forms of dependency are virtues that are needed as means to achieve productive ends, virtues such as, dare I say, industriousness, tidiness, and punctuality. Central to such dependency is creativity. Another form of dependence (call it the second sense) is defined by Michael Slote in terms of "dependent virtue," a virtue that attains "its full status as a virtue . . . only when accompanied by other desirable traits."[32] This feature of productive virtue is necessary to distinguish it from non-virtuous or vicious productivity such as exploitative productivity.

Productive virtue can now be understood as a broad-based virtue whose field relates to production or being productive. It is a virtue that is particularly dependent for its status as a virtue on a variety of other virtues such as justice, particularly in the form of not being exploitative. The nature of the virtues on which virtuous productivity depends is itself dependent on the nature of the practice, of which a form of production is an end. In the case of art, for example, production is not merely a virtue dependent on creativity in the first sense of "dependent," it is also dependent on creativity in the second sense. To exhibit the goods of excellence internal to art, art has to exhibit one's own creativity: it cannot be copied or merely be an imitation of someone else's work.

When productiveness is seen as a virtue and not simply as an activity or result, such as obtaining money or profit, a complex understanding of the end of business as *profit-exemplifying productive virtue* becomes possible. The fundamental distinction between virtues and vices of productivity in relation to the business purpose is one drawn by Rand between getting and making money. Getting money, in contrast to making money, does not display productive virtue but merely greed and parasitism. Making money for Rand is a legitimate result of being productive in a way exemplifying virtue. Not all ways of being productive are connected with making money, however; in Rand's *The Fountainhead*, Howard Roark is a character whose creative virtue, including integrity, moral courage, and independence of mind, does not for a long time bring him money.[33] He remains in poverty rather than sell out on the internal goods of excellence of the practice of architecture.

In the common view, greed as a vice is understood simply as a powerful *desire* for, or excessive love of, money. Here again we must distinguish between a desire to make money and a desire to get or acquire money. For Rand, the desire to make money, even when strong, is not a manifestation of a vice such as greed, self-indulgence or intemperance, for it is connected with the essence of humans as beings engaged in productive work. Indeed, in *Atlas Shrugged*, powerful love of money is described as a virtue on the assumption that money has value through its connection with (virtuous) production.[34] By contrast, desires to simply *get* money, by parasitical or unjust means, manifest greed as a vice, even when the desire for money is moderate.

Once profit is not confused with money as an external good, making money in the form of making profits can receive a rich understanding as an internal good of business practice. We have already noted one of the virtues on which virtuous productivity depends, independence. Certainly, Rand's valorizing of independence, understood as "one's acceptance of the responsibility of forming one's own judgments and of living by the work of one's own mind,"[35] a definition which is expanded upon in John Galt's speech in *Atlas Shrugged*, has caused her to be viewed by some as a "rugged individualist." But independence as a virtue must be integrated with other desiderata of a productive individual, one of which, of course, is the ability to deal with people, especially those on whom one's productive goals depend. Although seriously neglected in the analytic tradition because they are not thought of as "moral" virtues, conversational and dialogic virtue are central to a business life of productivity.

Amiability, regarded as a virtue by Aristotle—and also by Jane Austen—is a central background virtue on which productivity as a virtue depends (in both senses), provided the former is properly understood as an excellence. As such it is not a mere social agreeableness of manners but, as Austen recognizes, has at its heart a genuine love and concern for one's fellow human beings.[36] It should not be confused with a bland niceness, a feeble compliance, or failure to confront problems—indeed, it must be compatible with one of Solomon's business virtues, toughness. In particular, amiability must be joined with a no-nonsense toughness when dealing with non-performing suppliers, excuse making contractors, shirking employees, and dishonest professionals, a toughness that is displayed in *Atlas Shrugged* both by Reardon and Taggart.[37] At the same time, toughness integrated with amiability is not to be confused with (literally) vicious toughness (such as that allegedly displayed by certain executives of a certain Australian-based supermarket chain operating in New Zealand and under investigation there for employing stand-over coercive tactics towards its suppliers).

In *After Virtue*, MacIntyre claims that in practices, "human powers to achieve excellence, and human conceptions of the ends and goods involved, are systematically extended."[38] Practices, he notes, have a history, and the standards defining excellence are not "immune from criticism."[39] This is true in business practice where productive virtue is dependent not only on the non-exploitation of people but also on the non-exploitation of the environment. In the age of global warming and increasing sensitivity to the wonders of nature for its own sake, debate on green issues is particularly vibrant (and many would say not vibrant enough). The illumination of productive virtue in that case is an ongoing process.

To avoid confusion we must finally say something about the relation between exhibiting virtues on which the virtue of productivity are dependent, and right action. The details of my virtue-ethical account of right action and its application to role ethics are beyond the scope of this chapter, but the following points should be noted.[40] First, I have claimed, for instance, that amiability (properly understood as a virtue) is a background virtue on which productivity as a virtue depends; without that, for example, the virtue of toughness will descend into a vice of ruthlessness. But that is not to say that all actions in a business practice have to exhibit or express amiability to be right. Tough actions of sacking or tough talking, for example, may be called for, but it would be a stretch to say that these actions exhibit amiability or could be described as "amiable." To conform to productive virtue, however, those actions cannot be describable as unjust.

Second, the virtues inherent in and exercised within practices complicate the traditional distinction between categorical and hypothetical oughts. Crisp gives the following example: "If my art teacher tells me I ought to hold my brush differently, she is saying this on the assumption that I want to improve my technique. If I'm in the class just to get out of the house, however, her ought-judgment no longer applies to me."[41] The art teacher is making no such assumption, though. The "ought" in question is neither categorical nor hypothetical: rather it relates to the internal excellences of a practice of drawing and painting. Holding one's brush in a certain way is assumed by the teacher to be part of that excellence; it matters not what are the motives of the student.

4. CONCLUSION

I have argued that a virtue-centered conception of business can re-establish it as a practice, the internal good of which is the making of profits exhibiting productive virtue. MacIntyre is correct to claim that the undermining of standards of virtue in general, and role virtues in particular, occurs where institutions that should sustain practices, instead, pursue external goods. But this feature is not inevitable, not even for productive enterprises like business.

Corruption also occurs through incorrect conceptions of the internal goods of practices, conceptions often driven by global totalizing ideologies imposing external standards on particular institutions. Ironically, MacIntyre and Rand are on the same page here. The ideology attacked by Rand is, of course, socialism, and that attacked by MacIntyre is liberalism (or a certain conception of it). In the wake of these ideologies, the disappearance of *phronēsis* in favor of *technê* becomes likely, if not inevitable. Rand's political philosophy (as opposed to her virtue-centered ethics) also exhibits, in my view, the limiting perspective of ideology.

Where there is ideology or a domination of overly abstract moral ideas, virtues internal to practices vanish under the looming presence and pressure of a limited and powerful range of moral concepts, such as rights or equality, that are insufficiently nuanced by sophisticated conceptions of virtue. For example, MacIntyre argues that neither John Rawls' nor Robert Nozick's conceptions of justice make room for dessert.[42] But dessert too is a relatively thin concept unless it is embedded in a variety of virtue (and vice) concepts where distinctions can be drawn between, for example, overblown and legitimate senses of dessert-entitlement; resentment based on invidious self-referential comparisons and legitimate resentment based on culpable ignoring of dessert; respect for and overly rigid application of rules creating dessert claims; and so forth.

However, Rand and MacIntyre seem to be poles apart in their optimism regarding the capacities of individuals to rise above the insidious effects of technicist rationality with its attendant vices of greed, lack of integrity, dishonest manipulativeness, and pleasure-seeking. Rand's heroes are heroes of productive virtue, breaking away from or relatively immune to corrupting influences and therefore representing exemplars of virtue internal to practices, whether business or architecture. MacIntyre, by contrast, with his notion of character-role, often seems to believe that individuals inhabiting those roles are morally trapped by the weight of the cultural determinants of their normative conceptions of themselves.

In opposition to MacIntyre I hope to have shown in this chapter that his skepticism about business ethics can be rebutted. Business can be a practice-sustaining virtue that facilitates the achievement of goods internal to the distinctive practice of business. Profit must be seen not merely as an external good but a good internal to the practice of business. For this to be the case, productive virtue is necessary.

NOTES

1. Alasdair MacIntyre, *After Virtue: A Study in Moral Theory*, 3rd ed. (Notre Dame: University of Notre Dame Press, 2007).
2. Daniel H. Freedman, "A Formula for Economic Calamity," *Scientific American* 305(5) (2011): 76–9, at 78.
3. Ibid., 79.
4. MacIntyre, *After Virtue*, 187.
5. Ibid., 191.
6. Wim Vandekerckhove, "Virtue Ethics and Management," in Stan van Hooft (ed.), *The Handbook of Virtue Ethics* (Durham, NC: Acumen, 2013), 341–51, at 347.
7. Richard T. DeGeorge, *Competing with Integrity in International Business* (Oxford: Oxford University Press, 1993), 7, as quoted in John Dobson, "Virtue Ethics as a Foundation for Business Ethics: A 'MacIntyre-Based' Critique," 2nd International Symposium on Catholic Social Thought and Management Education, presented at the Catholic Social Thought and Management Conference, University of Antwerp (1997), retrieved from <http://stthomas.edu/media/catholicstudies/center/johnaryaninstitute/conferences/1997-antwerp/JohnDobson.pdf>.
8. Thomas Hurka, *Virtue, Vice, and Value* (Oxford: Oxford University Press, 2001).
9. Robert Solomon, too, argues that business is a practice in his *Ethics and Excellence: Cooperation and Integrity in Business* (New York: Oxford University Press, 1993), chapter 13, though I later question his distinction between goal and purpose, and he does not refer MacIntyre in his discussion of a practice.
10. MacIntyre, *After Virtue*, 30.
11. Ibid., 29.
12. Solomon, *Ethics and Excellence*.
13. See my "A Virtue Ethical Theory of Role Ethics," forthcoming in *Journal of Value Inquiry*.
14. Robert C. Solomon, *It's Good Business: Ethics and Free Enterprise for the New Millennium* (Lanham, MD: Rowman and Littlefield, 1997), 87.
15. Solomon, *Ethics and Excellence*, 118.
16. Ibid., 120–1.
17. Vandekerckhove, "Virtue Ethics and Management," 347.
18. MacIntyre, *After Virtue*, 194.

19. But even here there are difficulties since *technê*, as such mastery does not capture the nature of creativity. The relation between creativity and virtue or *phronēsis* is not my primary concern here.
20. Joseph Dunne, *Back to the Rough Ground: Practical Judgment and the Lure of Technique* (Notre Dame: University of Notre Dame Press, 1993), 1.
21. See in particular Heidegger, "The Question Concerning Technology," in *The Question Concerning Technology and Other Essays*, trans. W. Lowitt (New York: Harper & Row, 1997).
22. In Heidegger, *Poetry, Language, Thought*, trans. Albert Hofstadter (New York: Harper Collins, 1971), 17–76.
23. In recent times much academic work is encouraging a more sophisticated treatment of Rand's ethics as has already occurred with Nietzsche. See, for example, Alan Gotthelf (ed.), *Metaethics, Egoism, and Virtue: Studies in Ayn Rand's Normative Theory* (Pittsburgh: University of Pittsburgh Press, 2011).
24. Dunne, *Back to the Rough Ground*, 249.
25. Aristotle, *Nicomachean Ethics*, 2.2.
26. Ibid., 1144a24–27, cited in Dunne, *Back to the Rough Ground*, 271.
27. Dunne, *Back to the Rough Ground*, 265.
28. Ayn Rand, "The Objectivist Ethics," in *The Virtue of Selfishness: A New Concept of Egoism* (New York: Signet/Penguin, 1964), 13–39, at 25. She describes the distinction between the good life or "purpose" for each individual man and the "standard of evaluation" for the way that purpose is prosecuted thus: "that which is required for the survival of man *qua* man is an abstract principle that applies to every individual man." (Survival *qua* man means survival that is *proper* to man, in an Aristotelian sense that involves virtue.) "The task of applying this principle to a concrete, specific purpose—the purpose of living a life proper to a rational being—belongs to every individual man, and the life he has to live is his own," and "*his own life* is the ethical *purpose* of every individual man" (ibid., 27, my emphasis).
29. In Julia Annas, *Intelligent Virtue* (Oxford: Oxford University Press, 2011), 9n1, 105.
30. In Christine Swanton, "The Notion of the Moral: The Relation between Virtue Ethics and Virtue Epistemology," *Philosophical Studies* 171(2014): 121–34.
31. Martha Nussbaum, "Non-Relative Virtues: An Aristotelian Approach," *Midwest Studies in Philosophy* 13(1988): 32–53.
32. Michael Slote, *Goods and Virtues* (Oxford: Clarendon Press, 1983), 62.
33. Ayn Rand, *The Fountainhead* (Indianapolis: Bobbs-Merrill, 1943).
34. Ayn Rand, *Atlas Shrugged* (New York: Random House, 1957).
35. Rand, "The Objectivist Ethics," 28.
36. MacIntyre, *After Virtue*, 241, and more generally 239–43.
37. I am not saying here that these characters are fully virtuous *tout court*, including in their personal lives. Although my position suggests that there is integration between role virtue and virtue in other spheres, I am skeptical that there is full unity. See my "Pluralistic Virtue Ethics," in Lorraine Besser-Jones and Michael Slote (eds.), *The Routledge Companion to Virtue Ethics* (New York: Routledge, 2015), 209–21.
38. MacIntyre, *After Virtue*, 187.

39. Ibid., 190.
40. See in particular my "A Particularist but Codifiable Virtue Ethics," in Mark Timmons (ed.), *Oxford Studies in Normative Ethics*, Vol. 5 (Oxford: Oxford University Press, 2015) 38–63.
41. Roger Crisp, "Methods, Methodology, and Moral Judgement: Sidgwick on the Nature of Ethics," *Revue International de Philosophie* 4(2013): 397–419, at 411.
42. MacIntyre, *After Virtue*, chapter 17.

10

Virtues as Social Capital

David C. Rose

What is the nature of the connection between economics and the virtues? Although there are signs that change is in the air, most mainstream economists continue to think of economic behavior as being largely driven by enlightened self-interest and regulated by incentive compatibility. Yet most of the classical economists, as well as most of the American founding fathers, could not imagine a well functioning free market economy in the absence of a strong moral foundation, which would include the widespread inculcation of many of the virtues.[1]

The reason for such incredulity was rooted in the nature of the most fundamental unit of analysis of the free market economy: the voluntary transaction. When transactions are voluntary we do not have to transact if we do not want to, which allows us to expect that transactions are mutually beneficial. That, in turn, is the key to having more output per person, because to be mutually beneficial transactions must be positive sum in nature. If we cannot trust each other to transact in good faith, or we cannot sustain trust dependent institutions that reduce transaction costs in other ways, there will be fewer mutually beneficial transactions through which we can derive the gains from positive sum activity, and therefore fewer goods and services per person.

So it all comes down to trust, but trust has to come from somewhere. Classical economists and the founding fathers believed that such trust came from a society possessing a sufficiently strong moral foundation, although there was no unified position on precisely what such a moral foundation would look like. For them it was nevertheless obvious that virtues like honesty, integrity, and respect for others' property are required for a thriving market economy.

A natural way to explore the nature of the connection between economics and the virtues is to examine the historical record. If the virtues matter, then there should be economic phenomena that change in response to changes in widely abided virtues. The more important are the phenomena so affected, the more important are the virtues involved. Max Weber's famous argument that Protestant emphasis on industriousness helped launched the rise of capitalism is, of course, the most well known example of such efforts.[2]

Deirdre McCloskey has examined the relationship between the development of free market societies and the virtues.[3] McCloskey provides a compelling account for how the development of free market societies in the West was catalyzed by the spread of *The Bourgeois Virtues*. These virtues, she argued, did not merely keep a lid on the negative aspects of capitalism. Instead, "capitalism and the bourgeois life can be, and to some extent already are, virtuous. That is, bourgeois life improves us ethically, and would have even if it had not also made us rich."[4]

McCloskey's point was not that capitalism emerged because societies suddenly became moral, righteous, or virtuous. Instead, some virtues matter more than others, and economic development took off when those that mattered most appeared in sufficient measure. Moreover, these virtues were sustainable because they were not in conflict with free market economic activity and were, in fact, reinforced by it. McCloskey carefully considers the enormous literature on the virtues and boils them down to what she calls the "Western Seven": faith, hope, love, justice, courage, temperance, and prudence.

Most prior approaches to the analysis of the virtues culminate with the enumeration of a relatively short and comprehensive list of virtues. But to be exhaustive, each virtue must include a number of different attributes. The shorter the list, the truer this is. Short lists are certainly easier to remember than long ones, but I submit that the conflation of attributes has had the effect of obfuscating some important issues.

In what follows I consider virtues, more broadly and finely, as any quality or trait that is good for one to have, because it is good either for the individual who possesses it or for others in society (insofar as it encourages positive moral action or discourages negative moral action). Without getting into details about any specific virtue, in what follows I employ the following threefold categorization scheme for my discussion of virtues:

1. Those that increase the welfare of the individual in whose mind such virtues reside, I call the *prudential virtues*.
2. Those that increase the welfare of others by encouraging positive moral action, I call the *positive virtues*.
3. Those that increase the welfare of others by discouraging negative moral action, I call the *negative virtues*.

I will argue that all virtues function like capital as defined in standard economic theory. I will argue further that some virtues, principally the positive and the negative ones, also produce large *social* payoffs and are therefore also properly thought of as forms of *social* capital. Finally, I will argue that virtues that function as social capital require more investment than will be forthcoming from merely prudential incentives, and this is truest for the negative virtues. When we think of the virtues in terms of social capital, the question of achieving a *socially optimal* level of investment naturally presents itself. The idea of investment comports with standard economic theory about capital in general, which is a product of prior investment, and with virtue ethics, which focuses on the cultivation of character.

This presents us with an uncomfortable question. Few would argue that any of the best-known virtues should not be endorsed—but then what? Because inculcating virtues amounts to costly investment, and resources are finite, simply endorsing all of them is not likely to produce the best possible result regardless of how one defines the best possible result. When we think of virtues as capital that is a product of costly investment, we become keenly aware of the fact that, for any society that is serious about having a strong moral foundation for social behavior, choices have to be made about the relative importance of virtues.

To address the question of socially optimal investment, economists step back from the question of what constitutes the best possible result by focusing on factors that impede a society from automatically achieving such a result regardless of what that result might be. For example, economists know that a tax on a polluted effluent may improve social welfare without knowing what the socially optimal level of pollution is for a particular river. Here I apply standard welfare theory to explain why the virtues that are most accurately viewed as social capital—the positive and negative virtues—are also the most likely to receive inadequate attention if a society hopes to flourish by most fully supporting the development and operation of a free market economy. I then explain why the negative virtues satisfy the definition of a public good and are therefore the most likely to be subject to sub-optimal investment.

1. THE NATURE OF VIRTUES

Although I shall consider virtues in a less bundled fashion than is customary, I nevertheless define them rather conventionally, as qualities or traits that are good for one to have. The word *good* is meant to include the common good as well as that which is good for the individual alone. Virtues thereby produce the kind of person who is predisposed to take actions that are considered good and to refrain from taking actions that are considered bad. Often context and circumstance determines whether a given action or inaction is good or bad, which is why the word "predisposition" is more appropriate than "pre-programmed."

The more we think of virtues associated with an individual putting himself in a position to live a good life, the more such virtues are a matter of prudence. Prudence is a frequently enumerated virtue but it overlaps with a number of other enumerated virtues, all of which are beneficial. Everyone wants to have a good life and wants those they care for to have good lives, too. Few things are as miserable as a parent forced to watch an adult child live a life in misery resulting from an endless parade of imprudent decisions.

Ancient and traditional accounts of virtue stressed prudential aspects of virtue more than later accounts. Ancient and traditional accounts clearly comport with Plato's lesson that "our good" transforms when we become virtuous. This is a powerful and important point about what I call the prudential virtues. But we shall set this issue aside in what follows because it is not relevant to the arguments I shall be making.

The cultivation of the prudential virtues is in any child's long-term best interest, but the costs involved come early and are certain, while the benefits come later and are uncertain. So even the cultivation of what are ultimately self-serving virtues is an uphill battle against nature. It is likely that, as prudence became a more important margin for survival among humans, evolution drove up kindred affection to ease this uphill battle. But as bad as this is, the expected private return to the individual from investments in the positive and negative virtues that promote the common good is often very close to zero or even negative *at the margin*.

A large society with an additional person who puts the common good ahead of himself is not changed noticeably, but that individual's personal net payoff is likely reduced as he spends more on positive moral action, as he foregoes negative moral actions that would enrich him, and as he receives a smaller bequest from parents who invested more of their resources into his proper upbringing. A society filled with people who put the common good ahead of themselves, however, is a qualitatively different society altogether, and each individual's share in the bounty of such a society can be markedly higher than would prevail in a society where everyone puts self first. At some level we all know this, which is why for a very long time one of the greatest challenges to human flourishing has been solving this problem by effectuating the socially optimal level of investment in the kinds of virtues that qualitatively change society for the better. Indeed, the more we think of the virtues that predispose the individual to promote the common good, the more such virtues move from the practical to the moral, and the more they are of genuine public concern.

The obvious questions are: in attempting to build our children's moral character, what should we teach them, and how should we teach them? Even if there is no debate over the list of things that should be taught, in the real world there is no avoiding the iron law of economics, which is that teaching is costly and resources are finite, which forces us to choose among competing ends. So do some virtues matter more for a given set of ends and, if so, should more resources be directed to teaching them relative to other virtues? Similarly, do some virtues come very naturally to us so, even if they are very important, it is foolish to spend much time on them?

2. WHY SOME VIRTUES FUNCTION AS SOCIAL CAPITAL

Virtues are like a hammer. A hammer is still there at the end of the day: it is used but not used up and, as such, is a form of capital in the deepest sense of the word. In contrast, a carpenter's time (labor) and his bag of nails (inputs) are used up. As with a hammer being used to pound in nails, one's virtues are not used up when one engages in virtuous behavior. Because capital is that which is used but not used up in production, the virtues function like capital in the most fundamental sense of the word.

A well-known attribute of virtue is the concept of *arête*, which essentially means moral excellence. Moral excellence is a matter of degree, which suggests that greater efforts to invest in the inculcation of virtues will result in more virtuous behavior. This is also much like capital in general in that capital appears in greater measure or quality in response to greater prior investment. Having more or better capital obviously affects labor's ability to convert inputs into output. Similarly, virtues are built up over time by instruction and conditioning.

This is hardly an original way of thinking of virtues. Virtue ethics stresses virtue character and the need for effort to be put forth to inculcate virtues and, once instantiated, the need to reinforce them. The only difference is that here I have told the story more in terms of the economic concept of capital to facilitate what follows.

As a practical matter, for virtues to do their job one must invest resources to build up, refine, and reinforce neural pathways associated with having a virtuous predisposition. These pathways are physical realities. They remain after an instance of virtuous behavior is undertaken and might even be strengthened by that behavior. Since these neural pathways exist in the brains of individual humans, one can therefore properly think of virtues as *human* capital. Efforts to inculcate specific moral beliefs and to then drive up resolve to abide by them therefore amount to investment into an individual's human capital. Human capital is arguably the purest form of capital. Again, capital is that which is used but not used up in production. But while capital is not used up, physical capital still normally wears out with use. Even a hammer must be replaced eventually. But in most cases human capital does not wear out but, rather, improves with use. This is an oft cited attribute of virtues as well; for instance, Robert Frank has argued that people actually work on their virtuousness by practicing it, which is consistent with the idea that moral values or tastes function as a rather strong form of capital.[5]

Few ideas have had as widespread an impact on the social sciences as the idea of social capital. The literature on social capital is immense and continues to grow.[6] The concept of social capital is most closely identified with the work of James Coleman and Robert Putnam.[7] In particular, Coleman laid out the basic theoretical framework in an effort to close the gap between sociological approaches, which lack an "engine of action" such as rational choice provides for economics, and economic approaches, which ignore social context.[8] Robert Putnam, Robert Leonardi, and Raffaella Nanetti demonstrated the power of the concept of social capital in the book, *Making Democracy Work*, finding that measures of civic engagement were strongly related to the quality of local governments in Italy.[9] Then, first as an article titled "Bowling Alone" and then later in the form of an even more influential book of the same title, Putnam made a sweeping case for the existence of a disturbing downward trend in social capital in America since the 1950s.[10] Following the publication of *Bowling Alone* the literature on social capital mushroomed.

There is no shortage of definitions of social capital.[11] The work of Pierre Bourdieu is not as well known as that of James Coleman or Robert Putnam, but Bourdieu's definition of social capital explicitly accounts for one of the most important distinctions in social capital theory:

> Social capital is an attribute of an individual in a social context. One can acquire social capital through purposeful actions and can transform social capital into conventional economic gains. The ability to do so, however, depends on the nature of the social obligations, connections, and networks available to you.[12]

This early definition is surprisingly perceptive, rich, and durable. In a detailed review of social capital literature, Sobel employed a definition that closely followed Bourdieu's and argued that his "definition of social capital fits easily into strategic models of economic behavior."[13]

2.1 Individual social capital

Bourdieu's definition contains two distinct senses of social capital. The first sense is consistent with the work of Loury, and of Glaeser, Laibson and Sacerdote, which is to think of social capital as a characteristic of the individual.[14] In other words, *individual social capital* is the set of characteristics that enable an individual to be more effective in social settings, including but not limited to what is normally referred to as "social skills." The better are one's social skills, specifically in forming and maintaining social ties within and across social networks, the more social capital one has and therefore the more productive one will be. Individual social capital also refers to predispositions for a variety of pro-social behaviors. Among other things this includes moral dispositions to be trustworthy, to be public spirited, to be socially connected to other individuals and organizations, and to form, perform well in, and help sustain social networks.

These attributes can improve the quality of life for those who possess them, but the social benefits of these assets are often significantly greater than the private benefits. For example, an individual who is regarded as being trustworthy certainly benefits from having such a reputation, so parents have a strong incentive to inculcate virtues that support trustworthiness in their children. But that individual's transaction partners also benefit from having a trustworthy transaction partner. This means the social returns to inculcating virtues that produce a trustworthy individual are far greater than the private returns, an issue I will return to later.

2.2 Network social capital

Network social capital refers to external structures, usually in the form of networks that make social behavior more effective. These networks are sometimes formal, but many are informal and some spontaneously arise. The concept of network social capital emphasizes the study of community-level attributes and large-scale social structures.

The idea of network social capital is alluded to in the second part of Bourdieu's definition, "the nature of social obligations, connections, and networks available to you." This aspect of social capital does not pertain to the social skills possessed by individuals but, rather, to the nature of the social structures within which an individual lives and works. This sense of social capital is more consistent with the work of Mark Granovetter and Robert Putnam, whose approach to social capital emphasizes social connectedness, social ties, and "embeddedness" as the substrate of social networks.[15]

Trust can be both an input and an output of social networks. If everyone in a given social network is completely trustworthy, then the social network will function more effectively. But social capital theorists normally emphasize trust as an output of social networks. In others words, *A* and *B*'s common membership in a given social network makes it far easier for *A* to trust *B* and vice versa, because routine association casts a kind of "shadow of the neighborhood" in that being in the same social network socially connects *A* to *B*. At the same time, common membership also casts a kind of "shadow of the future" in that expulsion from a social network is very costly so members are careful not even to be suspected of cheating other members so as to protect expected future gains arising from continued membership. Members know this about each other so this allows them to transact with each other with greater confidence.

2.3 Virtues as social capital

Some virtues—the prudential virtues emphasized by the ancients—primarily benefit the individual within whose mind they reside, but by definition both the positive and the negative virtues go beyond this. Some of the spillovers involved are direct, such as the benefits enjoyed by others of transacting with a trustworthy and reliable person, while other spillovers are indirect, such as the benefit of living in a society with clear and robust standards for behavior that lead to lower transaction costs and thereby substantially increase general prosperity.

Positive virtues predispose individuals to undertake acts that improve the welfare of others. Positive virtues may also benefit the individual, but because the welfare of others is also improved by the actions engendered by positive virtues, the social benefits arising from having them clearly exceed the private benefits. Negative virtues predispose individuals to refrain from taking acts that reduce the welfare of others, and in the same way as positive virtues, the social benefits arising from having them clearly exceed the private benefits. So both the positive and the negative virtues are forms of human capital, but because they also produce social benefits beyond private benefits, they are also properly thought of as social capital.

Note that the evolution of virtues through human history has reflected an increasing emphasis on the positive and the negative virtues relative to the prudential virtues. This corresponds with the rise of large, complex, and prosperous market economies, and also that what the ancients taught us about virtue was necessary but not sufficient for building flourishing societies. Better human capital makes for a better life, but better social capital makes for a better society as well. I submit that the first step to helping people have good lives is having flourishing societies for them to live in, and flourishing societies ultimately require a great deal of social capital.

3. WHY *NEGATIVE VIRTUES* REQUIRE THE MOST ATTENTION

Public goods are goods whose consumption is both non-rival and non-excludable in nature. This presents two additional problems for the negative virtues. First, the non-rival nature of the social benefits arising from the negative virtues produces a stronger positive spillover problem than for the positive virtues. Second, when grounded in the internalization of the negative virtues, the ability to benefit from the moral restraint of others is inherently non-excludable.

3.1 The public good problem: Non-rival and non-excludable consumption

The positive virtues predispose one to take positive moral actions. Taking actions normally requires resources that could be used for other things, including taking other positive moral actions. The positive virtues therefore give rise to benefits that are inherently *rival* in nature. For instance, giving a dollar to one needy person precludes giving that dollar to another.

The negative virtues predispose one to refrain from taking negative moral actions. Unlike the positive action associated with positive virtues, refraining from acting normally does not require additional resources that might be used for other things. The negative virtues therefore give rise to restraint which is inherently *non-rival* in nature. Not lying to Bob does not preclude not lying to Joe or even to an entire society.

With the negative virtues, then, the non-rival consumption of the benefits accruing to others produces a positive spillover effect that is proportional to the number of people in the group. This is because the spillover is not from rival benefits that spill over to *some* others, but from consumption that is inherently non-rival in nature and therefore can benefit *all* others, no matter how large is the number of other people in the group, because restraint does not require additional resources at the margin.

So the larger is a given society, the larger the positive externality arising from non-rival consumption compared to that arising from positive spillovers whose consumption is rival in nature. This is a serious problem because the key to achieving general prosperity—what most would consider a necessary condition for human flourishing—is the ability to support trust and, therefore, low transaction costs in large group contexts in order to support the greatest scale and scope of economic activity.

The positive virtues predispose one to take positive moral actions. One can choose not to act, so positive moral action is inherently excludable, but things are very different for the negative virtues. People who refrain from lying as a manifestation of acting on an internalized negative virtue will not lie to others because of what it says about their character, so they will not lie even to those who lie themselves or refuse to invest the socially optimal level of resources into the moral training of children. Therefore, the benefit accruing to others from an individual abiding by any negative virtue is inherently non-excludable.

This non-excludability of moral restraint creates a free rider problem with respect to inculcating the negative virtues that give rise to that restraint. It is costly to inculcate the required negative virtues and children will not be able to demand payment for their moral restraint because it is non-excludable. The resulting spillover benefits therefore go unrewarded, so it makes more sense to leave the creation of a high-trust society up to others. Because this is true for all others, too, the result will be a socially insufficient amount of inculcation of the required negative virtues. Obviously the larger is the society, the less effect any individual's virtue will have on the society as a whole, and therefore the stronger will be the incentive to free ride.

This problem is largely unrecognized because the free-riding effect is rather obvious in small group settings and is therefore well managed in such settings.[16] But the larger the group involved, the stronger free-riding incentives will be, the less likely mutual monitoring will solve the problem directly or that free-riding will produce a self-enforcing effect on its own, because one's free-riding reduces total output but one's share of the reduction becomes so small that no one could possibly notice.

In general, the properties that make the negative virtues social capital, as well as the behavior supported by the negative virtues, produce benefits that are normally both non-rival and non-excludable, representing both halves of the public good problem. As such, there will likely be a substantial difference between the privately and socially optimal levels of investment in the negative virtues. Moreover, because the social benefit of positive spillovers arising from non-rival consumption and the social benefit of moral restraint both rise with group size, this difference rises with group size. This has important implications not only for understanding why some virtues matter more than others, but for understanding why some societies enjoy markedly higher levels of economic development than others. As we know from Adam Smith, general prosperity rises directly with a society's ability to sustain cooperation in large groups. But larger group size makes the public good problem associated with the negative virtues more difficult to solve, and therefore this public good problem acts as a brake on economic development and therefore human flourishing.

3.2 Two specific examples of the public good problem

To illustrate the connection between the negative virtues and social capital theory, I will now focus on two specific examples, involving individual social capital and involving network social capital, respectively.

The negative virtues that discourage opportunistic behavior simultaneously drive up trustworthiness. One who is trustworthy benefits from such a predisposition because a reputation for trustworthiness expands the range of transactions. But one who is trustworthy also produces direct spillover benefits to every transaction partner. These direct spillover benefits drive a wedge between the social and private returns to investment in the negative virtues involved.

The negative virtues that predispose one to be trustworthy comport well with the concept of *individual* social capital. Such negative virtues are obviously part of the individual's human capital, but because others benefit also, social benefits exceed private benefits, so this human capital is properly regarded as *individual* social capital.

Social networks create value through engendering trust by instantiating consistent behavioral expectations; a common set of standards for behavior therefore reduces transaction costs and thereby benefits those in the network. The positive virtues drive up moral resolve to take positive moral action, so their obedience is by nature a matter of degree. This makes them subjective and therefore unable to provide a clear standard for conduct. Two highly moral people can differ greatly on how much one should give to a needy person; there is simply no objective basis for determining moral adequacy.

In contrast, the negative virtues engender inaction, so obeying them is qualitative in nature. One either lies or does not. So unlike the positive virtues, the negative virtues produce clear lines of demarcation. Any negative moral action, such as lying, clearly crosses the line and is therefore qualitatively wrong. Moral adequacy is therefore well defined, producing crisp and universal triggers for disapproval. Similarly, if *A* discovers *B* to have lied, *A* can convey that information to others, who will understand what it means. Because one's social distance to either *A* or *B* does not affect the relevant objective information involved, these standards can work even in large groups within which transactions frequently occur between strangers.

This fits well with Adam Smith's account of how different moral standards emerge in different communities through approbation and disapprobation in *The Theory of Moral Sentiments*. Smith assumed that concern for what others think of us is part of our human nature. This facilitates the emergence of unique standards for behavior across groups that, in turn, produce harmony tailored to any given environment. This process works best when everyone in a community can conclude, at the same time, that something is to be approved or disapproved. Since positive moral actions are a matter of degree, they are less likely to produce universal expressions of approval or disapproval than negative moral actions, which are qualitative in nature.

The negative virtues are therefore more likely than the positive virtues to produce beneficial network effects that emerge at higher levels of social organization than bilateral interaction. If the negative virtues involved are instantiated with sufficient consistency and in sufficient measure across the whole of society, then the relevant network would be the entire society, which would benefit from lower transaction costs arising from more consistent standards for behavior, resulting in more real output per capita. However, because no individual's moral restraint can bring about this outcome (as it emerges only at the network level), it will not be accounted for in anyone's decision to invest in any other individual's moral character. This further widens the wedge between the privately optimal and socially optimal levels of investment in the negative virtues for any individual.

4. SUMMARY AND FINAL THOUGHTS

The very qualities that make any given virtue a form of social capital also inevitably lead to *socially* sub-optimal investment, which makes it a matter of public concern. Moreover, when we think of the virtues as products of prior investments in human capital, it becomes clear that the problem of socially sub-optimal investment in the virtues increases in severity as we move from the prudential to the positive and, finally, to the negative virtues. The problem of socially sub-optimal investment is the most extreme with the negative virtues because the benefits they produce for others amounts to consumption that is both non-rival and non-excludable in nature. Non-rival consumption produces an even stronger positive externality problem than is normally associated with the positive virtues, and non-excludable consumption adds the problem of free-riding with respect to adequately investing in virtue character. The public good nature of the negative virtues therefore drives the largest possible wedge between privately optimal and socially optimal levels of investment in virtue character. It follows that when considering the adequate provision of a cultural foundation for a free market society, the negative virtues warrant our greatest attention.

The prudential virtues are clearly more prominent than either the positive or the negative virtues in the earliest writings pertaining to the virtues. The historical record suggests that with the rise of the Roman Empire there was an increasing emphasis on the negative virtues (consider, for instance, the increasing formalization of the rule of law). With many setbacks along the way, this built up slowly over the next millennium, especially in Northern Europe.

Among many others, this was reflected in the writings of John Locke and the Scottish Enlightenment, particularly those of Adam Smith. Smith's conception of justice comports well with the negative virtues and he stressed the importance of justice over beneficence in *The Theory of Moral Sentiments*. The writings of the founding fathers echoed these views by emphasizing that the common good is best promoted indirectly through institutions that clarified the boundaries of civilized behavior rather than directing pro-social behavior, which is more about moral restraint than moral advocacy and therefore more dependent on having sufficiently strong negative virtues than sufficiently strong positive virtues.

With the rise of the industrial revolution and soaring real incomes per capita alongside growing income inequality, it was inevitable that there would be calls for an increasing emphasis on the positive virtues over the course of the nineteenth century, culminating with an effort to transform formal institutions with the rise of the progressive movement. Over the course of the twentieth century we also saw the rise of social justice theory and increasing evidence that an emphasis on the positive virtues had begun to crowd-out investment in the negative virtues. Were he alive today, I suspect that

John Rawls, who is often invoked by social justice advocates, would likely be alarmed by the extent of this crowding-out.[17]

In a recent book, I proposed a framework for analyzing the role morality plays in the functioning of a free market society.[18] Among other things, that analysis provided a demand-side story for the social value of the negative virtues. In a nutshell, it explained why trust is so important for the development and operation of a free market economy, and why the kind of trust that matters most requires moral beliefs that stress prohibitions against taking negative moral actions over exhortations for taking positive moral actions.

Obviously, those who have had extensive moral training that emphasizes the negative virtues relative to the positive virtues would be most predisposed to obeying prohibitions against negative moral actions. As such, the analysis presented here can be viewed as a supply-side story for the social value of the negative virtues. This is because those societies that stress the inculcation of the negative virtues are societies that are most likely to have prevailing moral beliefs for which prohibitions against negative moral actions take precedence over positive moral actions and therefore are most likely to enjoy the benefits of having a high-trust society.

As summarized above, measures of trust and social capital in general have shown a steady decline in the west since the 1950s. This suggests we may be doing more to promote something that is not very critical to our success at the expense of adequately promoting something that is very critical to it, and much more prone to socially sub-optimal investment. It remains an empirical question as to whether the decline in trust is a reflection of an increasing emphasis on the positive virtues at the expense of the negative virtues. But given the stakes involved, there is no question as to the importance of directing our attention to answering this question.[19]

NOTES

1. The classical economist of most relevance to this claim is Adam Smith, widely recognized as the father of economics and himself a moral philosopher. Smith emphasized five virtues in his *The Theory of Moral Sentiments*, D.D. Raphael and A.L. Mackie (eds.) (Indianapolis: Liberty Fund Press, 1759/1982). For an insightful discussion of Smith's treatment of the virtues in general, see Deirdre McCloskey, "Adam Smith, the Last of the Former Virtue Ethicists," *History of Political Economy* 40(2008), 43–71, as well as the chapter by Otteson in this volume. As for the founding fathers, consider Benjamin Franklin's famous list of thirteen virtues.
2. Max Weber, *The Protestant Ethic and the Spirit of Capitalism* (New York: Scribner's, 1904/1958).
3. Deirdre McCloskey, *The Bourgeois Virtues: Ethics for an Age of Commerce* (Chicago: University of Chicago Press, 2006), and *Bourgeois Dignity: Why Economics Can't Explain the Modern World* (Chicago: University of Chicago Press, 2010).

4. Deirdre McCloskey, "Bourgeois Virtues?" *Cato Policy Report*, May/June 2006, <http://cato.org/policy-report/mayjune-2006/bourgeois-virtues>. See also the chapter by Choi and Storr in this volume.
5. Frank, *Passions within Reason: The Strategic Role of the Emotions* (New York: W.W. Norton, 1988).
6. For extensive reviews of the social capital literature, see Alejandro Portes, "Social Capital: Its Origins and Applications in Modern Sociology," *Annual Review of Sociology* 24(1998): 1–24; Joel Sobel, "Can We Trust Social Capital?" *Journal of Economic Literature* 40(2002): 139–54; Elinor Ostrom and T.K. Ahn (eds.), *Critical Studies in Economic Institutions: Foundations of Social Capital* (Cheltenham, UK: Edward Elgar, 2003); and Steven N. Durlauf and Marcel Fafchamps, "Social Capital," NBER Working Paper No. w10485, May 2004.
7. For a brief review of what others have said regarding the origins of the term, see Charles F. Manski, "Economic Analysis of Social Interactions," *Journal of Economic Perspectives* 14(2000): 115–36. Most view the term as originating with James S. Coleman (*Foundations of Social Theory*, Cambridge, MA: Harvard University Press, 1990) or Robert D. Putnam, Robert Leonardi, and Raffaella Y. Nanetti (*Making Democracy Work: Civic Traditions in Modern Italy*, Princeton: Princeton University Press, 1993). Steven N. Durlauf ("The Case 'Against' Social Capital," *Focus* 20(1999): 1–5) credits Glenn Loury ("A Dynamic Theory of Racial Income Differences," in P.A. Wallace and A. Le Mund (eds.), *Women, Minorities, and Employment Discrimination*, Lexington, MA: Lexington Books, 1977, 153–88), while Edward Glaeser and colleagues ("Measuring Trust," *Quarterly Journal of Economics* 115(2000): 811–46) credit Jane Jacobs (*The Death and Life of Great American Cities*, New York: Random House, 1961). Ostrom and Ahn (*Critical Studies in Economic Institutions*) say the idea can be traced back to Alexis de Tocqueville (*Democracy in America*, Vol. I, New York: Vintage, 1835/1990).
8. Coleman, *Foundations of Social Theory* and "Social Capital in the Creation of Human Capital," *American Journal of Sociology* 94(1998): S95–S120.
9. Putnam, Leonardi, and Nanetti, *Making Democracy Work*.
10. Putnam, "Bowling Alone: Americas Declining Social Capital," *Journal of Democracy* 6(1995): 65–78, and *Bowling Alone: The Collapse and Revival of American Community* (New York: Simon & Shuster, 2000).
11. See Durlauf and Fafchamps, "Social Capital," for a review of the most influential definitions.
12. Pierre Bourdieu, "Forms of Capital," in John G. Richardson (ed.), *Handbook of Theory and Research for Sociology Education* (Wesport, CT: Greenwood Press, 1986), 241–60. Coleman was apparently unaware of Bourdieu; he states flatly in "Social Capital in the Creation of Human Capital" (S95) that "in this paper, the concept of social capital is introduced" and he does not cite Bourdieu. It is surprising how close their conceptions of the idea come to one another and may be taken as an indication of the validity and importance of the idea, that it was a "multiple" and therefore almost an inevitable next step to be taken in the social sciences given the questions that remained unanswered and the state of the existing paradigm.
13. Sobel, "Can We Trust Social Capital?" 139.

14. Loury, "Dynamic Theory of Racial Income Differences," and Edward Glaeser, David Laibson, and Bruce Sacerdote, "An Economic Approach to Social Capital," *Economic Journal* 112(2002): 437–58.
15. Mark S. Granovetter, "The Strength of Weak Ties," *American Journal of Sociology* 78(1973): 1360–80, and "Economic Action and Social Structure: The Problem of Embeddedness," *American Journal of Sociology* 91(1985): 481–510; Putnam, "Bowling Alone" and *Bowling Alone*, as well as Putnam, Leonardi, and Nanetti, *Making Democracy Work*. Although Coleman emphasizes the role played by social capital in the creation of human capital in "Social Capital in the Creation of Human Capital," his definition of social capital itself does not comport with the individual social capital approach of Loury and Glaeser, Laibson and Sacerdote (see Note 14). In other words, he does not view social capital as a form of human capital, but rather, as the connectedness and networks emphasized in aggregate social cost theory. Specifically, Coleman states, "unlike other forms of capital, social capital inheres in the structure of relations between actors and among actors. It is not lodged either in the actors themselves or in physical implements of production" ("Social Capital in the Creation of Human Capital," S98).
16. See Ostrom and Ahn, *Critical Studies in Economic Institutions.*
17. Rawls' *A Theory of Justice* (Cambridge, MA: Harvard University Press, 1971) is, of course, one of the most influential books in all of moral philosophy, but his arguments are considerably more complex and subtle than is recognized by many who invoke him. His position clearly and fundamentally reflects an appreciation for what I have defined here to be the negative virtues.
18. For an explanation for why moral restraint is more important than moral advocacy for supporting free market activity by creating and sustaining a high-trust society, see David C. Rose, *The Moral Foundation of Economic Behavior* (New York: Oxford University Press, 2011).
19. This work was supported by the Earhart Foundation, the Templeton Foundation, and the International Studies and Programs Center at the University of Missouri-St. Louis. The author also benefited from comments and suggestions from Kenneth Arrow, Robert Frank, Jonathan Haidt, James Otteson, and Robert Putnam.

11

Can Trust, Reciprocity, and Friendships Survive Contact with the Market?

Seung (Ginny) Choi and Virgil Henry Storr

The market is a tool. It is a social machine that links prospective buyers with prospective sellers. It is a social arena where prospective buyers compete with one another to secure the goods and services that they desire, and where prospective sellers compete with each other to attract customers for their wares. If a buyer and a seller agree on the terms of the trade (including the price), the buyer gives the seller something of value (for example, money or a money equivalent) in exchange for the good or service that the seller is offering. Buyers succeed in the market when they secure the goods and services that they want at the price that they are willing to pay (when the utility they gain from the good is greater than the utility that they gain from what they must give up to purchase the good). Sellers succeed in the market when the selling price is greater than the cost (when they earn a profit).

Like any tool, the market can be used for good or for ill. A hammer can be used by a carpenter to build a house and can also be used by the murderer to crack the skull of his victim. A computer can be used to do homework and can be used to bully a classmate. A radio can be used to transmit vital information about evacuation routes in the hours before a major storm and can be used to direct armed militia intent on genocide to their next victims. In each of these cases, it would be a mistake to praise or blame the tool for the praiseworthy or blameworthy purposes that they were used to advance. Instead, in each of the cases above, it is the person and their purposes and not the tool that should be praised or blamed. The same is true of the market. The market can be used to buy books, food and homes, and it can also be used to purchase sex and illicit drugs.

Nonetheless, individuals must often have certain skills or be in possession of certain knowledge in order to effectively use certain tools. To effectively wield a hammer to hit a desired object with a desired level of force, you must have a minimum level of strength and hand–eye coordination. To effectively use a computer to accomplish a particular function, you must possess a certain level of computing knowledge. Moreover, the more that you use a tool to perform a certain function, the more facility you gain with the tool and the more dexterous you become with it. In the case of social tools, the skills that you are likely to develop are social skills, and some of these social skills are socially relevant moral habits or virtues.

The market, then, is a social arena where individuals not only pursue their material goals but also exercise their moral selves. The goods and services that market participants desire and offer, the trading partners with whom they are willing to exchange, and the manner in which they conduct themselves during their market dealings, are all shaped at least in part by their morality. Moreover, to the extent that market participants prefer to deal with certain kinds of people and demand to be treated a certain way by would be trading partners, success in the market will incentivize actors to exhibit certain character traits.

In related work, Storr discusses the moral teachings of the market, that is, the moral sentiments individuals are likely to acquire and develop as they engage in the market.[1] As he writes, "For the market to promote vice it would have to expose us to circumstances where vice received praise and was thought to be praiseworthy, where the individuals that we encountered were relatively more vicious than the individuals we tended to encounter in other contexts, and where we were rewarded for immoral behavior. None of this appears to be the case in the market."[2] Rejecting the notion that the market is amoral or that it has negative moral consequences, Storr argues that the market is a moral teacher that tends to punish vices and reward virtue. It places them in circumstances where they are forced to interact with diverse others in a way where they have to be concerned with their desires. Moreover, not only can social bonds survive their contact with the market without being corrupted, but the market can encourage the development of meaningful social bonds.[3] As such, the market makes individuals morally better people.

This is, of course, not a novel view: as McCloskey writes, "Capitalism has not corrupted our souls. It has improved them."[4] It is also not an uncontroversial view: for instance, it has been argued that markets can destroy individual judgment and conduct,[5] weaken societal and corporate morality,[6] hurt altruism and cooperation,[7] and have unintended adverse effects on social norms and informal institutions.[8] This chapter is an attempt to push back against these complaints and to further the argument that the market is a moral teacher. Specifically, we argue that the market depends on and promotes trust and trustworthiness as well as fairness and reciprocity. Additionally, we argue that the market is an arena where meaningful social bonds characterized by trust and trustworthiness can and do develop.

Summarizing the arguments offered by Michael Sandel, Section 1 briefly engages a common but often persuasive critique leveled against the market that market dealings are unfair and corrupting. Sections 2 and 3 use evidence from the experimental literature to highlight the important roles that trust and trustworthiness, as well as fairness and reciprocity, are likely to play in successful market exchanges. Section 4 explores the notion that injecting market values into social relationships is necessarily damaging to those relationships and argues, as has been suggested elsewhere, that the market is a social space where meaningful social bonds can and do develop. Section 5 offers concluding remarks.

1. THE MARKET'S MORAL LIMITS

Michael Sandel has argued that markets undermine morality and, in particular, worries about the recent expansion of markets and market values.[9] Although he believes that an increase in greed has undoubtedly accompanied this "market triumphalism," the most worrisome consequences of this growth of markets has been "the expansion of markets, and of market values, into spheres of life where they don't belong."[10] There are perverse moral consequences, he argues, associated with our moving to a world "where everything is up for sale." Specifically, as Sandel explains, "markets leave their mark on social norms. Often, market incentives erode or crowd out nonmarket incentives."[11] Moreover, Sandel argues that markets in certain goods and services under certain scenarios are likely to be unfair and corrupting.

As Sandel explains, "the fairness objection points to the injustice that can arise when people buy and sell things under conditions of inequality or dire economic necessity."[12] This suggests that market exchanges are not always fully voluntary and that desperation can force people to buy or sell goods and services that otherwise they would not buy or sell if they were in less dire economic circumstances. "Market choices," Sandel explains, "are not free choices if some people are desperately poor or lack the ability to bargain on fair terms. So in order to know whether a market choice is a free choice, we have to ask what inequalities in the background conditions of society undermine meaningful consent."[13] Think here of the child forced to work in a sweatshop, the woman forced into prostitution, and the man forced to sell an organ, because each is extremely poor; think also of the indigenous producer of some export commodity in the developing world who is not able to bargain for fairer terms for her product when transacting with her certainly richer and potentially more sophisticated trading partners in the developed world. As Sandel explains, "a peasant may agree to sell his kidney or cornea to feed his starving family, but his agreement may not really be voluntary. He may be unfairly coerced, in effect, by the necessities of his situation."[14]

In addition to his fairness concerns, Sandel also worries that market relationships can be corrupting in some circumstances, an objection that "points to the degrading effect of market valuation and exchange on certain goods and practices. According to this objection, certain moral and civic goods are diminished or corrupted if bought and sold."[15] This suggests that giving away certain goods and services can be morally neutral or even virtuous while exchanging the same goods and services for money can be morally problematic. This also suggests that introducing money into certain relationships can pervert or poison those relationships. Think here of the monetization of certain activities, like sex in the case of prostitution, which many view as being inherently degrading to both the buyer and the seller. Think also of the sister who charges her brother for doing a favor and the attempt to buy a friendship rather than earning it; both types of relationships, according to Sandel, would be damaged by the introduction of market dealings. He also mentions the selling of blood, which he claims ends up reducing rather than increasing the availability of blood relative to the current system that relies on donations.

Sandel, thus, suggests that certain transactions are likely to be unfair or corrupting because of either the nature of the goods being exchanged or the relationships between the parties to the deal. In a sense, Sandel's claims are not controversial. Going where you do not belong is bound to have perverse consequences or at least unfortunate or unhappy consequences. There are, however, reasons to worry about his claims. For instance, whether or not Sandel draws the line correctly around where the market should and should not go remains an unsettled question. Moreover, his rationale for drawing the boundaries where he does draw them is arbitrary at best and appears to be based on tradition or his subjective perception that certain goods ought to be widely available and that certain goods should not be for sale.

However, even if we were to accept Sandel's claims, several key questions remain unanswered. First, what is the moral character of market transactions and values when they occur in spheres where, in his perspective, they *do* belong—that is, where the exchange is truly voluntary and the good is not corrupted by being sold? Are market transactions involving the appropriate goods or the injection of market values between appropriate parties also likely to be unjust and corrupting? Second, are injustice and corruption the only possible, likely, or even dominant morally relevant outcomes of transacting in goods that "should not be traded" and of transactions between individuals who "should not trade" with one another? Is it possible that engaging in market activity and adopting market values can be virtuous even when they occur where and when they should not occur?

Section 2 attempts to answer these questions, albeit indirectly. Markets, we argue, depend on, as well as engender, trust and trustworthiness, and fairness and reciprocity. Absent trust and trustworthiness, market transactions can become prohibitively costly, and absent fairness and reciprocity, market transactions can become prohibitively uninviting. Moreover, rather than corrupting social bonds, markets benefit from and can encourage the emergence of meaningful social friendships.

2. TRUST AND TRUSTWORTHINESS IN MARKET DEALINGS

By trust we mean the belief that others will not betray us and might even act beneficently towards us in uncertain or risky situations when they are not required to do so and when it is not in their short-term interest to do so.[16] To be trustworthy is to prove deserving of trust by keeping your promises and not betraying confidences or commitments. There is a great deal of research that speaks to the important roles that trust and trustworthiness play in economic activity as well as how economic activity can engender trust and trustworthiness.

Economic agents are said to have either game-theoretic or preference-based reasons to trust (in any context). The former equates trust with an individual's prior belief that his opponent will act cooperatively in a repeated game. The latter motivation (that is, preference-based reasons) presupposes that individuals have preferences for fairness and cooperation. Here, individuals trust anonymous partners even in one-shot games because they expect the same behavior from them. Together, they suggest that markets depend on and engender trust.

The idea that markets depend on trust is not new. As Arrow explained, "virtually every commercial transaction has within itself an element of trust, certainly any transaction conducted over a period of time. It can be plausibly argued that much of the economic backwardness in the world can be explained by the lack of mutual confidence."[17] Studies of prosperous societies highlight the pivotal role of trust in economic performance.[18] For example, La Porta and his colleagues showed that the proportion of trusting people was negatively correlated with inflation rates and positively correlated with GDP growth across countries.[19] Zak and Knack found the positive correlation between generalized trust, GDP growth and investment levels.[20] Dyer and Chu examined whether trust generates economic value and found that the level of supplier trust in a buyer was correlated with greater (confidential) information-sharing between the exchange partners and also resulted in lower (ex post) transaction costs (such as monitoring costs) and substantively better financial performance.[21] Guiso, Sapienza and Zingales discovered that greater bilateral trust between two countries is associated with higher volumes of trade between the countries.[22] Zaheer and colleagues investigated how firm performance is influenced by interpersonal and inter-organizational trust and found that negotiation costs were a function of interpersonal and inter-organizational trust: where interpersonal trust between employees of partner firms was low, inter-organizational trust remained high and accounted for the low negotiation costs.[23] Furthermore, higher trust societies are also associated with other factors that influence economic success like less crime,[24] efficient judicial systems,[25] high quality government bureaucracies,[26] less government intervention,[27] as well as less corruption and better financial markets.[28]

Trust matters in a market setting for two main reasons. First, as suggested above, trust has the propensity to lower transaction costs since it can complement and substitute for contractual and bureaucratic mechanisms for cooperation.[29] Firms often devote a large amount of resources while engaging in expensive negotiations before entering business together to screen for unreliable or untrustworthy partners (that is, ex ante and ex post opportunism).[30] Vetting all possible partners each time an individual wishes to engage in trade is costly, however, and conducting business with traders with good reputations (or with whom others have had "good" personal experience) can reduce the uncertainty arising from the risk inherent to the reliability of partners. As such, individuals have incentives to build lasting relationships with trustworthy others. In addition, there are added benefits to forming such relationships. For example, two trusted partners may not need written contracts and, even when there is one, may not need to stipulate every possible contingency. Furthermore, citizens in high-trust societies are less likely to devote a large amount of resources to protect themselves from violations of their property rights or criminal acts, whether they are in the form of private security or bribes.

Second, trust can inspire not only information-sharing between trading partners (and even competitors) but also confidence in the information that is shared. Through information-sharing, trust can shift focus from short-term returns to long-term returns and thereby encourage investment (in physical and human capital), innovation and specialization. Moreover, entrepreneurs would have more time to engage in ventures and streamline existing processes if they could spend fewer resources on monitoring potential wrongdoings by partners and their employees because they trust them. Additionally, trust can promote greater efficiency by enabling each party to be more flexible in responding to changing market conditions and in reaching a mutually beneficial solution; after all, individuals can be assured that their partners would reciprocate in the future if they compromise first.[31]

Markets not only depend on trust and trustworthiness but also promote them. As Granovetter notes, "individuals with whom one has a continuing relationship have an economic motivation to be trustworthy."[32] Several studies, for instance, have suggested that the greater the individuals' exposure to markets, the more likely they are to be trusting and trustworthy. One implication of these studies is that commercial activities—including labor market participation—train individuals to trust and to act trustworthily. Henrich and colleagues, for instance, concluded that market integration explains a large portion of the behavior variation across societies that are observed in economic experiments.[33] The more the market is integrated into a community the higher levels of prosociality they exhibit in ultimatum games. Tracer also found that there was some (albeit weak) support for the notion that a greater level of market integration at both the community and individual level leads to greater prosociality.[34] Ensminger found that exposure to markets was a predictor of offer size within ultimatum and dictator games.[35] Tu and Bulte explored the links between trust and market integration and concluded that trust (as measured using a trust game) is positively associated with labor market participation.[36] Fehr and List observed a significantly higher display of trust and trustworthiness by coffee mill executives than students in their experiment in Costa Rica.[37] Using a market-priming task followed by a trust game, Al-Ubaydli and colleagues concluded that market priming (encouraging subjects to adopt a market mindset) significantly increased levels of trust and trustworthiness.[38] Finally, Choi and Storr found that individuals develop relationships characterized by trust and trustworthiness in market settings.[39]

3. FAIRNESS AND RECIPROCITY IN MARKETS

By fairness we mean not only impartiality and equanimity but also treating others in a manner that is consistent with how they "deserve" to be treated. To treat someone fairly is, thus, to treat them justly. The existing empirical and experimental research suggests that fairness concerns shape market activity and that, in turn, market activity promotes and encourages people to be concerned with fairness. This should not be surprising, for (at least) two reasons. First, the most profitable businesses are those that are able to develop relationships with trading partners and so encourage repeat business with customers and suppliers. Because people are likely to avoid dealing with those that they believe have treated them unfairly (so long as alternatives exist), businesses have an incentive to deal fairly with their trading partners. Second, it has been well established that norms (regardless of their content) color economic behavior. We should, therefore, expect market activity and outcomes to be impacted by fairness concerns to the extent that norms of fairness exist within a particular culture.

Concerns about fairness can have an impact on market competition, cooperation, and incentives.[40] Ample empirical evidence suggests that fairness motivates firm and individual behavior. Kahneman, Knetsch and Thaler, for instance, reported that the public has strong feelings about what constitutes a fair price (set by firms), about firms adjusting their prices in the short-run in response to changing market circumstances, and about firms exploiting their market power (in particular, monopoly status).[41] Franciosi and colleagues have suggested that buyers who expect to be treated fairly believe that prices should only rise when a seller's production costs rise.[42] Sellers who accept this fairness norm will not raise prices in the short-run unless the price rise can be justified by an increase in their production cost.

Likewise, employees' perception of fair wage constrains the firms' ability to freely set its wages and their willingness to lower them when market conditions decline.[43] Bewley explained that persistent downward wage rigidity for both existing and new employees during recessions was the result of employers' beliefs about employee motivation and morale.[44] Specifically, data collected from interviews suggested that employers want employees to identify with their companies and their objectives and to encourage positive cooperation with their colleagues and supervisors. Refusing to cut wages is not only consistent with the practice of rewarding good performance but also with keeping good worker morale and with maintaining social cohesion and productivity within the firm.

Additionally, experimental research based on a simple bilateral bargaining game called the ultimatum game also illustrate that a non-trivial number of participants do not care solely about monetary payoffs. In this game, the first mover is asked to divide a given monetary endowment between himself and the second mover, who has the right to take or reject the division. If the division is rejected, both players earn nothing. Game-theoretic predictions dictate that the self-interested first mover should offer as little as possible to the second mover, who, likewise, should accept even the minimum amount offered. This asymmetric division, however, tends to appear unfair to many people, and dozens of replications of ultimatum games support this view. Typically, first movers offer an average of 40 per cent of the endowment to second movers and second movers frequently reject offers of less than 20 per cent. This observation holds even at higher stakes of $100 and $400.[45] One interpretation of second mover rejections is that some players respond to unfair treatment with negative reciprocity (that is, by harming the person who treated them unfairly even at their own expense). Undoubtedly, negative reciprocity can be observed in social settings (such as ugly friendship breaks and divorces) as well as economic settings (such as boycotts).

Dozens of ultimatum games from around the world corroborate the general observations from the small-stakes games conducted in the United States. Cross-cultural comparisons of behavior in ultimatum games revealed similarities in offer distributions and acceptance rates between student populations in America, Japan, Slovenia, and Israel.[46] These cross-cultural similarities suggest that an "overwhelming market influence [may be dominating] any cross-cultural notions of fairness or norms of exchange."[47] Supporting this view, Henrich and colleagues concluded that the levels of market integration and fairness—even in brief, one-shot exchanges—are positively correlated, based on data collected from basic experimental games (including the ultimatum game) administered over fifteen distinct small-scale societies.[48]

4. THE SOCIALITY OF COMMERCIAL EXCHANGES

Zelizer has criticized what she describes as the "separate spheres" and "hostile worlds" views of the relationship between economy and society.[49] The separate spheres view holds that the two arenas of social life, one characterized by sentiment and mutuality and the other characterized by rationality and exchange, can co-exist peaceably alongside one another. The "hostile worlds" view, however, suggests that these two spheres inevitably "contaminate" each other if and when they intersect: "penetration of rational calculation into the sphere of sentiment would disrupt solidarity, just as the penetration of sentiment into the sphere of rationality would disrupt [rational] efficiency."[50]

Interestingly, Hayek seemed to endorse the "hostile worlds" view, writing that

> we must constantly adjust our lives, our thoughts and our emotions, in order to live simultaneously within different kinds of orders according to different rules. If we were to apply the unmodified, uncurbed, rules of the micro-cosmos (that is, of the small band or troop, or of, say, our families) to the macro-cosmos (our wider civilisation), as our instincts and sentimental yearnings often make us wish to do, we would destroy it. Yet if we were always to apply the rules of the extended order to our more intimate groupings, we would crush them.[51]

Zelizer has rejected this style of thinking in favor of "a more fully social conception of economic activity."[52] The dichotomy between the world of the family and the world of the firm, she suggests, is a false one.

It is possible for social relationships to survive contact with the market without being corrupted. In fact, as suggested above, social relationships can facilitate economic activity. Stated another way, economic activity is embedded within a context of ongoing social relations and individuals can utilize their social connections as they pursue their economic goals. Additionally, it is possible for social relationships to develop within market contexts and for commercial relationships to develop into social friendships. Indeed, the market is a social space where meaningful social connections do occur and meaningful social bonds do deepen. Even if Sandel is correct that the introduction of market values do sometimes and under certain circumstances corrupt social bonds, it does not appear to be the case that the introduction of market values *necessarily* corrupts social bonds. Moreover, there appears to be the potential that market activity can be enhanced by social relationships and that social relationships can be deepened by market activity.

4.1 The concepts of embeddedness and social capital

"Actors," Granovetter writes, "do not behave or decide to behave as atoms outside of social structure, nor do they adhere slavishly to a script written for them by the particular intersection of social categories that they happen to occupy."[53] Instead, economic action is embedded within social structures. Specifically, he argues that concrete relationships reduce transaction costs by engendering trust and reducing the likelihood of malfeasance.[54] Elsewhere, Granovetter has likewise discussed the persistence of large family firms and ethnic trade groups in advanced economies.[55] More recently, he has pointed out that social structures can affect and influence a variety of economic phenomena including prices, productivity and innovation.[56]

Others have profitably employed the concept of embeddedness to explain how social structure affects economic activity.[57] Uzzi and Lancaster, for instance, have discussed how firms' embedded relationships can affect the prices of both standard and complex legal services.[58] Similarly, Uzzi has argued that firms are embedded in organizational networks that can both promote and retard economic performance.[59] Romo and Schwartz have made the case that the market and non-market relationships that develop within regional economies eventually create dependencies that work to constrain the migration of manufacturing firms out of the region, even when migration would result in monetary savings.[60]

The social capital literature has, similarly, discussed how individuals utilize their social relationships as they pursue their economic goals. Coleman, for instance, has explained that "social capital is productive, making possible the achievement of certain ends that in its absence would not be possible."[61] Like other forms of capital, it is a tool that is heterogeneous, with some social capital better suited for some purposes, and some better suited for other purposes.[62] Social capital, Coleman explains, exists within and is inextricable from "the structure of relations between and among actors."[63] According to Coleman, social capital comes in several different forms, including mutual trust, information channels, norms, and effective sanctions.[64] For instance, as he describes, social ties between Jewish diamond traders in New York act as a kind of insurance, eliminating the need for purchasing expensive insurance devices, lowering transaction costs, and therefore facilitating transactions that would not otherwise be possible. Similarly, social capital within the family and within the community can act as a resource that facilitates the attainment of human capital by children. The closer the relationships between parents and children and the closer knit the community to which they belong, he concludes, the less likely it is that these children will drop out of school.

Others have used the concept of social capital to explain how individuals deploy their social networks and the resources embedded within their social networks as they pursue their economic goals. Granovetter, for instance, has described how individuals rely on weak ties in order to secure employment.[65] Podolny and Baron have described how peoples' informal ties within an organization affect their advancement.[66] Uzzi has found that social relationships between corporate bankers and borrowers can lower loan prices by facilitating the flow of information and the establishment of informal enforcement mechanisms.[67] Torsvik has likewise found that social capital as social norms reduces transaction costs in the economic sphere and, so, promotes social cooperation.[68] Also, Knack and Keefer found that economic performance and social capital in the form of norms of civic cooperation and interpersonal trust are positively related.[69]

Although there is some discussion in the literature on the possible costs associated with belonging to particular networks,[70] most studies tend to focus on how social relationships, and the resources that individuals can access through their social networks, affect economic performance. Moreover, when they do discuss the formation of social relationships within the economic sphere, scholars tend to focus on the formation of weak ties within commercial organizations and not on the possibility that strong ties can and do develop within commercial places.[71]

4.2 Social relations as economically conditioned

Even though studies within the embeddedness literature tend to focus on how these relationships affect individual or organizational economic performance, some point to the possibility of social bonds developing between participants in a market setting.

While Ingram and Roberts, for instance, focus on the economic function of the relationships that can develop between competitors, they nonetheless acknowledge the possibility that these relationships can form.[72] Similarly, Granovetter is aware that social action can be economically conditioned: as he acknowledges, "business dealings [sometimes] spill over into sociability... especially amongst business elites."[73] Additionally, in explaining why consumers tend to trust and prefer "our own past dealings" as sources of information, Granovetter notes "continuing economic relations often become overlaid with social content that carries strong expectations of trust and abstention from opportunism."[74] Although he stops there and does not tease out the implications of his observation that social feelings often grow out of commercial relationships, the observation that market relations often develop into relationships characterized by trust is important in itself.

Indeed, as Adam Smith argued, "the necessity or convenience of mutual accommodation very frequently produces a friendship not unlike that which takes place among those who are born to live in the same family. Colleagues in office, partners in trade, call one another brothers; and frequently feel towards one another as if they really were so."[75] More generally, as Silver discussed, commercial society can actually promote meaningful social connections.[76] Seabright has pointed out that markets work because human beings in market contexts and governed by market institutions are "willing to treat strangers as honorary friends."[77] As Storr observed, markets can be social spaces "where both economic and extraeconomic relationships are developed and maintained."[78] By extraeconomic relationships, Storr is referring to social relationships that begin as economic or commercial relationships (that is, relationships between co-workers, employers and employees, mentors and apprentices, and so on) that morph into genuine social friendships characterized by deep bonds of trust and affection. As he continues, "markets are not only embedded in the community but can also promote and sustain the community.... Many meaningful conversations beyond negotiations occur within the conversation of the market."[79]

There are a few studies within the industrial sociological and management studies literature that speak to the potential of commercial relationships to morph into social friendships as well as the potential benefits and negative aspects of deep commercial friendships. For instance, many have described how strong bonds develop between workplace friends because of their common experiences and circumstances.[80] Think of co-workers on the factory floor who invite each other over for barbeques on the weekends, or office workers who reconvene after work for happy hour before heading home. These relationships, it turns out, are not only important for job satisfaction but can also represent deep social bonds. Similarly, other studies have discussed how workplaces can facilitate office romance because co-workers often have similar backgrounds and so much time is spent at work associating with colleagues.[81] Also, as yet others describe, even principal–client and seller–buyer relationships can develop into close friendships.[82] Again, the trust that is necessary for their work relationships to function well and the trust fostered during their non-work interactions can reinforce one another. As Price and Arnould found, "commercial friendships, similar to other friendships, involve affection, intimacy, social support, loyalty and reciprocal gift giving."[83]

Admittedly, these commercial relationships may not be as deep as the social bonds that develop in other contexts. The social unions between neighbors, schoolmates, church members, or lodge brothers may very well be closer, by their very nature, than workplace friendships.[84] And, of course, family ties may trump any relationship that might ever develop in the workplace. The point in highlighting these relationships is not to privilege them over non-commercial friendships but merely to suggest that these relationships can play important roles in people's lives.

In addition to being spaces where commercial friendships are formed, businesses also provide spaces where non-commercial relationships grow and develop. Amongst the range of goods and services that businesses provide, one key and easily overlooked one is the provision of environments where social bonds that developed in, say, the synagogue, church, university, or the neighborhood playground, can be cemented. That two friends can spend a Saturday afternoon at the mall, that a family can share a meal on Sunday night at their favorite restaurant, that friends at different firms can find places to meet for lunch in the middle of a busy work day, that a couple can go out to dinner, dancing and a movie on a Friday night, are important aspects of what businesses provide in addition to goods and services. To be sure, friends, couples, and family members found spaces for conviviality before there were restaurants and shopping malls. Indeed, homes, churches, parks, and museums remain important social spaces. The point is simply to emphasize that market spaces can serve a similar function.

5. CONCLUSION

There has been a long-standing debate around the sociality and morality of markets. On the one hand, markets are said to be socially and morally problematic. Market dealings are said to be inherently unfair and potentially corrupting. On the other hand, markets are said to have an ameliorative effect. Commerce, it is argued, engenders gentle manners (the "doux commerce thesis"),[85] cordializes mankind,[86] and enhances virtues.[87] This chapter attempted to indirectly engage this debate by discussing how trust, reciprocity, and friendships are affected by market dealings. Specifically, we argued that markets engender trust and trustworthiness as well as fairness and reciprocity. Moreover, we argued that the market is a social space where meaningful social relationships characterized by trust and reciprocity can and do develop. Rather than trustworthiness, fairness, and friendships being put at risk when individuals engage in market activity, the market crucially depends on and actively encourages their development.

NOTES

1. Virgil Storr, "The Impartial Spectator and the Moral Teachings of Markets," David Schmidtz (ed.), *Oxford Handbook of Freedom* (Oxford: Oxford University Press, in press).
2. Ibid.
3. Virgil Storr, "Why the Market? Markets as Social and Moral Spaces," *Journal of Markets and Morality* 12(2009): 277–96.

4. Deirdre N. McCloskey, *The Bourgeois Virtues: Ethics for an Age of Commerce* (Chicago: University of Chicago Press, 2006), 23. See also Albert Hirschman, *The Passions and the Interests* (Princeton: Princeton University Press, 1997), and Paul J. Zak, *Moral Markets: The Critical Role of Values in the Economy* (Princeton: Princeton University Press, 2008). For additional discussions of this view, see Virgil Storr, "Why the Market? Markets as Social and Moral Spaces," *Journal of Markets and Morality* 12(2009): 277–96; Ryan Langrill and Virgil Storr, "The Moral Meanings of Markets," *Journal of Markets and Morality* 15(2012): 347–62; and Chapter 12 by Brennan in this volume.
5. For example, Thorstein Veblen, *The Theory of the Leisure Class* (London: Penguin Books, 1899/1994), and Armin Falk and Nora Szech, "Morals and Markets," *Science* 340 (2013): 707–11.
6. For example, Karl Marx, "On Authority," in Robert Tucker (trans.), *Marx-Engels Reader* (New York: W.W. Norton, 1872/1972), 730–3; Andrei Shleifer, "Does Competition Destroy Ethical Behavior?" *American Economic Review* 94(2004): 414–18.
7. For example, Samuel Bowles, "Endogenous Preferences: The Cultural Consequences of Markets and Other Economic Institutions," *Journal of Economic Literature* 36(1998): 75–111.
8. For example, Bruno S. Frey and Felix Oberholzer-Gee, "The Cost of Price Incentives: An Empirical Analysis of Motivation Crowding-Out," *American Economic Review* 87(1997): 746–55; Edward L. Deci, Richard Koestern and Richard M. Ryan, "A Meta-Analytic Review of Experiments Examining the Effects of Extrinsic Rewards on Intrinsic Motivation," *Psychological Bulletin* 125(1999): 627–68; Armin Falk and Michael Kosfeld, "The Hidden Cost of Control," *American Economic Review* 96(2006): 1611–30; Michael Sandel, *What Money Can't Buy: The Moral Limits of Markets* (New York: Farrar, Straus and Giroux, 2012).
9. Sandel, *What Money Can't Buy*, 7. Sandel's view is not all that different than the arguments advanced by Alasdair McIntyre: "the tradition of virtues is at variance with central features of the modern economic order and more especially its individualism, its acquisitiveness, and its elevation of the market to a central social place" (*After Virtue: A Study in Moral Theory*, 3rd ed., Notre Dame: University of Notre Dame Press, 2007, 254). McIntyre worries that the profit motive and competition, both essential elements of the market, undermine virtue.
10. Sandel, *What Money Can't Buy*, 7.
11. Ibid., 64.
12. Ibid., 111.
13. Ibid., 112.
14. Ibid., 111.
15. Ibid.
16. Margaret Foddy and Toshio Yamagishi, "Group-Based Trust," in Karen Cook, Margaret Levi and Russell Hardin (eds.), *Whom Can We Trust?* (New York: Russell Sage Foundation, 2009), 17–41.
17. Kenneth Arrow, "Gifts and Exchange," *Philosophy and Public Affairs* 1(1972): 343–62, at 357.
18. For example, see Robert Putnam, *Making Democracy Work: Civic Traditions in Modern Italy* (Princeton: Princeton University Press, 1993); Francis Fukuyama, *Trust: The Social Virtues and the Creation of Prosperity* (London: Hamish

Hamilton, 1995); Stephen Knack and Philip Keefer, "Does Social Capital Have an Economic Payoff? A Cross-Country Investigation," *Quarterly Journal of Economics* 112(1997): 1251–88; Paul J. Zak and Stephen Knack, "Trust and Growth," *Economic Journal* 111(2001): 295–321.

19. Rafael La Porta, Florencio Lopez-de-Silanes, Andrei Shleifer, and Robert W. Vishny, "Trust in Large Organizations," *American Economic Review* 87(1997): 333–8.
20. Zak and Knack, "Trust and Growth."
21. Jeffrey H. Dyer and Wujin Chu, "The Role of Trustworthiness in Reducing Transaction Costs and Improving Performance: Empirical Evidence from the United States, Japan, and Korea," *Organization Science* 14(2003): 57–68.
22. Luigi Guiso, Paola Sapienza and Luigi Zingales, "Cultural Biases in Economic Exchange?" *Quarterly Journal of Economics* 124(2009): 1095–131.
23. Akbar Zaheer, Bill McEvily and Vincenzo Perrone, "Does Trust Matter? Exploring the Effects of Interorganizational and Interpersonal Trust on performance," *Organization Science* 9(1998), 141–59.
24. William J. Wilson, *The Truly Disadvantaged: The Inner-City, the Underclass and Public Policy* (Chicago: University of Chicago Press, 1987).
25. Niclas Berggren and Henrik Jordahl, "Free to Trust: Economic Freedom and Social Capital," *Kyklos* 59(2006): 141–69.
26. Putnam, *Making Democracy Work.*
27. Philippe Aghion, Yann Algan, Pierre Cahuc and Andrei Shleifer, "Regulation and Distrust," *Quarterly Journal of Economics* 125(2010): 1015–49.
28. La Porta et al., "Trust in Large Organizations"; Guiso, Sapienza and Zingales, "The Role of Social Capital in Financial Development," *American Economic Review* 94(2004): 526–56.
29. Diego Gambetta, *Trust: Making and Breaking Cooperative Relations* (Cambridge: Blackwell, 1998).
30. For example, A. Michael Spence, "Time and Communication in Economic and Social Interaction," *Quarterly Journal of Economics* 87(1973): 651–60; Oliver Williamson, *Markets and Hierarchies* (New York: The Free Press, 1975); Amy Farmer and Andrew W. Horowitz, "The Engagement Game," *Journal of Population Economics* 17(2004): 627–44.
31. For example, Richard E. Walton and Robert B. McKersie, *A Behavioral Theory of Labor Negotiations* (New York: McGraw-Hill, 1965); Ronald Dore, "Goodwill and the Spirit of Market Capitalism," *British Journal of Sociology* 34(1983): 459–82; Dyer and Chu, "The Role of Trustworthiness."
32. Mark Granovetter, "Economic Action and Social Structure: The Problem of Embeddedness," *American Journal of Sociology* 91(1985): 481–510, at 490.
33. Joseph Henrich, Robert Boyd, Samuel Bowles, Colin Camerer, Ernst Fehr, and Herbert Gintis (eds.), *Foundations of Human Sociality: Economic Experiments and Ethnographic Evidence from Fifteen Small-Scale Societies* (Oxford: Oxford University Press, 2004); Joseph Henrich, Robert Boyd, Samuel Bowles, Colin Camerer, Ernst Fehr, Herbert Gintis, Richard McElreath, Michael Alvard, Abigail Barr, Jean Ensminger, Natalie Smith Henrich, Kim Hill, Francisco Gil-White, Michael Gurven, Frank W. Marlowe, John Q. Patton, and David Tracer, "'Economic Man'

in Cross-Cultural Perspective: Behavioral Experiments in 15 Small-Scale Societies," *Behavioral and Brain Sciences* 25(2005): 795–855.

34. David P. Tracer, "Market Integration, Reciprocity, and Fairness in Rural Papua New Guinea: Results from a Two-Village Ultimatum Game Experiment," in Joseph Henrich et al. (eds.), *Foundations of Human Sociality* (Oxford: Oxford University Press, 2004), 232–59.
35. Jean Ensminger, "Market Integration and Fairness: Evidence from Ultimatum, Dictator, and Public Good Experiments in East Africa," in Henrich et al., *Foundations of Human Sociality*, 356–81.
36. Qin Tu and Erwin Bulte, "Trust, Market Participation and Economic Outcomes: Evidence from Rural China," *World Development* 38(2010): 1179–90.
37. Ernst Fehr and John List, "The Hidden Costs and Returns of Incentives-Trust and Trustworthiness Among CEOs," *Journal of the European Economic Association* 2(2004): 743–71.
38. Omar Al-Ubaydli, Daniel Houser, John Nye, Maria Pia Paganelli, and Xiaofei Sophia Pan, "The Causal Effect of Market Priming on Trust: An Experimental Investigation Using Randomized Control," *PLOS One* 8(3), 2013, e55968. doi:10.1371/journal.pone.0055968
39. Seung (Ginny) Choi and Virgil Storr, "The Emergence of Social Relationships in Markets," working paper, 2014.
40. Ernst Fehr and Urs Fischbacher, "Why Social Preferences Matter: The Impact of Non-Selfish Motives on Competition, Cooperation, and Incentives," *Economic Journal* 112(2002): C1-C33.
41. Daniel Kahneman, Jack Knetsch, and Richard Thaler, "Fairness as a Constraint on Profit Seeking: Entitlement in the Market," *American Economic Review* 76(1986): 728–41.
42. Robert Franciosi, Praveen Kujal, Roland Michelitsch, Vernon Smith, and Gang Dong, "Fairness: Effect on Temporary and Equilibrium Prices in Posted-Offer Markets," *Economic Journal* 105(1995): 938–50.
43. For example, Alan S. Blinder and Don H. Choi, "A Shred of Evidence on Theories of Wage Stickiness," *Quarterly Journal of Economics* 105(1990): 1003–15; Jonas Argell and Per Lundborg, "Theories of Pay and Unemployment: Survey Evidence from Swedish Manufacturing Firms," *Scandinavian Journal of Economics* 97(1995): 295–308; Trumen F. Bewley, "A Depressed Labor Market as Explained by Participants," *American Economic Review Papers and Proceedings* 85(1995): 250–4.
44. Bewley, "A Depressed Labor Market."
45. Elizabeth Hoffman, Kevin McCabe, and Vernon Smith, "Social Distance and Other-Regarding Behavior in Dictator Games," *American Economic Review* 86(1996): 235–57; John List and Todd Cherry, "Learning to Accept in Ultimatum Games: Evidence from an Experimental Design that Generates Low Offers," *Experimental Economics* 3(2000): 11–29.
46. Alvin E. Roth, Vesna Prasnikar, Masahiro Okuno-Fujiwara, and Shmuel Zamir, "Bargaining and Market Behavior in Jerusalem, Ljubljana, Pittsburgh, and Tokyo: An Experimental Study," *American Economic Review* 81(1991): 1068–95.

47. Michael Gurven, "Does Market Exposure Affect Economic Game Behavior?", in Henrich et al., *Foundations of Human Sociality*, 194–231, at 195.
48. Joseph Henrich, Jean Ensminger, Richard McElreath, Abigail Barr, Clark Barrett, Alexander Bolyanatz, Juan Camilo Cardenas, Michael Gurven, Edwins Gwako, Natalie Henrich, Carolyn Lesorogol, Frank Marlowe, David Tracer, and John Ziker, "Markets, Religion, Community Size, and the Evolution of Fairness and Punishment," *Science* 327(2010): 1480–4.
49. Viviana A. Zelizer, *Economic Lives: How Culture Shapes the Economy* (Princeton: Princeton University Press, 2011).
50. Ibid., 5.
51. Friedrich von Hayek, *The Fatal Conceit: The Errors of Socialism* (Chicago: The University of Chicago Press, 1988), 18.
52. Zelizer, *Economic Lives*, 387.
53. Granovetter, "Economic Action and Social Structure," 487.
54. Granovetter, "Economic Action and Social Structure," 490.
55. Mark Granovetter, "The Strength of Weak Ties: A Network Theory Revisited," *Sociological Theory* 1(1983): 201–33.
56. Mark Granovetter, "The Impact of Social Structure on Economic Outcomes," *Journal of Economic Perspectives* 19(2005): 33–50.
57. See Greta R. Krippner and Anthony S. Alvarez, "Embeddedness and the Intellectual Projects of Economic Sociology," *Annual Review of Sociology* 33(2007): 219–40 for a discussion of the research that applied and extended the concept of embeddedness.
58. Brian Uzzi and Ryon Lancaster, "Embeddedness and Price Formation in the Corporate Law Market," *American Sociological Review* 69(2004): 319–44.
59. Brian Uzzi, "The Sources and Consequences of Embeddedness for the Economic Performance of Organizations: The Network Effect," *American Sociological Review* 61(1996): 674–98.
60. Frank P. Romo and Michael Schwartz, "The Structural Embeddedness of Business Decisions: The Migration of Manufacturing Plants in New York State, 1960 to 1985," *American Sociological Review* 60(1995): 874–907.
61. James S. Coleman, "Social Capital in the Creation of Human Capital," *American Journal of Sociology* 94(1988): S95–S120, at S98.
62. Coleman, "Social Capital in the Creation of Human Capital"; see also Emily Chamlee-Wright, "The Structure of Social Capital: An Austrian Perspective on its Nature and Development," *Review of Political Economy* 20(2008): 41–58.
63. Coleman, "Social Capital in the Creation of Human Capital," S98.
64. Ibid., S101.
65. Mark Granovetter, "Strength of Weak Ties," *American Journal of Sociology* 78(1973): 1360–80, and "The Strength of Weak Ties: A Network Theory Revisited"; see Ted Mouw, "Social Capital and Finding a Job: Do Contacts Matter?" *American Sociological Review* 68(2003), 868–98.
66. Joel M. Podolny and James N. Baron, "Resources and Relationships: Social Networks and Mobility in the Workplace," *American Sociological Review* 62(1997): 673–93.

67. Brian Uzzi, "Embeddedness in the Making of Financial Capital: How Social Relations and Networks Benefit Firms Seeking Financing," *American Sociological Review* 64(1999): 481–505.
68. Gaute Torsvik, "Social Capital and Economic Development: A Plea for the Mechanisms," *Rationality and Society* 12(4) 2000, 451–76.
69. Knack and Keefer, "Does Social Capital Have an Economic Payoff?"
70. For example, Uzzi, "The Sources and Consequences of Embeddedness"; Mauricio Rubio, "Perverse Social Capital: Some Evidence from Colombia," *Journal of Economic Issues* 31(1997): 805–16; Michael Woolcock, "Social Capital and Economic Development: Toward a Theoretical Synthesis and Policy Framework," *Theory and Society* 27(1998): 151–208; Alejandro Portes, "The Two Meanings of Social Capital," *Sociological Forum* 15(2000): 1–12.
71. For more on social capital and virtue, see Chapter 10 by Rose in this volume.
72. Paul Ingram and Peter W. Roberts, "Friendships among Competitors in the Sydney Hotel Industry," *American Journal of Sociology* 106(2000): 387–423.
73. Granovetter, "Economic Action and Social Structure," 495.
74. Ibid., 490.
75. Adam Smith, *The Theory of Moral Sentiments*, D.D. Raphael and A.L. Mackie (eds.) (Indianapolis: Liberty Fund, 1976), 223–4.
76. Allan Silver, "Friendship in Commercial Society: Eighteenth-Century Social Theory and Modern Sociology," *American Journal of Sociology* 95(1990): 1474–504.
77. Paul Seabright, *The Company of Strangers: A Natural History of Economic Life* (Princeton: Princeton University Press, 2010), 12.
78. Storr, "Why the Market?" 143.
79. Ibid.
80. For example, Michael Argyle and Monika Henderson, *The Anatomy of Relationships: And the Rules and Skills Needed to Manage Them Successfully* (London: Penguin, 1985); Patricia Zavella, "'Abnormal Intimacy': The Varying Work Networks of Chicana Cannery Workers," *Feminist Studies* 11(1985): 541–57; Keenan Bridge and Leslie A. Baxter, "Blended Relationships: Friends as Work Associates," *Western Journal of Communication* 56(1992): 200–25; and Randy Hodson, "Group Relations at Work: Solidarity, Conflict, and Relations with Management," *Work and Occupations* 24(1997): 426–52.
81. Christine L. Williams, Patti A. Giuffre, and Kirsten Dellinger, "Sexuality in the Workplace: Organizational Control, Sexual Harassment and the Pursuit of Pleasure," *Annual Review of Sociology* 25(1999): 73–93; and Charles A. Pierce, Donn Byrne and Herman Aguinis, "Attraction in Organizations: A Model of Workplace Romance," *Journal of Organizational Behavior* 17(1996): 5–32.
82. Linda L. Price and Eric J. Arnould, "Commercial Friendships: Service Provider–Client Relationships in Context," *Journal of Marketing* 63(1999): 38–56; and Diana L. Haytko, "Firm-to-Firm and Interpersonal Relationships: Perspectives from Advertising Agency Account Managers," *Journal of Academy of Marketing Science* 32(2004): 312–28.
83. Price and Arnould, "Commercial Friendships," 50.
84. Yet these non-commercial relationships, when soured, could be more malicious and vindictive than commercial relationships. We often hear of irreconcilable

family feuds, ugly divorces, vindictive ex-best friends, and ostracism of former members of religious groups.

85. Charles Montesquieu, *De l'esprit des lois* (Paris: Garnier, 1748/1961); Hirschman, *Passions and the Interests.*
86. Thomas Paine, *The Rights of Man* (New York: Penguin Books, 1791/1984).
87. Smith, *Theory of Moral Sentiments*; Maria Pia Paganelli, "The Moralizing Role of Distance in Adam Smith: The Theory of Moral Sentiments as Possible Praise of Commerce," *History of Political Economy* 42(2010): 425–41.

12

Do Markets Corrupt?

Jason Brennan

Market societies enjoy higher standards of living and greater material prosperity.[1] But many people worry that all this filthy lucre comes at the expense of our souls.

Both friends and foes of market society say that markets recruit "low-grade motives" to produce publicly "beneficial ends."[2] Some friends say that markets *economize* on virtue—they function well even though people are not saints.[3] The average economics textbook claims that one virtue of markets is that they work fairly well even if people are predominantly selfish.[4]

Critics take this one step further. They worry that markets do not merely economize on already scarce virtue, but in fact crowd out altruism and make virtue even scarcer. Markets encourage the "hypertrophy" of greed and selfishness.[5] Even when we work to benefit others, we are "essentially indifferent" to others' welfare.[6] Markets cause us to regard everyone else either as customers or competitors. We care about them only insofar as they can help us or get in our way, but we do not care about them for their own sake.

Suppose I rescue a toddler who was drowning in the Potomac River. The media rushes to call me a hero, but I confess, while being interviewed, that the only reason I rescued the toddler was that I hoped it would make me famous. In that case, the action I performed was precisely what a noble or virtuous person would do, but my motivation was not virtuous. In this case, I did the right thing, but I'm really a jerk.

The Marxist philosopher G.A. Cohen worries that markets are turning all of us into such jerks. Sure, he says, markets induce to produce things others want, but, according to this worry, we do so only because we want to serve ourselves.[7] Adam Smith tells us, "It is not from the benevolence of the butcher, the brewer, or the baker, that we expect our dinner, but from their regard to their own interest. We address ourselves, not to their humanity but to their self-love."[8] In markets, the best way for a person to pursue her self-interest is to produce goods and services others want at prices they can afford to pay.

Critics of markets believe that markets tend to encourage us to have immoral motivations and vicious or defective feelings. As Cohen summarizes:

> The immediate motive to productive activity in a market society is . . . typically some mixture of greed and fear. . . . the motives of greed and fear are what the market brings to prominence, and that includes greed on behalf of, and fear for the safety of, one's family. Even when one's concerns are thus wider than those of one's mere self, the market posture is greedy and fearful in that one's opposite-number marketeers are predominantly seen as possible sources of enrichment, and as threats to one's success. These are horrible ways of seeing other people . . .[9]
> Markets, he claims, corrupt us.

In a related complaint, Benjamin Barber claims that markets are dangerous for a country's civic life. Capitalism induces citizens to be more concerned with procuring consumer goods for themselves than with their common civic life. Markets draw people away from the public forum and towards the market.[10]

In this chapter, I argue that the critics are probably mistaken. This chapter considers and rebuts two major arguments purporting to show that markets are corrupting:

1. *The Selfishness Objection*, which claims that exposure to and involvement in markets tends to make people more selfish and less altruistic.
2. *The Civics Objection*, which claims that markets and commodification threaten civic engagement, because markets draw people away from active participation in politics.

Contrary to the Selfishness Objection, I argue that the available empirical evidence indicates that markets make us *more*, not less, altruistic. As far as we know, they make us more trusting, trustworthy, honest, respectful, tolerant, and benevolent. Contrary to the Civics Objection, I argue that markets not only fail (as far as we know) to make us participate less in political life, but markets also provide new opportunities to serve the common good. I further argue that markets tend to encourage tolerance, and, finally, that the wealth markets generate makes it easier for us to be virtuous. A virtue of markets is that they reduce one major impediment to virtue.

One note about this chapter: I will be evaluating certain social scientific results and explaining what these say about how markets affect our behavior. However, how these results are best accommodated into any particular *theory* of virtue, from Stoicism to Aristotelianism, goes beyond the scope of the chapter. Instead, I will stick closely to ordinary, commonsense moral thinking. A proper theory of virtue needs to be informed by the discussion here, but I will not try to say just how Stoics or Aristotelians should accommodate these results.

1. THE BURDEN OF PROOF

To know whether markets corrupt, we need the tools of the social sciences. Philosophy can tell us what counts as moral corruption, but it cannot tell us what causes what in the world. Those who claim that markets corrupt us owe us proper empirical evidence that such corruption does in fact occur. Proponents must supply us with the kind of sustained empirical analysis that would merit publication in a social scientific academic journal. Most critics of market society, including Jean-Jacques Rousseau, Karl Marx, G.A. Cohen, and Michael Sandel, dispense with this step. Accordingly, most of their accusations remain little more than accusations.

People who argue that markets corrupt us must discharge their burden of proof. They assert a controversial empirical claim, namely, that certain kinds of exposure or involvement in certain markets cause certain kinds of bad character. They must prove their hypothesis, the same way that medical researchers who claim that a chemical causes cancer must prove their hypothesis. Otherwise, in the absence of substantive empirical evidence, we are by default justified in being skeptical of the claim that markets cause bad character, just as we are by default justified in being skeptical of a claim that some chemical causes cancer.

It is easy to think of examples of money incentivizing people to do wrong. Of course, incentives incentivize. But people have also performed wrongful acts for sex, love, religious grace, academic prestige, knowledge, community, status, and political power. Almost anything people want or care about can cause them, in some circumstances, to act badly. To support the thesis that markets corrupt, it is not enough to show that sometimes money incentivizes people to do wrong, or that some businesspeople are bad. Almost everything corrupts sometimes. Instead, we need to know what the general trend is. Does exposure to markets tend to corrupt people, or not? Does putting a person in a market society tend to make him have worse or better character? Finally, to what alternatives are we comparing these cases?

Critics must also distinguish between two claims: the market *causes* people to have worse character or preferences, and the market *reveals* people's base character or preferences. Consider: you might find certain markets, such as vending machines selling used schoolgirls' underwear, perverse or gross.[11] For the sake of argument, suppose your revulsion is justified, and that such markets really do display a kind of perversion. But the existence of such markets does not show us that the markets *cause* people to be perverts; these markets might just be catering to (or giving a specific form to) pre-existing perversions. Even if these "perversions" are cultural rather than innate or genetic, it is again not clear the market is *causing* this culture rather than responding to it. Critics might assert the market manufactured these wants, but, again, we need evidence, not assertion.

Finally, it is not enough to show that participating in the market reduces certain virtues. One still needs to show that markets are corrupting on *net*. After all, it is possible that the market degrades some virtues but improves others. So, for the sake of argument, suppose that filial piety is a virtue, and that it turns out that, empirically speaking, markets tend to reduce filial piety. Even if so, it might also turn out that the market simultaneously increases people's tolerance and openness. We might determine, on net, that the trade-off in terms of character alone is worth it, that the market reduces some desirable character traits but improves others and the improvements outweigh the losses. If we are going to focus on character, we need to focus on the *whole* character.

2. THE SELFISHNESS OBJECTION

The most obvious objection to markets is that they make us more selfish, that is, that they induce us to have an objectionably high degree of self-concern and an objectionably low degree of concern for others. G.A. Cohen, for instance, claims that capitalism "work[s] on the basis of the development, and, indeed, the hypertrophy of selfishness."[12] Michael Sandel worries that if markets "economize on virtue," they will cause "civic virtue and public spirit [to] atrophy with disuse."[13] It is possible that they are right, but they do not offer us any evidence for this claim. At any rate, we cannot settle this kind of issue from the armchair by doing a priori philosophical or economic analysis. We need to conduct historical, sociological, and psychological research on what exposure to markets does to people and what happens when markets are replaced by something else.

One way to test this hypothesis is through experimental economics. Economists like to conduct experiments, using large amounts of real money, in which participants have the opportunity to cheat and swindle each other or to play fairly. In one game, the Dictator Game, one player (the "dictator") is given a sum of money. The dictator is then asked whether he is willing to donate part of that money to an anonymous second player, one with whom the dictator will have no further interaction, and who must accept the offer. In another game, the Ultimatum Game, one player (the "proposer") is given money and must then propose splitting the money with a second player (the "respondent"). If the respondent accepts the split, both players receive the proposer's proposed payoff; if the respondent rejects the split, both players get nothing. In yet another game, the Trust Game, one player is given money and may then elect to give some of it to a second player. Whatever amount he gives to the second player is then multiplied by three. The second player can then decide to give some of that money back to the first player, or keep it all for himself. Each of these games tests some motive or character trait, such as unconditional beneficence, a sense of fairness, the willingness to incur a personal loss to punish unfair behavior, trust, or reciprocity.

Joseph Henrich, Herbert Gintis, and others have tested a large number of variables to see which factors tend to make people play fair or cheat in games such as these. These studies strongly disconfirm the thesis that markets make people more selfish overall. In fact, markets make people less selfish in these games. As Gintis summarizes these studies:

> Movements for religious and lifestyle tolerance, gender equality, and democracy have flourished and triumphed in societies governed by market exchange, and nowhere else.
>
> My colleagues and I found dramatic evidence of this positive relationship between markets and morality in our study of fairness in simple societies—hunter-gatherers, horticulturalists, nomadic herders, and small-scale sedentary farmers—in Africa, Latin America, and Asia. Twelve professional anthropologists and economists visited these societies and played standard ultimatum, public goods, and trust games with the locals. As in advanced industrial societies, members of all of these societies exhibited a considerable degree of moral motivation and a willingness to sacrifice monetary gain to achieve fairness and reciprocity, even in anonymous one-shot situations. More interesting for our purposes, we measured the degree of market exposure and cooperation in production for each society, and we found that the ones that regularly engage in market exchange with larger surrounding groups have more pronounced fairness motivations. The notion that the market economy makes people greedy, selfish, and amoral is simply fallacious.[14]

Contrary to the hypothesis that markets make people more selfish, it turns out, empirically, the strongest cultural predictor that participants will play fairly with strangers is how market-oriented their society is. The claim that markets make people selfish is a testable hypothesis, and insofar as it has been tested, it is not merely false, but backwards.

Other studies produce similar results. Paul Zak and Stephen Knack have shown that market societies also tend to be high-trust societies, while non-market societies tend to be low-trust societies.[15] Omar Al-Ubaydli, Daniel Houser, and colleagues have shown that "priming" people with words related to markets and trade makes them more trusting, trustworthy, and fair in experiments—that is, when we get people into the market mindset, they become nicer.[16] Mitchell Hoffman and John Morgan found, contrary to everyone's expectations, that "adult populations deliberately selected from two cutthroat internet industries—domain trading and adult entertainment (pornography)" are "more pro-social than [undergraduate] students: they are more altruistic, trusting, trustworthy, and lying averse."[17]

Another study by Gabriele Camera and his colleagues finds slightly more ambiguous results. Camera and his colleagues played a series of experimental

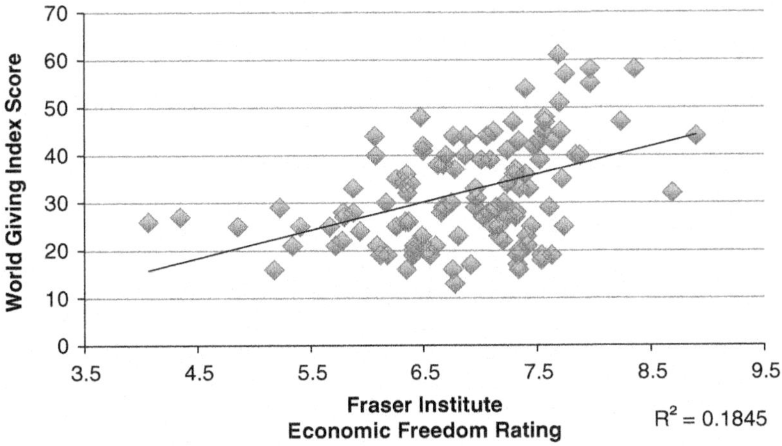

Fig. 12.1. Markets and Generosity

games in which people could choose to cooperate or not, and could choose to be generous or selfish when cooperating.[18] They found that introducing fake money-like tokens into small groups made players more selfish and less cooperative, but, at the same time, that introducing fake money-like tokens into large groups made them less selfish and more cooperative.

The Charities Aids Foundation World Giving Index measures how likely people in different countries are to give money to charity, to help strangers, and volunteer.[19] Figure 12.1 illustrates that the positive relationship between how market-oriented a society (as measured by the Fraser Institute's Index of Economic Freedom) is and how "giving" it is.

Another way to test the hypothesis that markets are corrupting is to see whether there is a relationship between how market-oriented a society is and how much political corruption there is. As Figure 12.2 shows, contrary to what the Selfishness Argument predicts, there is a robust positive correlation between countries' degree of economic freedom (as measured by the Fraser Institute's economic freedom ratings) and countries' lack of corruption (as measured by Transparency International's Corruption Perceptions Index).[20] Note also that the most marketized societies tend also to be significantly above the trend line. These findings also support the arguments of institutionalist economists, who often argue that market exchange does not rely upon self-interest alone, but also upon—and at the same time tends to reinforce—mutual trust, reciprocity, and trustworthiness.[21]

These studies or correlations, independently or collectively, are not definitive on their own. I would not expect a market skeptic to look at Figure 12.1 and say, "well, that settles it. Markets make us nice." My point here is to shift the burden of proof. There is a wealth of empirical studies trying to test what

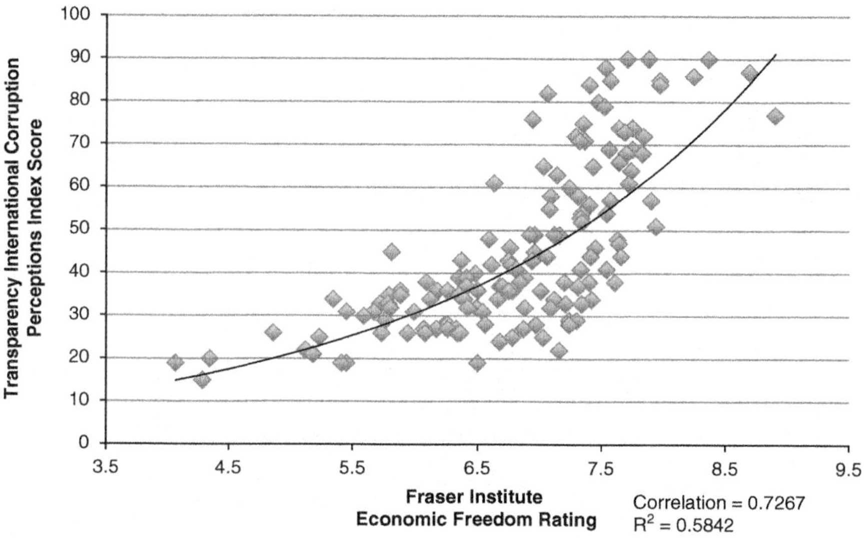

Fig. 12.2. Economic Freedom vs. Corruption

effect, if any, exposure to markets or living in a capitalist society has on people's character. The majority of these studies find ameliorative effects. While the Selfishness Objection seems plausible at first glance, the available evidence undermines rather than supports it. Of course, it is possible that the Selfishness Objection is true, but we seem to lack sufficient grounds right now to believe it.

3. DOES BASIC MICROECONOMICS PREDICT THAT MARKETS CORRUPT US?

These empirical findings might seem surprising. After all, it seems like we can argue that markets corrupt us on the basis of basic microeconomic reasoning. The argument might go something like this:

Reduced Supply Argument

1. Markets economize on virtue.
2. By economizing on virtue, markets thus reduce the value of virtue.
3. By reducing the value of virtue, all things equal, markets thus reduce both the supply and demand of virtue.
4. By reducing the supply and demand of virtue, all things equal, markets thus reduce the total amount of virtue.

In premise 1, by "virtue," I mean nothing more than morally good motivation and the propensity to act on these good motivations. You can feel free to fill in the details with whatever you regard as the correct theory of virtue. Michael Sandel, recall, expresses a worry like this in his *What Money Can't Buy*. He worries that markets make it so we need less virtuous motivation, and so we are less likely to act upon such motives, and as a result, these motives will atrophy.[22] While we have already seen in the previous section that the extant empirical work shows that markets do not reduce virtue, it is worth investigating further just where this theoretical argument goes wrong.

There a number of problems with this argument. First, even if it were a sound argument, it does not tell us how *much* the supply of virtue is reduced. That is, it does not tell us what the elasticity of the supply curve is. Second, the "all things equal" qualifier is important. It remains open that markets tend to reduce virtue because they reduce the need for it, but, at the same time, it might be that markets cause greater virtue in some other way not considered by the argument. For instance, it might turn out that because markets tend to bring people from different religions or regions together to trade, they increase the virtues of tolerance and openness, and this offsets whatever effect the argument above is meant to predict. (I will examine this point in the next section.)

More fundamentally, this argument rests on a deep mistake. It moves from the claim that markets "require" less virtue than some other arrangements to function properly, to the claim that the markets therefore *exhibit* less virtue.

To see why this is a mistake, consider the following parody:

1. All things equal, the supply of any good increases as the value of that good increases and supply decreases as value decreases.
2. Drunken fraternity parties provide the opportunity for men to sexually assault women. Military invasions provide the opportunity for men to murder, plunder, and assault. Accordingly, the value of virtuous motivation is much higher during drunken fraternity parties and during military invasions than in, say, a normal market transaction.
3. Therefore, the supply of virtue will be higher in drunken fraternity parties and during military invasions than in normal market transactions.

This parody argument reveals what is wrong with the Reduced Supply Argument. The problem is that the Reduced Supply Argument ignores the question of *who* bears the benefits and costs of virtue and vice. Frat parties and military invasions increase the value of virtue, but they in fact encourage vice, not virtue—and the reason they do so is that frat boys and soldiers can *externalize* the costs of their vice onto their victims. And whether supply and demand predicts that markets will reduce virtue depends on these same issues. In a market, how much can people *externalize* the costs of their vice onto others? In a market, how valuable is my virtue *to me?*

In fact, markets tend to make us *internalize* the costs of our behavior. Markets punish bad behavior and bad character because, in a normally functioning market, no one is forced to make trades with strangers. Anyone can walk away from a bad deal or from a suspicious deal. Thus, my ability to make trades on the market depends upon my reputation. In a market, people do not have to trade with me; they can go to one of my many competitors instead. Accordingly, if they think I am not trustworthy, I lose business. If they think my competitors are slightly more trustworthy than I am, all things equal, I lose business. Thus, I have every incentive to appear trustworthy. In fact, just as I have an incentive to compete by lowering my prices, or offering higher quality for the same price, I have an incentive to compete by demonstrating that I am more trustworthy than my competitors.

As David Gauthier and David Schmidtz have pointed out, faking truthworthiness over the long term is difficult.[23] Psychology shows that most of us are bad at lying, and it takes a large amount of effort.[24] Those of us who are not sociopaths find it stressful to lie. Further, it turns out that lying is hard—one has to invent details on the spot and find ways to work these details into the true details of one's life. It is also difficult to maintain lies under questioning. To illustrate this, each year, in one of my classes, I conduct an informal experiment in which students try to detect each other's lies. Students form pairs and each student then tells her partner one true story from high school and one fictional story, made up on the spot. The partner may then ask five questions and must then guess which story is true and which is false. As it turns out, students detect the lie about two-thirds of the time, which is better than chance. This illustrates what psychologists have already found: lying is hard. For most of us, the most economical and efficient way to *appear* trustworthy is to actually *be* trustworthy.

4. COMPARED TO WHAT?

Markets do not perfectly internalize the costs of vice, of course. Some people do in fact get away with being vicious or wicked. However, when discussing how much markets internalize or externalize virtue and vice, we need to ask—we *have* to ask—*compared to what?* Can people externalize the costs of their vice *more* in markets than they can in other arrangements?

Consider an alternative to the market: a democratic socialist system in which all property is collectively owned and every decision is made democratically. The system might require more virtue than a market society, but that does not mean it will supply it.

After all, suppose we are about to vote on a particular economic proposal. Any individual's vote makes a difference only in changes to the outcome of the collective vote. But, as economists have long known, the probability that an individual vote will be decisive, even in a small election, is vanishingly small.[25] While what the collective decides makes a big difference, the way any individual in that collective votes makes no difference.

In particular, suppose that we democratic socialists are about to decide whether to build a tire factory or to build a new hospital. Suppose that there is an objectively right answer that can be expressed in monetary terms: it turns out the hospital is worth $10 billion more to my countries' well-being than the tire factory is. Furthermore, suppose I am perfectly altruistic. However, suppose I am one of ten million voters, and that, going into the referendum, I know that my fellow citizens are not evenly split. One side (it does not matter which) has a tiny lead: about 50.1 per cent of my fellow citizens say they favor it, although they might change their minds. In that case, while it's worth $10 billion for the country to pick the hospital over the tire factory, it is not even worth one penny for me to even *vote* for the hospital over the tire factory.[26]

Accordingly, regardless of whether individuals have selfish or altruistic motives, they have no incentive to be well-informed about the decision, and they have no incentive to overcome their biases or to think rationally about the decision. They are thus expected to remain ignorant and to think irrationally about the decision.[27] In fact, this is just what political scientists tend to find in democratic decision-making: most voters are spectacularly ignorant about basic politics,[28] and they process political information in an extremely biased way.[29] Democratic socialism needs virtue more than a market does, but in fact it incentivizes vice.

Socialist philosopher G.A. Cohen, in his book *Why Not Socialism?* has us imagine an ideal socialist society.[30] In that society, everyone acts out of love, kindness, and a sense of community. There are no divisions, and no one ever acts on a motive that anyone could find objectionable. Cohen then asks us to imagine that this society starts exhibiting the behaviors of a modern capitalist state. People start being greedy and self-serving. Almost every reader concurs with Cohen that this makes the society worse, not better. As the society becomes more capitalist, it becomes more corrupt.

Cohen's criticism seems powerful, but it rests on a mistake. What Cohen is asking us to do is to imagine an ideal socialist society in which everyone is stipulated to have morally perfect character and pure motives. He then asks us to compare this to a realistic capitalist society, in which people have whatever motives they in fact have. Of course moving from an imaginary world of perfect virtue to our realistic world of imperfect virtue means an increase in vice. But that does not show that capitalism causes vice more than socialism does. The problem here is not capitalism—it is that we are comparing a daydream to the real world. Cohen's socialist society full of saints is better than real-world capitalism not because it is socialist, but because it is full of saints.

One could just as easily ask Cohen to imagine a utopian market-oriented society, in which everyone is stipulated to have morally perfect character and pure motives.[31] We could then compare this to a realistic socialist society, such as Cambodia or the Soviet Union, in which people have whatever motives they in fact had. Realistic socialist societies, of course, fall far short of the virtue exhibited in imaginary utopian capitalist societies, but that does not show that socialism causes vice compared to capitalism.

People in realistic societies have less virtue than people in imaginary societies where we purposefully imagine everyone to have perfect virtue. These thought experiments do not show us that the institutions in the imaginary societies cause virtue, or that our institutions in the real world cause vice. Rather, all they show us is that we are good at imagining perfectly virtuous people living under a wide variety of different institutional structures. This is no substitute for genuine social scientific investigation.

5. MARKETS AND TOLERANCE

Most people think markets make us more selfish and less trustworthy. However, as we just saw, the available empirical evidence speaks against this. In fact, markets make us more trusting and trustworthy, and more cooperative.

Might markets have other ennobling effects? As Voltaire wrote in 1733,

> Go into the London Stock Exchange—a more respectable place than many a court—and you will see representatives of all nations gathered there for the service of mankind. There the Jew, the Mohammedan, and the Christian deal with each other as if they were of the same religion, and give the name of infidel only to those who go bankrupt. There the Presbyterian trusts the Anabaptist, and the Anglican accepts the Quaker's promise. On leaving these peaceful and free assemblies, some go to the synagogue, others go to drink . . . others go to their church to wait the inspiration of God, their hats on their heads, and all are content.[32]

Here, Voltaire asserts that markets make us *less* rather than more inclined to discriminate against one another.

More recently, economist Gary Becker argued that the market tends to eliminate unjust discrimination.[33] He asks us to suppose that people have a "taste for discrimination"—they prefer to hire white workers instead of equally high quality black workers. This will tend to reduce blacks' wages. However, this gives firms willing to hire blacks an advantage as black labor becomes cheaper than white labor, and firms who hire blacks can sell their products for less and make higher profits. The more other people discriminate against blacks, the more a white factory owner would benefit from hiring them. The market thus *punishes* taste for discrimination by making it come at the expense of people's other selfish interests.

Becker's argument is not mere theoretical speculation; there are a number of real world experiences that illustrate his analysis. For example, economist Linda Gorman presents South Africa as a test case. In the early 1900s, despite threats of violence and legal sanctions, white mine owners fired highly paid white workers in order to hire lower paid blacks. The South African government had to pass the apartheid laws to *stop* the white mine owners from hiring blacks.[34]

Also, consider the Jim Crow Laws: economist Jennifer Roback says the economics of the streetcar business weighed heavily against providing separate compartments. Jim Crow was expensive because train companies lost money by having to run extra train cars and lunch counters lost money by having to supply twice as many restrooms. Southern states thus *required* private companies to mistreat blacks. The laws were there because many businesses did not discriminate until forced to do so. If you read old newspaper editorials from the Southern states under Jim Crow, you will find editors frequently complaining about how greedy businessmen just chase the dollar and are unwilling to uphold the moral ideal of segregation.[35]

Roback adds that the Southern states had a wide range of laws designed to stop blacks from competing for work. Enticement laws forbade white farm owners from trying to hire black farmworkers away from other farmers during the planting or harvesting season. Black farmworkers who tried to leave their jobs for higher-paying jobs could be thrown in jail. Vagrancy laws required blacks to be employed at all times. Any unemployed black man was considered a vagrant and could be put on a chain gang. Thus blacks could not search for better employment; they had to stick with whatever job they had. Emigrant-agent laws forbade white recruiters from enticing laborers to leave their current cities or states to take jobs elsewhere. These and other laws and regulations were created in order to *stop* the market from helping blacks.

Capitalism gives people an economic incentive to overlook their differences and instead work together. Furthermore, empirical studies show that once people work together, they tend to *stop caring* about those differences. It is not merely that people put up with those whom they hate in order to make a buck; rather, they tend to stop hating their trade partners. This is why market societies are also usually the most tolerant societies.[36] Competitive market pressures and the desire for profit push people to see past racial or religious divides. This explains Voltaire's observation that at the London Stock Exchange, people of all races and creeds came together to do business.[37]

6. MAYBE MONEY BUYS MORALITY

In 2006, the Gallup World Poll surveyed 130,000 people from 90 different countries, being careful to ensure that they surveyed a properly representative sample of people from each country. (Previous studies in the 1960s had failed to be so careful and generated misleading results.) Economists Betsey Stevenson and Justin Wolfers used the survey data to show that, contrary to what had been the received wisdom before then, money does indeed buy happiness.[38] As Daniel Kahneman summarized their results, "Humans everywhere, from Norway to Sierra Leone, apparently evaluate their life by a common standard of material prosperity."[39] That is, on average, as people have absolutely higher levels of income, their happiness increases.

However, one often overlooked finding from Stevenson and Wolfers is how money also appears to buy respect. The survey asked, "Were you treated with respect all day yesterday?" Stevenson and Wolfers find a very strong correlation between a country's GDP per capita and a "yes" answer to that question.[40] Apparently, people in richer countries are more likely to respect one another.

This does not necessarily mean that increasing prosperity makes us more respectful of one another. It could instead be that being respectful of one another makes us more prosperous. Alternatively, it could be that there is a virtuous circle, with respect causing prosperity and prosperity in turn causing respect; or it could be that a common factor causes both.

That said, we can at least explore why prosperity might lead to greater respectful behavior, even if we do not know for sure that it is causing it. Consider a parallel finding. Worldwide, we have seen the following trend. As countries start to develop and become richer, they do more and more damage to their environment. However, at a certain "turning point," such as $9,000 GDP per capita, countries often start to pollute less rather than more.[41] Economists call this the "Environmental Kuznets Curve," as shown in Figure 12.3.

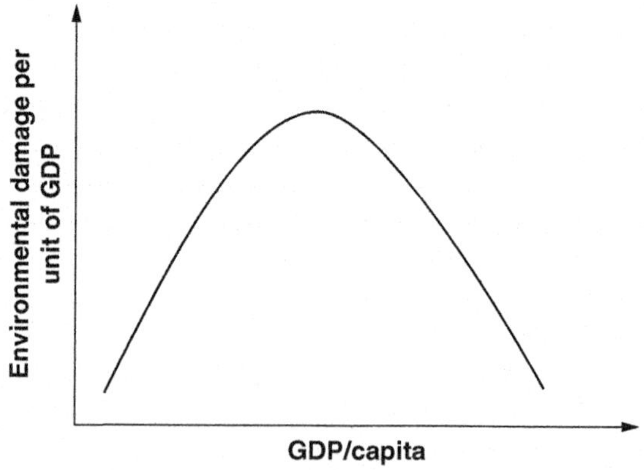

Fig. 12.3. Environmental Kuznets Curve

One possible reason for this trend is that environmental quality seems to be what economists call a "superior good," a good that is pursued more strongly by those with higher incomes.[42] The idea here is that wealth enables us to think in a more long-term manner. When people are desperately poor, they have little incentive to think long-term, and instead focus on meeting their basic needs. But, as people become richer, they become more willing to make trade-offs in environmental quality—they are more willing to forego additional material benefits to enjoy a cleaner environment. Few people are willing to let their kids starve to keep the air clean, but most people are willing to pay a little extra for catalytic converters in their cars to keep the air clean.

Psychologist Abraham Maslow proposed that most people have a hierarchy of needs.[43] The items at the bottom of the hierarchy include immediate physical needs, such as bodily integrity, security, food, and water. At the top of their hierarchy are more spiritual goods, such as self-actualization, respect, transcendence, and a range of higher moral pursuits. The items at the bottom of the list are more urgent, while the items at the top are more important. Accordingly, we tend to pursue the needs at the bottom first, and we go for the higher-level needs only after we have met the needs at the bottom. If Maslow's hypothesis is roughly accurate, this helps to explain why markets appear to be ennobling rather than corrupting: market societies are richer societies, and richer people can afford to focus on higher moral concerns.

7. MARKETS AND CIVIC VIRTUE

Like Rousseau before him, Benjamin Barber complains that market societies tend to draw people away from public, civic life, inducing citizens to be more concerned with procuring consumer goods for themselves. In other words, markets draw people away from the public forum and towards the market.[44] In principle, this is a testable hypothesis, something that can be studied by the social sciences. However, it is a difficult question to study because one needs to find a way to operationalize the degree to which a society is market-oriented and also what counts as political participation. In addition, one needs to look for and control for other possible variables that affect political participation.

One quick measure would be to see if the more marketized countries worldwide also have lower rates of political participation. Figure 12.4 charts major democratic countries, showing the relationship between their degree of economic freedom and their voter turnout for elections for a country's lower national legislative house.[45] In fact, the correlation is very weakly positive, rather than negative, contrary to what Barber or Rousseau might expect.

Of course this is not the final word on the matter. It is just a piece of a larger puzzle. In fact, the question of what determines turnout is quite complicated,

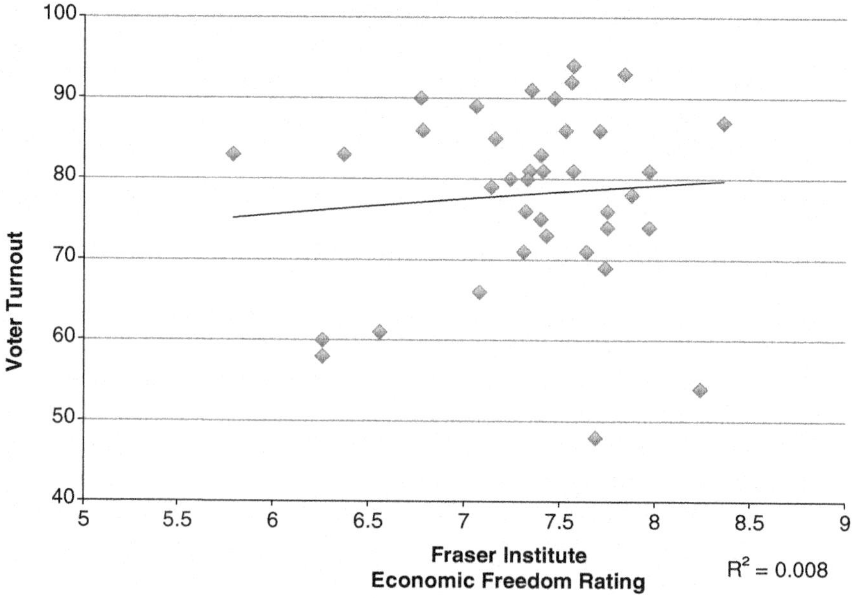

Fig. 12.4. Market Societies and Voter Turnout

and there is a large empirical literature on this.[46] However, I can find no empirical literature showing that market societies tend to have less political engagement, or that increasing the degree to which a society is market-oriented makes it less participatory.[47]

So far, I have taken Barber's view of civic engagement for granted. Perhaps I should not. Barber has a narrow conception of citizenship, in which being a good citizen means being engaged in political and quasi-political activities, such as voting, deliberating, running for office, serving in the military, and volunteering. But there is an alternative, broader conception of civic virtue, in which being a good citizen can instead mean working at a productive job, creating art, being a good parent, or pursuing knowledge.

Consider, by analogy, two views of "courage." The ancient Greeks—that is, the Greeks who lived at the time the *Iliad* was supposed to have taken place—had a narrow view of courage. For them, courage was largely a martial and manly virtue, a virtue that could properly be exercised only by men, and only during conflict and battle. However, most of us now reject this narrow conception of courage. We instead subscribe to a broad view of courage, by which to be courageous is to have an appropriate recognition of danger and risk and to be willing to confront that danger and risk when called for. Once we realize that this is what courage is all about, we recognize that courage can be exercised by both men and women, and also that it can be exercised almost everywhere, not just on the battlefield. A woman can exercise courage in childbirth just as much as a man can exercise courage in war. (Also, a man can exercise courage in childbirth just as much as a woman can exercise courage in war.) Just as we have adopted a broad conception of courage, we should also adopt a broad conception of civic virtue, or so I will briefly argue here.

Philosophers almost universally define civic virtue as the disposition to promote the common good of society over purely private ends.[48] But this leaves open just *how* and *where* one can exercise civic virtue. Civic virtue is the disposition to promote the common good, and political participation can certainly promote the common good. However, many other things can promote the common good as well. Michelangelo contributed to the common good of society by making art. Thomas Edison promoted the common good by making light bulbs. Marie Curie promoted the common good with her scientific discovery. And, in my view, a typical baker does much more to promote the common good by baking and selling bread than he does by voting or writing letters to his elected officials. While Barber sees the move from the forum to the market as a loss of civic virtue, I see it as a potential gain. In my view, the market is as good or better a place to exercise civic virtue than the forum.

I will illustrate this point with a thought experiment.[49] Imagine you could wave a magic wand that would instantaneously make everyone fifteen times richer, and to that extent dramatically improve everyone's standard of living. Most people would conclude that this counts as promoting the common good.

Now suppose your magic wand's power is not instantaneous, so that it takes 200 years for incomes to increase fifteen-fold. While this second magic wand is not as good as the first, waving the wand would still serve the common good.

Next, suppose the slow-acting magic wand is imperfect. Though it systematically improves conditions over time, it causes some important problems, people sometimes get hurt, and it needs to be supplemented by government activity to really maximize its contribution to the common good and to correct the problems it causes. Even then, the magic wand serves the common good, only imperfectly.

Now suppose that, instead of the slow-acting magic wand, we have a noble philosopher-queen, who determines that if we work together, divide up various tasks, and so forth, we can increase our incomes by fifteen times over the next 200 years. The philosopher-queen issues various instructions and offers some rewards for good work and punishments for bad work. Unfortunately, the queen is imperfect in exactly the same way the magic wand was. Even then, the philosopher-queen serves the common good. More importantly, those of us who follow her directives and work for her would, in general, be helping to serve the common good. If any of us have the goal of serving the common good, one strategy would be to work for the philosopher-queen, to do whatever job she recommends you do.

Finally, suppose that, instead of the imperfect philosopher-queen, you have a market economy that issues the same directives, offers the same rewards and punishments, and produces the same results. While the queen might have had written or verbal commands, the market economy uses prices instead. While the queen might have issued monetary rewards or fines, the market economy offers profits, losses, and consumer surpluses. Yet, otherwise, the system is the same. Again, as with the queen, the market economy serves the common good. In a sense, the market economy *just is* the philosopher-queen, and those of us who follow its directives and work for it would, in general, be helping to serve the common good, just as we would have been in working for the philosopher-queen. If any of us have the goal of serving the common good, one good strategy for satisfying that goal would be to work inside the market economy, doing whatever is profitable. In a robust, well-functioning market economy, a highly altruistic person who understood economics would regard for-profit business activity as one of the best available means to serve the common good.

Mainstream economic theory claims the market economy is, fundamentally, the same as the imperfect philosopher-queen or the slow-acting, imperfect magic wand.[50] If so, then productive work in the market—including for-profit business activity—will generally promote the common good. In the hypothetical land governed by the wise philosopher-queen, a person with a high degree of civic virtue would just ask the queen how he could be most useful, and do what the queen asks. Since the market just is the philosopher-queen, a person of civic virtue in a market society can similarly do what the market deems useful.

If a person is motivated to promote the common good and to serve others, it does not follow that she must pursue political activities or must avoid the market. Rather, each of us will have a unique set of options in how we can contribute to the common good. For some of us, that means specializing in political or quasi-political activity. For some, it means specializing in non-political activities. For others, it means doing a mix of political and non-political activities. Contrary to Barber, then, we cannot automatically treat a reduction in political participation as a reduction in citizens' civic-mindedness.

8. CONCLUSION

Moral philosophers excel at the analysis of normative concepts. They can find relationships among ideas about morality and discover what is packed into our intuitions about moral virtue. Philosophers can devise theories of virtue and help us see reasons to accept, say, an Aristotelian theory of virtue over a Stoic theory (or vice versa). They can also help identify what the requirements of virtue are.

That said, however, they have no special expertise in discussing how different institutions or practices affect our character. Most arguments about whether an institution or practice helps or hinders our character require not just having a good theory of virtue in hand, but having access to proper empirical data about what these institutions or practices actually do to us.

The research on how institutions affect our character is small but growing. There is a robust literature in the field of institutional economics and a growing literature in the fields of moral psychology and experimental economics. As the literature grows, the balance of the evidence might change. However, as things now stand, the charge that markets are corrupting is not only ungrounded or unsupported by the evidence—instead, the evidence shows that markets improve our character.

Markets are not a panacea, and there is little reason to think that even perfectly functioning markets would transform us all into perfectly virtuous people. However, that is no more reason to blame markets for vice than it is to blame Advil for headaches. Advil does not cure all headaches, but it tends to help. Markets do not cure all vices, but they tend to help.

NOTES

1. David Schmidtz and Jason Brennan, *A Brief History of Liberty* (Hoboken: Wiley-Blackwell, 2010), 121–2; Tyler Cowen, *Creative Destruction* (Princeton: Princeton University Press, 2002) and *In Praise of Commercial Culture* (Cambridge, MA: Harvard University Press, 2010).
2. G.A. Cohen, *Why Not Socialism?* (Princeton: Princeton University Press, 2009), 78.
3. Geoffrey Brennan and Alan Hamlin, "Economizing on Virtue," *Constitutional Political Economy* 6(1995): 35–56.
4. For example, Gregory Mankiw, *Principles of Economics*, 6th ed. (New York: Cengage, 2011), 14–17.
5. Cohen, *Why Not Socialism?* 58.
6. Ibid., 50.
7. Ibid., 39.
8. Adam Smith, *The Wealth of Nations*, R.H. Campbell and A.S. Skinner (eds.) (Indianapolis: Liberty Fund, 1776/1982), 26–7.
9. Cohen, *Why Not Socialism?*, 39–40.
10. Benjamin Barber, *Consumed* (New York: W.W. Norton, 2008), 118–65, especially 131–2.
11. In Japan, *buru-sera* vending machines do just that.
12. Cohen, *Why Not Socialism?* 58.
13. Michael Sandel, *What Money Can't Buy: The Moral Limits of Markets* (New York: Farrar, Straus, and Giroux, 2012), 128.
14. Hebert Gintis, "Giving Economists Their Due," *Boston Review*, May/June 2012, <http://new.bostonreview.net/BR37.3/ndf_herbert_gintis_markets_morals.php>.

15. Paul Zak and Stephen Knack, "Trust and Growth," *Economic Journal* 111(2001): 295–321. For more on trust, see Chapter 11 by Choi and Storr in this volume.
16. Omar Al-Ubayli, Daniel Houser, John Nye, Maria Pia Paganelli, and Xiaofei Sophia Pan, "The Causal Effect of Market Priming on Trust: An Experimental Investigation Using Randomized Control," *PLoS One* 8(2013): e55968.
17. Mitchell Hoffman and John Morgan, "Who's Naughty? Who's Nice? Experiments on whether Pro-Social Workers are Selected Out of Cutthroat Business Environments," Rotman School of Management Working Paper, 2013. Available at SSRN, <http://ssrn.com/abstract=2345102>.
18. Gabriele Camera, Marco Casari, and Maria Bigoni. "Money and Trust among Strangers," *Proceedings of the National Academy of Science of the United States of America* 110(2013): 14889–93.
19. See the Charities Aids Foundation, *World Giving Index* 2013.
20. Transparency International, *Corruption Perceptions Index 2012*, <http://cpi.transparency.org/cpi2012/results>.
21. For example, Elinor Ostrom (ed.), *Trust and Reciprocity: Interdisciplinary Lessons from Experimental Research* (New York: Russell Sage Foundation, 2003); Hernando De Soto, *The Mystery of Capital* (New York: Basic Books, 2002); Douglass North, *Institutions, Institutional Change, and Economic Performance* (New York: Cambridge University Press, 2000).
22. Sandel, *What Money Can't Buy*, 128.
23. David Gauthier, *Morals by Agreement* (New York: Oxford University Press, 1986); David Schmidtz, *Rational Choice and Moral Agency* (Princeton: Princeton University Press, 1995).
24. Dan Ariely, *The Honest Truth about Dishonesty* (New York: Harper Perennial, 2013).
25. Geoffrey Brennan and Loren Lomasky, *Democracy and Decision* (New York: Cambridge University Press, 1993), 56–7, 119.
26. Ibid., 57.
27. Ilya Somin, *Democracy and Political Ignorance* (Stanford: Stanford University Press, 2013); Bryan Caplan, *Myth of the Rational Voter* (Princeton: Princeton University Press, 2007).
28. Michael X. Delli Carpini and Scott Keeter, *What Americans Know about Politics and Why It Matters* (New Haven: Yale University Press, 1996); Somin, *Democracy and Political Ignorance.*
29. Dennis Chong, "Degrees of Rationality in Politics," in Leonie Huddy, David O. Sears, and Jack S. Levy (eds.), *The Oxford Handbook of Political Psychology* (New York: Oxford University Press, 2013), 96–129.
30. Cohen, *Why Not Socialism?* 3–9.
31. I make an argument like this in *Why Not Capitalism?* (New York: Routledge, 2014).
32. Letter 6 in Francois Marie Arouet Voltaire, *Letters on England* (1733), available at <http://gutenberg.org/ebooks/2445>.
33. Gary S. Becker, *The Economics of Discrimination* (Chicago: University of Chicago Press, 1957).

34. Linda Gorman, "Discrimination," *The Concise Encyclopedia of Economics*, Library of Economics and Liberty, 2008, <http://econlib.org/library/Enc/Discrimination.html>.
35. Jennifer Roback, "The Political Economy of Segregation: The Case of Segregated Streetcars," *Journal of Economic History* 56(1986): 893–917.
36. For example, see Niclas Berggren and Therese Nilsson, "Does Economic Freedom Foster Tolerance?" *Kyklos* 66(2013): 107–207; Saumitra Jha, "Trade, Institutions, and Ethnic Tolerance: Evidence from South Asia," *American Political Science Review* 107(2013): 806–32.
37. Jha, "Trade, Institutions, and Ethnic Tolerance."
38. Betsey Stevenson and Justin Wolfers, "Economic Growth and Subjective Well-Being: Reassessing the Easterlin Paradox," *Brookings Papers on Economic Activity* 39(2008): 1–102.
39. Daniel Kahneman, "The Sad Tale of the Aspirational Treadmill," *Edge: World Question Center*, 2008, <http://edge.org/q2008/q08_17.html>.
40. Stevenson and Wolfers, "Economic Growth and Subjective Well-Being," figure 23.
41. Gene M. Grossman and Alan B. Krueger, "Economic Growth and the Environment," *Quarterly Journal of Economics* 110(1995): 353–77.
42. Jeffrey A. Frankel, "The Environment and Economic Globalization," in Michael W. Weinstein (ed.), *Globalization: What's New* (New York: Columbia University Press, 2005), 129–69.
43. Abraham H. Maslow, "A Theory of Human Motivation," *Psychological Review* 50(1943): 370–96.
44. Barber, *Consumed*, 118–65, especially 131–2.
45. Turnout rates from Mark N. Franklin, "Electoral Participation," in Richard Niemi and Herbert Wiesberg (eds.), *Controversies in Voting Behavior*, 4th ed. (New York: CQ Press, 2001), 83–99.
46. For a review of this literature, see Sarah Birch, *Full Participation* (Manchester: University of Manchester Press, 2009).
47. See, for example, Pippa Norris, *A Virtuous Circle: Political Communications in Postindustrial Societies* (New York: Cambridge University Press, 2000).
48. Richard Dagger, *Civic Virtues* (New York: Oxford University Press, 1997), 14; Brennan and Hamlin, "Economizing on Virtue."
49. This argument follows Jason Brennan, "For-Profit Business as Civic Virtue," *Journal of Business Ethics* 106(2012): 313–24.
50. See, for example, Paul Krugman and Robin Wells, *Economics*, 2nd ed. (New York: Worth Publishers, 2009); David Weil, *Economic Growth* (New York: Prentice Hall, 2009).

Index

CPSIA information can be obtained
at www.ICGtesting.com
Printed in the USA
BVOW06*1424081217
502238BV00005B/25/P

9 780198 701392